ANTHROPOLOGY AND ETHICS

THE QUEST FOR MORAL UNDERSTANDING

REVISED EDITION

MAY EDEL
AND
ABRAHAM EDEL

CLEVELAND
THE PRESS OF CASE WESTERN RESERVE UNIVERSITY
1968

Revised Edition

First edition published by Charles C Thomas, 1959.

PREFACE

Anthropology and ethics, first published in 1959, began as an experiment in collaboration between two fields. It aimed to clarify the theory of morality in the work of both disciplines. But it was not addressed solely to professionals; it sought to provide an orientation to morality itself in a world in which human problems are becoming extremely complex and have to be confronted directly as moral.

The book was no mere juxtaposition of fields. In its original preparation every chapter was worked over critically by both authors and subjected to a succession of rewritings, and the result was the product of continual dialogue. Now that *Anthropology and Ethics* is being reissued, almost a decade after it was written, it would have been appropriate to assess what has been going on in both fields, in the light of the theses put forth in the book. Since my wife is no longer alive, my own reflections cannot be the product of the same persistent dialogue. They are not, however, without some nourishment in the discussion we carried on and the work we did in the intervening years. What I have done is to append an essay reflecting from a philosophical standpoint on the enterprise—on its logic, on the grounds for its theses, and more particularly on the revolution it calls for in the methods of moral philosophy.

There is an almost paradoxical character to the recommendations to anthropologist and philosopher which are made in the book. The anthropologist is advised to make a more independent study of morality, the philosopher to stop treating it as an isolated field. But the paradox is only on the surface; for when two people face in opposite directions, the recommendation that they get together involves about-face for both.

To the anthropologist the book in effect says: You take morality for granted. The anthropological treatment of it rarely asks the direct question of what it is; a consideration of morality appears incidentally in some other inquiry, whether into religion or economics, law or education, and it is seen sometimes as an additional sanction, sometimes as a means of social control, sometimes as an abstract value (like charity or benevolence), sometimes as a sentiment that binds men together. It is strange that anthropology—which most among the social sciences has developed an integrated way of looking at the whole of the life of a people and at the same time of exploring the structure of each phase in its detailed socio-cultural relations—should have so markedly overlooked morality. Why not focus on it directly as an independent area for investigation, as itself one of the great institutions of society or departments of a culture? Such an experiment needs a working concept of morality at least as well developed as the working concept anthropology has furnished of religion—one that is comprehensive and opens up whole new areas of investigation, yet keeps them together in some systematic way. Take a leaf from the philosopher's book; you may find some assistance in his methods of analyzing concepts and many clues in his conceptual grappling with the problems of ethical theory.

To the philosopher, the book says: You have dealt with morality as an isolated self-contained domain, cut off from relations to psychological and cultural processes. Its vocabulary has been explored as though the field were separate and meaningful in total isolation, as though its processes of justification were utterly unique and unrelated to processes in knowledge generally, and a conceptual chasm has been created between fact and value to preserve the distinctive character of moral judgment. And what has resulted is often described by contemporary philosophers as a deadlock or impasse in ethical theory. Why not experiment in the reverse direction? Take a leaf from the anthropologist's book and try to understand morality itself in its fuller cultural and social relations. Help fashion a working philosophical concept of morality which itself reveals these relations in all their complexity rather than disguises them. Then see whether you cannot break through the present impasse by refining the theoretical questions so as to make fresh kinds of answers possible, without jeopardizing the integrity of moral judgment.

Those whose interest in morality is general and practical, not theoretical and professional, have also a stake in this kind of enterprise—the more systematic description of moralities and the wedding of cultural insight with ethical theory. For only in this way can they make sense of their moral experience and see that what they grapple with as inner personal issues are often conflicts in their culture and revolutions in their social conditions. Or, again, they will understand why what they have taken for granted as social duties flare up as critical inner decisions of basic principle. Or, again, why traditional moral rules may fade away, and others, quite contrary, take their place.

There has, for example, been a revolution during the past half-century in the principles of social organization and in the related conceptions of social justice, which have moved from an emphasis on individual responsibility (and individual charity) to a position stressing collectivized or social responsibility for one aspect after another of human well-being. Organized through techniques of social insurance and utilizing the power of the state, the shift has been made possible by the incredible increase of production resulting from successive waves of technological and scientific change. For a long while carried on in relation to the stark opposition of capitalism and socialism, this revolution has only in recent years emerged as a common trend, reflecting common problems, of all social systems. How far our morality of social justice has been transformed can be seen in the extent to which left and right and center today move toward a concept of a guaranteed annual minimum income for all people.

An opposite shift is seen in the rise of civil disobedience as a problem of individual conscience. In matters of war, in questions of racial injustice, men have become less accepting of legality and obedience to social regulation. Conscience now often demands that we say "No" in some active way to what we ultimately cannot live with. While in part this attitude has emerged as a reaction against the discredit which states have brought on themselves by oppression (as in the case of organized Nazi brutality), it also has deep socio-cultural roots in the contemporary world; for the whole structure of basic loyalties and group identifications has been shaken, and the place and relation of individual, family, nation, and mankind as a whole are undergoing transformation in the present unification of the globe in economy, communication, and culture contact.

The shift in traditional moral rules is perhaps most clearly evident in the so-called sexual revolution. The changes that have taken place in this area of human conduct are no longer regarded simply as the inroads of immorality, but as indications of a revolution in morality which would like to tackle the whole problem of body and spirit in human relations, and do so in frankness rather than shame. The understanding of the sexual revolution involves not merely the advance of knowledge in techniques of birth control, but the whole treatment of sex in our traditional culture and the extent to which repression has been a typical mode of resolving problems of personal relations. And its evaluation involves a further appreciation of what will be its cultural consequences.

How great the need is for understanding in morality today can be seen by what is happening to traditional modes of justification—that is, to the relationship between religion and morality—in our culture. It has finally become apparent in this last decade that the unsettled moral problems of our age emerge as problems *within* each religion too. The   ʰake-up in Catholic thought is
only more pron   ⁿ of the traditional authori-
tarian clarity oⁱ   ιt the lesson is the same in
all religions. ʿ   the religious had moral
answers whilⁱ   ʰad moral problems—
so pervasive i   ιished. Moral problems
have to be f   ᵉvery outlook, and in
the modern   ɔral problems.
    On tʰ   ality, the thesis of
this book   systematic understanding   ˢce for practice.
Such unι   better what jobs
morality haˢ   ʰat have been its
successes and faˏ   ᵉ desirable. We
can come to understˎ..   ιly after the fact,
but while change is taking plˎ   t our very under-
standing can help us do the work ot ᴍorality more self-consciously, with greater enlightenment and greater effectiveness.

A.E.

New York
January, 1968

CONTENTS

ANTHROPOLOGY AND ETHICS

Chapter I

STAKING THE FIELD

The COLLABORATION of philosophy and anthropology in the effort to understand ethical theory and develop its implications for modern life seems a natural one. Philosophy runs a speculative-analytical workshop and anthropology has a flourishing descriptive-comparative laboratory. Each would seem to have some need of the other. Philosophy has become sensitive to the relativity of different modes of thought; it is haunted by the suspicion that human phenomena whose universality it has taken for granted may turn out to be localisms, that even cherished modes of interpretation may be culture-bound. Anthropology, for its part, has been reaching out for greater conceptual and methodological refinement; and just as it has profited in the development of problems and hypotheses by its relation with such fields as psychology, so it may likewise find much it can use in the accumulated philosophical tradition and in the techniques of philosophical analysis.

There has, however, been strong resistance on both sides to collaboration in the field of ethics. Philosophers have not wholly neglected the descriptive-explanatory enterprise: some have done a careful job of phenomenological description, and even offered causal hypotheses for moral phenomena. But on the whole they have preferred to take the province of *what ought to be* for their analysis, leaving the description of *what is* and its theoretical and causal explanation for the sciences to distribute among themselves. Meanwhile anthropology, pushing away evaluative responsibilities with the assertion that its business is to describe and understand, for a long time tended to disregard the whole field of ethics, even in its descriptive research. It is true that in a great deal of its material—in accounts of family quarrels, in details of the instructions given youths at initiation schools, between the lines of a speech in honor of a returning warrior— there is buried a wealth of data on moral rules and moral attitudes, on sanctions and justifications, and the way morality operates in relation to daily living. But apart from a few early attempts set in an evolutionary framework (e.g., Westermarck, 1906) these data have rarely been organized and analyzed around themes relating to ethics. One can look at the general index of such a representative publication as the *American Anthropologist* for the whole period from 1888 to 1938, and find only four references to articles on morals or ethics—and nothing at all under virtues, or right, or good, or character, or sin, sense of; not even conscience, guilt or shame.

In the last two decades, however, conscience and guilt have begun to move into a field of central interest, along with goals and value orientations. This marks a return to problems which are certainly relevant to the field of ethics. There are occasional analyses of whole moralities and discussions of ethical issues like ideas of justice, as well as reconsiderations of ethical relativity, in recent publications. Philosophy, too, is undergoing a hesitant broadening. In addition to looking for moral essences or proposing analyses of moral terms, it has reopened older questions of the structure of moral experience. Even its typically 20th century concern with the language of morals has moved into the wider exploration of contexts of actual usage. And some philosophers have begun to approach the anthropological materials directly, not only in the library (MacBeath, 1952) but even in the field (Brandt, 1954; Ladd, 1957).

The tendency to preserve sharp lines in any scientific partnership is still strong in philosophy today, but the present writers believe that some of the lines that are drawn are arbitrary ones, which interfere with the full formulation of common problems. Even if philosophy is primarily concerned with *analysis* and *evaluation*, it cannot neglect the material or empirical elements in its analysis, nor the factual conditions which make one line of analysis more fruitful than another. And though science may be more concerned with *description* of fact and *causal* investigation, scientific work cannot prudently neglect analysis of concepts nor founder among vague questions. The enterprises of description, analysis, causal investigation and evaluation certainly have to be kept distinct, but not as separate provinces to be parcelled out to philosophers and social scientists. It is possible for philosophy to use the psychological and social science materials without blunting its analytic precision or confusing subtle phenomenological description with causal explanation, and without violating the integrity of evaluation. And it is possible for anthropology to study values without becoming arbitrary and "subjective," to speculate on alternative models and tentative possibilities, without becoming less scientific.

It is a cooperative partnership of approaches with different traditions, different information, different data and different ways of posing problems, that we suggest and will try to carry out in this admittedly very exploratory survey. We do not propose the merger of anthropology and philosophy, but rather a working partnership which avoids any jostling for primacy, or quarrels over vested rights in either methods or problems. We hope by such an enterprise to establish "coordinates" for the more systematic mapping of particular moralities, to explore more explicitly the relations of morality to cultural patterns and social processes, and to see how philosophic issues of ethical theory become refined and reformulated when their cultural content is made manifest.

Chapter II

THE MARK OF THE MORAL

THERE IS, of course, some sense in which we all know what we are talking about when we talk about morality. But this is not adequate for comparative study. How can we be sure that what we have in mind is what we find in other peoples; or that translation in familiar moral terms is true to their language? By what mark shall we know "the moral"?

In this area the anthropologist has no definite guide-posts of his own. He may use the term "moral" occasionally, but if he does, he does so without precise analysis, sometimes to imply strong emotional bonds or religious support, sometimes to refer to public opinion as a major sanctioning mechanism, and so forth. Anthropology has no established definitions of the moral, nor even any body of common ascriptions. Indeed, to anthropologists morality has, perhaps, seemed more a dimension or aspect of living than a separate department with institutions of its own. Certainly, we do not find specialized groups to carry it out, nothing to correspond to a priesthood or a police force. There are no buildings for ethics, nor visible tokens of it like shell money or a witch's herbal bag. Apart from education, it is hard to find common institutional forms peculiarly dedicated to it. Perhaps Chinese anthropologists, with the books of Confucius as their guide, might have been quicker to single out morality for attention and

7

more able to identify it than we westerners have been; in any case we certainly have not done so.

Philosophers, on the other hand, have plenty of definitions. The trouble is, they have too many; controversy permeates the very starting-points. Some look for a quality in consciousness to be taken as the mark of the moral experience—for the *absoluteness* with which the moral overrules all other considerations in human feeling, or for the *authoritativeness* of conscience or precept; or, in a quite different direction, for the *sense of aspiration,* of being drawn to an ideal. Some find the mark of the moral in an *intellectual* experience of the *meaning* of ethical terms. Others look to indefinable *intuitive* particular *judgments* of right and wrong. Still others turn to an *evaluative reckoning,* taking moral judgment to be an appraisal of means to a specified end—happiness, or resolution of problems, or liberating growth. Some use specific emotions to mark the moral, while others stress some requiredness in the field of awareness. There are ethics social and ethics individual, ethics rigid and ethics critical, ethics negative and ethics positive.

The diversity of trends in assigning the mark of the moral may fruitfully be put into two broad categories, which we shall call Ethics Wide and Ethics Narrow. These seem to involve divergent broad hypotheses about the place of moral phenomena in human life.

Ethics Wide assumes that moralities are part and parcel of the whole field of human endeavor and striving. It poses inquiry conceptually in terms of the search, either by the individual or the group, for man's *good* in the sense of what he aims at, what goals he finds worthwhile, what values appear and are stabilized in his experience. There are all sorts of human "values"—any interest, any pleasure, any conception of the desired and the desirable, anything fitting or attractive or serviceable may come to rank as a value for human beings. Moral values constitute simply one part of the field. They may be differentiated by their reference to personal character, and their special relevance to desirable forms of interpersonal relations or social organization. Or they may be the values that play an organizing role in the whole field. Or they may have no particular unity beyond some broad servicing role in the achievement and maintenance of fundamental individual and social well-being.

Ethics Wide, therefore, stresses the investigation of the widest possible context. It expects that accounts of virtues, obligations, sanctions, feelings and so forth, will be geared in the long run to descriptions of human values and modes of achieving or realizing them. It sets no initial barrier to the domains into which one may have to go in tracking down the nature and tasks of ethics. Any account of man, whether it comes from biology or theology, may present itself as a candidate for providing insight into morality.

Ethics Narrow, on the other hand, limits the scope of inquiry into moral phenomena. Conceptually it pushes to the fore the idea of *obligation* or *duty*. Values, it says, are far too broad, far too promiscuous. Only those that *ought to be* or *ought to be realized* come within the scope of morality. Beyond, there may be questions of interest, even of importance for human needs and goals, but these are not morality. Descriptively, Ethics Narrow focusses on the moral experience, moral judgment, moral feelings, of the individual. It wants a systematic picture of these sentiments and responses. At times this has meant construing man's moral feelings as complex sympathy reactions, at times as finely-drawn conscience-responses. Ethics Narrow is more prone than Ethics Wide to insist on a unique defining mark or characteristic of the moral in terms of personal consciousness—though there has been no agreement on exactly what this mark is to be.

The complaint most often found in Ethics Narrow against Ethics Wide is that it is not faithful to the phenomena of human experience, that it shifts to the description of the causes or functional relations of the moral, or to ways of supporting and justifying it once it exists, but that such questions can properly be pressed only after the moral has been specifically identified descriptively in a way true to experience and to common usage. Causal inquiry and the study of wider role relations are thus kept off at arm's length and their moral relevance considered suspect. Ethics Wide, on the other hand, is suspicious of the diversity of descriptions in Ethics Narrow. Instead of trying to get agreement on an initial definition, it prefers to plunge in anywhere and go on, because it believes that a systematic picture will come only in seeing the relations of the wider context.

In the long run it will probably be found that Ethics Wide is too wide, but Ethics Narrow is clearly too narrow. It furnished a useful corrective against widespread reductive tendencies, and has properly stressed the need for careful phenomenal description, but it has nevertheless misconceived the precise relations of phenomenal qualities, functions and causes, and has thus unduly isolated the study of morality. The search for causes and functions can often help us identify and distinguish more sharply the variety of qualities involved in consciousness, prompting us to press for distinctions where uniformity was taken for granted. It is just as in the search for the mark of health. One can start with pain as the obvious, even blatant experience that is to constitute a mark of ill-health, and then trace the way it functions as a warning-signal of underlying disturbances. But there is also the glow of health, and the ability to function in a variety of "normal" activities without "undue" fatigue. The doctor's diagnostic skill may be needed to distinguish the glow of health from the flush of fever. And decades of psychological labor have been required to establish that certain forms of anxiety are marks of ill-health, quite as reliable as the stab of pain. Or again, only the growth of medical knowledge shows what painless inner changes may bring the body to death's door. What merit would contemporary theory find in a controversy as to whether pain is to be regarded as the primal mark of ill-health?

So too in morals. We cannot jump to the conclusion that there is a single qualitative mark of the moral and debate whether it is the pointing finger of duty or the glow of the ideal. For there are other and more complex possibilities among which only investigation can decide. For example, there might be a family of personally and culturally variable experiences, culled from the whole array of human emotional possibilities, combining different elements in complex configurations. And they might be a family either by resemblance or by being made out of the same components or even only because they have taken turns at doing a similar job of keeping human conduct from straying too far away from what is socially necessary. Perhaps also in each people it has mattered less what was the distinct combination doing the job than that the distribution converged to get the job done. If such possibilities are not to be ruled out, then Ethics Narrow may be misleading, running the risk of narrowing the image of man's morality to what a given culture can see when it looks into the mirror!

It is interesting to note that in three recent books in ethical theory by philosophers who have worked with anthropological data, there are three different marks of the moral employed. MacBeath, in *Experiments in Living* (1952), underscores concern with the whole of life, not merely one fragmentary part or purpose, as a central mark. Brandt gears his investigation of the Hopi (1954) to mapping the quality of individual moral experience. Ladd, analyzing Navaho ethical structure (1957) in terms of their ethical discourse, uses as the mark of the ethical that its prescriptions have "superiority" and "legitimacy." The significant thing, however, is that despite their starting with different conceptions, each is led in practice to cast a very wide net, and to come up with a great deal of refined moral description, covering far more of life than the initial definition or analysis suggested would be relevant.

We too shall cast a wide net, erring on the more inclusive side wherever there is doubt about dividing marks. The problem of how sharply distinctions can be made in different areas between the moral and the non-moral—say between moral prohibitions and religious tabus, between moral sanctions and different kinds of social ostracism, between sheer desires and goals that are moral ends, between downright anger and moral indignation, and so on—is itself one of the questions to be explored on a comparative basis, not to be settled in advance. At the present point the greater danger is that of a narrowing ethnocentrism—of forcing the criteria and selective patterns of one morality, upon those of another. By comparison, there is less harm in operating with multiple criteria which may stretch too far. Moreover, marking out our field for ethical inquiry is not so difficult as surveying its exact borders. The area is there if not the formal pinpoint; and even what different philosophers discuss but rule out wins a place in the field by its mere candidacy. At worst we shall have scooped in material that may in a later systematization of the whole field be sent packing as beyond bounds.

Fortunately we do not embarrass the anthropologist by giving him such initial freedom. He has an excellent example to follow right in his own domain. The use of an inclusive concept rather than a narrow criterion has proved fruitful in the highly comparable field of religion. If the anthropologist interested in primitive religion had limited his inquiries to cultures whose religions fit some definition narrowly modelled on special aspects of our own religion, he would have had to limit his studies to very few cultures indeed—those which had a belief in a single god, or at most several clearly personalized gods; or to religions that were in some significant sense "spiritual," concerned with morality and the search for goodness, or with love and faith. And many people take such a stand, regarding other people as "superstitious" rather than religious. Instead, using a very wide implicit working definition, something like "everything having to do in any way with man's relation to and reliance on some sort of supernatural forces," anthropologists have discovered an amazing variety in man's religious practices and religious experiences. They have described and analyzed the trance of the temple dancer in Bali and the shaman in Siberia, the ecstatic possession of the priestess in West Africa, the personal vision experience of Plains Indians, and the carefully memorized chant of the garden magician in Melanesia. They have seen fear and friendship, mechanical acceptance and near-contempt line up beside our "awe and wonder" as acceptable religious emotions. They have found gods who can be manipulated, bribed, cajoled as well as implored, and religious behavior based on concepts of the supernatural that have no gods or spirits at all, only a generalized power as impersonal as electricity. They have found religions which were oriented to success in the hunt, or to fertility, to health or long life. But through it all they have found emerging a general pattern of religion as supportive of man in his areas of greatest weakness and necessity, a bulwark against the unknown, and a support to social institutions. They have thus been able to find some unity underlying the multiplicity of what seemed initially quite different phenomena.

Anthropologists will have to follow a parallel path to resolve the dilemma in ethical inquiry. They will not be confused by the fact that other peoples do not observe our moral codes. Naive commentators, finding cannibalism, or infanticide, or a great deal of permitted premarital sexual license, were prone to say that many primitive peoples had no moral codes. This was reenforced by the discovery that most of these "savages" had no obvious concern with saving their souls, no anxious worry over guilt and sin, and had gods who didn't seem to mete out praise and blame—indeed were sometimes themselves guilty of the most indecent behavior. Yet strangely enough even these supposedly cruel and immoral savages were also reported to be gentle and considerate of their friends, hospitable, generous and extremely trustworthy. Their codes might differ from ours, and from each other's, but each apparently was loyally subscribed to. It is true that they might scalp their enemies, but only according to the strictest rules of war; and they fed the hungry, respected the aged, and lent their wives to fellow-tribesmen with the most gracious good-will.

Under these conditions, it makes more sense to think of such patterns as constituting different moral codes, rather than as not being moralities at all. Certainly, they overlap our morality in many respects. For each code involves honorable behavior, orderly and sometimes even sensitive behavior, concerned with doing right according to some accepted standards, and judging others by the same code; it involves approved traits of character, virtues and vices, as well as rules of good and bad behavior, and ideas concerning the whys and wherefores of at least some of the principles involved. There is often considerable group involvement in maintaining the code, including educating children in conformity with it, and treating conformists and offenders with required degrees of reward, punishment, social praise or blame. We cannot exclude any such behavior from our survey in advance because the rules are not the same as our own, or because the immediate appeal in support of conformity is to the needs of the group or the standards followed by the ancients, rather than the salvation of individual souls. Instead, we must explore precisely these varieties, to see how different they really are from our own, and what order we can discover underlying them. If we want to know whether there is any limit to the possible range of rules and sanctions that men in society have hit upon as basic guides, or whether there are any causal or functional relations between different parts of a morality, or between moralities and other aspects of culture, we cannot limit ourselves in advance to such behavior as is given the cachet of approval by the gods, or concerns man's conscience, or is set apart by any other simple single criterion. For it is precisely our desire to discover whether the structure of man's conscience has everywhere the same twinge of remorse, or whether there are other ways in which man weighs his duties, or seeks to build a good life, and how cultures function where it is men rather than the gods who are believed to determine the right and the good.

What topics then shall we take as falling within the description of the morality of a people? Certainly, we should look for injunctions and prescriptions about what is or is not to be done, that is, for rules of required or approved, prohibited or disapproved behavior. We should look for character-traits and attitudes that are praised or blamed, as well as goals of conduct that are regarded as acceptable or unacceptable, experiences that are taken to be desirable or undesirable. (These are the types of content that in our morality are referred to as rules of right and wrong, virtues and vices, goods and evils and ideals.) We should look for the way in which such content is structured in the life and thought of the people. For one thing, we may expect that each morality will mark out its membership—those who are to count in its reckonings and take part in its proceedings. We should want to see what marks it employs in this delineation. Again, we should look for the terms and concepts that carry on the business of enjoining or prescribing, prohibiting and approving, praising and blaming, finding desirable and undesirable. Having found these, we should see how moral discourse is shaped and systematized, what standards are articulated and what form they take. We should want to probe for what people say when pressed about their judgments in this domain, what justifications they use. We should want to find out what sanctions operate in the development and maintenance of the conduct that is enjoined, what specific feelings carry the job of sanctioning or of identifying acceptable or unacceptable paths. Finally, we should want to see how this whole aspect of life coheres or holds together, and how various kinds of rules and structures are related to other aspects of the life of the community.

Such studies span a number of areas that are sometimes distinguished terminologically, though not in any very precise or generally standardized way. There is, for example, a kind of division of labor between "morality" and "ethics." It is customary to use the term "morality" for the content-description of a moral code, reserving the term "ethics" for the more reflective probing of structure and basic principles. Both can be used in a descriptive way, as when we speak of the morality of a given people and of its ethical principles. Or both can be used in a normative way by those who are asserting their own moral commitments or are engaged in actual valuation and critical evaluation. In recent times there has emerged a concept of "meta-ethics." Originally used for an analytic study of the logical-linguistic structure of ethical theorizing, it has tended to be assimilated to any over-and-above study of ethical processes—a kind of science *of* ethics, just as one has a science of religion and a science of science itself. In this widest sense, meta-ethics would include the psychology of ethics and the sociology of ethics as well as the analysis of logical structure in ethics, and probably embrace comparative ethics as well. In this respect it would not be very different from ethical theory broadly conceived as involving all possible perspectives that could throw light on the phenomena, and might scarcely warrant a terminological addition. In any case, our present studies will follow problems of content and structure without special regard for provincial boundaries with terminological signs. For it is an integral part of our task to see how far the interpenetration of areas is required to illuminate the materials and issues.

We shall be concerned at first primarily with the content of moralities. We shall consider questions which have been raised about the extent of uniformity and the meaning and significance of divergence in human morality. Selected examples of moral rules and virtues and principles will be explored in the attempt to work out the ways in which moral content is to be understood in the context of on-going human living. Then we shall go on to take apart the structure of moralities, and see what methods of analysis can throw light on this and what kinds of researches are needed to understand it better. While some questions of evaluation will be dealt with throughout, Chapter XV will attempt to draw some lessons for problems of ethical evaluation in the contemporary world. And Chapter XVI will offer retrospective philosophical reflections on the enterprise in which we have been engaged throughout the book.

Chapter III

THE RANGE OF MORAL DIFFERENCES
AND THE QUEST FOR UNIVERSALS

THE IMPACT of anthropology has been felt very sharply in our ordinary thinking about morality. It has become a matter of common knowledge that people's standards, their actual moral rules and ideas about good and bad behavior, vary enormously. Just as our more or less literate children today all know that the Eskimo rub noses as a sign of greeting and affection, so we—their more sophisticated elders—know that Eskimo ideas of marital fidelity are different from our own, that they exchange their wives freely, lending bed and wife with equal hospitality to visiting friends. We know that such contraventions of our attitudes—toward adultery or lying or killing or toward virtually any rule we accept—are extremely common among the peoples of different cultures of the world. We know that not all people are shocked and indignant at the things which shock us. A little less confidently, we realize that they may instead be shocked at some aspects of our behavior which seem to us either desirable or "natural" and morally neutral—like our failing to share our daily bread with all our needy friends and neighbors, or allowing old people to waste away of painful diseases.

The actual range of the differences anthropology has discovered is enormous, and we cannot even begin to chart it here. There are societies in which it is required that you eat your deceased friend or brother to show your respect for him; others in which a cannibal feast on an enemy is an everyday event, and supplying this special game for the larder a required mark of adult status. There are societies where to eat your own crops, grown in your own garden, or the game bagged by your own hunting efforts, is out of the question, wrong in all the ways in which stealing is wrong in our own morality— offensive to gods and men, indicative of a generally bad character, ringed around with evil consequences both social and supernatural—in short, a form of wickedness so wrong that for the average man it is not usually even an admitted temptation. And there are other societies where a man will die of some compound of shame, guilt, remorse or fear if he finds that he has carelessly eaten a guinea hen with a forbidden pattern of markings on its feathers. There are societies where the young are permitted far more sexual freedom than we would allow, but where no man may decently eat in the presence of anyone but a very close relative. And others where extra-marital sex relations between mature adults are ordinarily of no moral import whatsoever—matters entirely of the desires and preferences of the parties involved—but become horrifying scandals if they are engaged in at some disapproved time or place.

The same kind of variety that is found in peoples' rules of behavior is found in their ideals of character, in their concepts of virtue and vice and in their goals of life. Anger and shouting may be offensive, abominable to the gods and dangerous; or they may be an admired demonstration of strength of character, pointed to for children to emulate as a model of respected masculine behavior.

Plains Indian honors go to the young warrior brave enough
to go through the lines of an enemy encampment to steal
a tethered horse. To a warrior in another part of the
world that would be foolhardy; his own bravery can include ambush, or sudden treachery, and most certainly
the good sense of running away from danger. Others
abhor fighting altogether and do all they can to minimize
it. Among the Trobriand islanders of the South Pacific
a basic code of mutual obligation is so ingrained that a
man will abandon a day's highly paid pearl diving for a
puzzled white trader in order to do a day's fishing for an
inland neighbor in return for a few yams or other farm
produce, because the obligations to a trading partner must
always be fulfilled. But their neighbors from the nearby
island of Dobu who also live by a complicated system of
trade relations, consider any cheating one can actually get
away with as a mark of the greatest shrewdness, an admired
stepping-stone to success. To have enough to eat, to have
sons, and to die in respected old age on one's own ancestral land, is the conscious goal of some peoples' striving,
while others are concerned with wealth or glory or power,
and will see such pursuits as the proper aim of a good life.

Anthropologists have found that differences go far
beyond these matters of specific rules and regulations, or
even goals and values. They reach into any and every part
of the phenomena and structure of morality. There are
different kinds of sanctions to support moral codes. In
one society shame and ridicule may be open weapons, and
public opinion a highly charged deterrent pressure, while
in another a man's neighbors will be very little concerned
with his breaches of the moral code, shrugging them off
with "Well, what can you do? That's just the kind of
man he happens to be." There are differences in the

systematizations, the justifications and rationalizations which people use, and in the basic values and world attitudes which underlie or elaborate their codes. Some people have gods who are malicious, and unconcerned with human morals, while others worship supernaturals who have the same kind of concern with men's behavior that we traditionally consider appropriate. For some people moral issues are explicit, verbalized, central; for others they are seldom considered central in decision situations. The structure of conscience itself, it now appears, may not be quite the same for all people; perhaps some mechanisms of pure fear, and prudence, combined with a total lack of concern with internal standards, may be the picture for at least some of the societies in the world.

We shall concern ourselves later with more detailed examination of some of these areas of difference, and their significance for ethical theory. Meanwhile, however, we must note that this picture of sweeping differences to be found in any part of the moral field on which the student sets his sights was one of the first contributions anthropology made to the pool of knowledge of the developing human sciences during the early part of the twentieth century. Of course it was not really a new discovery. The ancients had known it all along, and careful thinking about European morals over the centuries from classic times through the Middle Ages and the rise of modern times had perforce to note that there had been great changes in moral standards—from the condemnation of usury to the elevation of finance capitalism, from status-acceptance (the idea of filling the station to which one had been "called") to the ideal of competitive individual success. The ethical theories of the western world also reveal a vast array of differences. The good life of

Aristotle, with its harmonious balance, would seem insipid to a Nietzschean in his pursuit of the heroic; stoical inner peace, in the sense of playing one's role whatever the cost, would seem folly to a Hobbesian who sees man's morality as a compromise in the predatory quest for power, wealth and prestige. The rational temper of Socratic virtue contrasts markedly with the pious humility of the Christian, the loyalty and gratitude attitudes of the feudal order, the sobriety and thrift of the early Protestant ethic, or the industriousness, prudence, and often calculating beneficence of the Benthamite.

But somehow the significance of differences in moral standards did not deeply color modern thought until recently. The philosophical differences were obscured by the fact that each morality in turn claimed to be the true one, and each theory the correct one. Eighteenth century thinking was concerned with establishing the natural rights and properties of men. Rousseau, for example, had written of a romanticized "noble savage" who had our virtues undistorted by the corruption of civilization. The nineteenth century, more inclined to see the differences, tended to disregard them, either holding the "savage" to be altogether outside the domain of moral and religious feelings until the missionary came to convert him; or, in its more reflective expressions, assuming that he was somehow at a lower evolutionary stage.

In any case, the shock effect of the anthropological writings with their emphasis on the sweep and range of cultural differences, coupled with the insistence that these data were relevant to any thinking about human nature and human society, was very great. It was felt in sociology, in psychology, in the whole field of the social sciences. Sumner's thinking (1906) —"the standards are in the mores," and "the mores can make anything right"—a complete kind of cultural relativism, became quite pervasive. Anthropologists wrote of different "patterns of culture" and textbooks of social psychology threw out their lists of instincts to write instead of the differences between the Zuñi Indians, or the Kwakiutl, and ourselves. Popular attitudes to morality, at that time in a state of flux, seized upon and reflected these positions. If different people are angry and disapproving about different things, what validity can there be about any one of them? Why bother to be angry or disapproving about anything? If chastity is not a universal value, why value it at all? If the Samoans practise premarital promiscuity, why should we not experiment with it too?

Clearly anthropology was not uniquely responsible for the recasting of the various disciplines in these relativist terms. The mutual influence among the human sciences which were carving out their respective areas and charting their positions in the study of man was, of course, great, and it all tended in this direction. Behaviorist psychology in an extreme form was making a very similar point, discarding human nature as a theoretical construct, and starting instead with a concept of a person as beginning as a perfectly clean slate, a being who must learn all that he would ever know, including the shape of all his feelings and sentiments, through rather mechanical learning experiences, particularly repetitive association. At the same time, philosophy was expressing a sharp positivist trend, discarding as metaphysical nonsense a great part of traditional abstraction, and consigning all value assertions to the domain of simple emotional expression. Sociology was going through a similar phase of new discovery, a process of housecleaning marked more by a tearing down than a building up. All together contributed to a growing picture of mankind and his ways as the result of chance historical circumstances, largely random and whimsical, perhaps even unintelligible.

Of course this is not the only, nor necessarily the most sensible, way to look at differences. The discovery that there are other ways than our own, and that these seem pretty well grounded in other peoples' attitudes and habits, need not make us say, "Our ways, if not absolute and obvious, are no good, and neither for that matter are any one else's." We might instead say, "Whatever other peoples' different views, our own are best." This, as a matter of fact, is a view that some among us have always held to. And it is the reaction in most other cultures to the awareness of differences. Or we might take the more sophisticated view so well expressed by a Hopi Indian in his autobiographical discourse (Sun Chief, 1942, p. 178): "I could see that the old people were right when they said that Jesus Christ might do for modern Whites in a good climate, but that the Hopi gods had brought success to us in the desert ever since the world began." In short, each people has different ways, and does best to stick to its own. That indeed was the path anthropology tended to take for a while, emphasizing the need to respect different cultures' varying ways as "equally valid patterns of life" (Benedict, 1934a, p. 278). Or we might take the most difficult path of all: critical assessment.

We cannot here examine the conditions in our own culture that made the general revolt against absolutes so appealing in the earlier part of the present century. Moral rigidities and changed social conditions, the disillusionment of the generation that followed World War

I, a sense of the failure of dominant institutions to ensure progress, the doubt cast by the rapid growth of knowledge on many a cherished belief—all of these no doubt played a part. In similar fashion, the extremes of economic depression, the conflict with the Nazi world view, the failure to achieve peace after World War II and the intensity of ideological issues since that time, combined with the menace of atomic warfare, have provoked an insecurity that has become a base for a renewed search for absolutes. This has had its effect on the popular scene in a trend toward conformity and a search for safe anchors for ethics. In the sciences of man there has also been a renewed interest in looking for uniformities, for some common human elements that lie beyond the differences. The possibly wishful aspect in this new direction of inquiry does not invalidate the search—for the prior emphasis on differences may very well have been excessive—but it does suggest the need that it be conducted with great care. And indeed there is a greater sophistication about it which suggests the possibilities of a sober reckoning rather than a purely pendular swing (cf. A. Edel, 1955).

In this renewed inquiry the sciences of man have profited jointly by the advances in their various branches. The psychologist who has discarded his outmoded lists of specific instincts takes up his search for the common human at the level of common dynamic processes and potentialities, rather than simple uniformities of behavior. He works to integrate historically conditioned, learned ways of thinking, feeling and wanting into his accounts of human nature. The anthropologist and sociologist too, while still interested in differences, emphasize the "common denominators" of culture and "invariant properties of social interaction" (cf. Kluckhohn,

1953). They are engaged in renewed attempts to understand the trends of culture history and the causal and functional principles that operate in it. In morality particularly, many are reasserting the common meanings and common goals that may be seen beneath the differences in moral codes and moral patterns. This is of course not altogether a new approach.

Franz Boas himself, often presented as the arch-demon of relativism in anthropology—largely because of his supreme distaste for making generalizations in history that were too sweeping to be supported by verifiable evidence —pointed out that the ethics of the in-group provide a kernel of common moral motivation beneath the surface variety of behaviors. For, he wrote (1930), "The social obligations that develop in intimate family life . . . may be observed everywhere." Despite differences in the way groups treat outsiders, "the standard of ethical behavior toward members of one's own group is regulated by subordination of the individual to group interests and by recognition of the rights of other members of the group." And Ruth Benedict, certainly steeped in a relativist perspective, wrote (1934b), "Mankind has always preferred to say, 'It is morally good,' rather than 'It is habitual' and the fact of this preference is matter enough for a virtual science of ethics." And she went on to say, "It is quite possible that a modicum of what is considered right and what wrong could be disentangled that is shared by the whole human race."

This kind of view is now moving to a position of central interest and concern. Although some anthropologists—Melville Herskovits, for example—are sceptical of the very quest for a common human morality, as itself culture-bound (cf. 1958), many do share the view that some common base can be found. A few have even tried to pinpoint some actual areas of common content. Linton (1952), for example, has argued that "societies everywhere have moral principles in common but with different emphases." All societies, he says, "deplore incest and rape," demand "loyalty to some social group," and hold "disloyalty a vice," control aggression to some extent, expect truth in certain situations, as when oaths are taken, and expect people to meet obligations involved in exchange of goods and services. And Kluckhohn in a similar vein (1955, p. 672) writes, "Every culture has a concept of murder . . . The notions of incest and other regulations upon sexual behavior, of prohibitions upon untruth under defined circumstances, of restitution and reciprocity, of mutual obligations between parents and children—these and many other moral concepts are altogether universal."

Others, working in related disciplines, have also looked in various ways for common moral bases. Mac-Beath (1952, ch. 2), approaching anthropological data as a philosopher, does not believe that one finds specific moral rules or principles that all societies have in common, but he does claim that one can see, in the varying "operative ideals" which act as guides to conduct in the world's varying cultures, a common "formal ideal," a striving for a very general common human goal of satisfaction or fulfillment. And Morris Ginsberg (1957, ch. 7) analyzes some of the ways in which differences in moralities may be reduced by recognizing that they are often different means to similar ends, different weightings assigned to common principles, or based on differences in social contexts. However, he maintains that there are some fundamental differences that remain, differences in levels of moral sensitivity, in the "conception of the human person as such," and total rejection of cruelty per se, which are emergent developments of recent social history, rather than merely wider applications of older principles. Similarly, Karl Duncker (1939), examining moral experience from the perspective of Gestalt psychology, postulates the existence of common human valuations, which can be discovered by probing under the variations in the meaning and institutional settings of acts. People who condone or require infanticide, he maintains, are not disagreeing about the wrongness of killing babies. They just do not consider what they are doing as baby-killing. For them, the new-born are not human until they have breathed, or undergone some ritual treatment; or a malformed infant is held to be an evil spirit. Anthropologists have seen too much variety in human moral attitudes to accept such uniform moral perceptions as established. They agree, of course, that one must look for varying meanings and interpretations; contextual interpretation is their basic methodological stock in trade. But they are sceptical of finding behind *every* cannibal rite some moral altruism, behind every sadistic practice an offering to a—regrettably—demanding god, behind every war the feeling of a holy cause. There are such cases, of course, but they are inclined to wonder if this does not prove merely that man is prone to paint himself in pleasant colors, to disguise cruelty rather than abjure its practice, in short that man is, perhaps, less moral than moralizing.

The anthropologist then does not find it fruitful at this point to look for common moral perceptions and instinctive moral reactions. Instead, in looking for universal moral rules and for an understanding of differences, he pursues a mode of analysis which combines psychological with biosocial and historical factors. His general argument is somewhat as follows. The patterns of human social interaction, however deep their biological and psychological roots, are not simply direct instinctual expression, or the playing out of a built-in psychological drama. They are, as Kluckhohn puts it (1953, p. 520), "somewhat distinct answers to essentially the same questions posed by human biology and by the generalities of the human situation." They are complex answers, ways which have been built up over time, "experiments in living," to use MacBeath's telling phrase, that different cultures have worked out, in the course of which new and varying needs have themselves been generated. There is room for wide variety in the kinds of lives men build for themselves, but certain minimal standards must be met if these "experiments" are to be successful at all. Each culture must provide patterns of motor habits, social relations, knowledge and beliefs, such that it will be possible for men to survive. Everywhere there must be techniques for making a living, patterns of mating, of mutual help, ways of defining who is a friend and who a foe, and of dealing with each, ways of coping with sickness and old age and death—and means for learning all of these ways. And there are not only common requirements imposed by common problems, but common psychological processes and mechanisms through which they operate and on which they react (cf. Malinowski, 1944). Birth and death, love and sorrow and fear are the lot of all men; all are capable of desires and dreams, and use symbolic thinking, identification, reaction-formation. This common human nature sets limits to the forms that any experiments

in living can take, to the possible techniques of motivation, the scope of sympathy, the effectiveness of sanctions.
Common needs, common social tasks, common psychological processes, are bound to provide some common
framework for the wide variety of human behaviors that
different cultures have developed. And part of this framework includes the need for a certain measure of cooperation and conformity in the behavior of the members of
any society. Those who live and work together must go
along the paths charted by the customs and expectations
of the group not just through external coercive pressures
but through motivations which are to some degree built
into their habits and attitudes. The members of a society must share some common values and accept some bond-
age to their common goals and goods. "No man is an
island" nor can be, for to survive means to have grown
up and to live in society, to share its pressures and to share
in the "direct experience of the inevitability of interdependence between men in society" (Fortes, 1949, p. 346).
And so it is not unreasonable to expect nor surprising to
find that among all men, amid all the historically developed cultural diversity, there is not only a nuclear
family and some extended kinship, work and dancing, art
and religion—but also *morality*. And morality includes
common structural patterns, common mechanisms, and,
where social institutions are parallel, some detailed similarity in content.

Such a general approach as we have been describing is not so much a particular hypothesis as what has
sometimes been called a hypothesis-schema. It does not
give us a quick touchstone for discovering common moral
traits, nor for understanding all moral differences; it is,
rather, a suggestive guide to formulating hypotheses

about morality in relation to human needs. The anthropologist working in a sophisticated vein from such a perspective would not start with a ready-made check-list of biosocial demands. He knows that such a list would need to be constantly revised, both because of our increasing knowledge about the nature of man,—as in the increasing evidence of the role of emotional factors in health and disease,— and because new developments in technology or group living and population aggregation change the structure of human needs—as in the past land-space demands changed with the abandonment of a hunting economy, or irrigation agriculture posed new problems about access to water. The anthropologist knows that he has to study the actual, and changing, character of such needs, not merely to assume them. Nor can he assume any specific fixed role in the moral domain for needs of different sorts. He knows that the same end may be sought through differing means, and the pursuit of the same means may represent different goals; that men's actual paths of life may be compromises or resultants of the convergence of values whose subtle interplay may not easily be read off from the observed results; and that he must understand his data in a context of possible change, rather than permanent stability. How malleable different needs may actually prove to be; how they will intermesh with each other, and with historically-developed institutions and goals; whether their respective sweep in affecting moral development will be vast or small, determining, limiting, or merely exacting of a high price if violated, are empirical questions to be investigated, not prejudged. It is such questions which this general approach suggests as problems to be formulated for empirical research.

This complex task has certainly not been accomplished for the study of morality. It has, rather, barely been begun. We can deal here with only a few indications of the way it may be attempted on a comparative basis. We propose in the next few chapters to do an exploratory survey of some familiar areas of moral concern, to see how far this kind of method promises to carry us in understanding the content of moral prescriptions and proscriptions.

Chapter IV

ON BEING A GOOD MOTHER

Let us take as our first sample exploration a common human moral obligation which is deeply grounded in human needs, biological, physiological and social—the moral obligation for a mother to take care of her children. This is a universal imperative, and very pervasive in its moral implications, for it serves as the groundwork not just for restrictions, but for positive ideals and virtues. The idealized picture of mother-love which flourishes in our culture is only one instance of the way in which this area can generate moral sentiments.

The absolute character of the need that is served is obvious. Children need the sheltering care of a mother if they are to grow up at all; and we know too that the dependent human infant requires more than physical sustenance. It has emotional needs as well, which must be met if it is to grow to any kind of human adulthood. No society which failed to provide all these elements in the care of its children could possibly survive; and on the whole it seems that this must be provided by a mother or a very nearly equal mother surrogate. Despite the existence of adequate forms of artificial feeding, no modern experimental substitute of nursery or creche has thus far proved satisfactory.

It is obvious that the moral precept, "Mothers should take good care of their children," has a further special status. For it is rooted not only in the child's needs, but also in what are clearly a rich set of positive values for the mother herself. We do not have to determine at this point just how far biological drives carry us toward an actual human "maternal instinct." This kind of question was debated very earnestly twenty years ago; anthropologists and psychologists then tended to agree that in the simplest mechanical sense, as of an untutored cat knowing how to lick her first brood into shape, human beings were without an "instinctive" endowment. A human mother needs to be shown how to cut the umbilical cord, and follows the arrangements peculiar to her particular culture about how and when to give her baby its first feeding, whether to suckle it randomly from either breast, or alternate them at different feedings, whether to offer a finger dipped in gruel for a young infant to suck, or to thrust a bolus of premasticated food into its passive mouth from her own, when it is a few months old; whether to carry it tied to her back, or in her encircling arms, or swaddled on a cradle-board; whether to treat it as tough or tender, how much to fondle it, and so on (cf. Mead, 1949, ch. 3).

How much this variation is refutation of instinct in the more flexible and sophisticated sense in which that term is now being used, how much we are dealing with a natural hormone-stimulated drive taking socially-cultivated outlets, how much indeed maternal behavior does depend on a girl's *learning* her role as a woman, need not really concern us here. It is enough for our purposes to recognize: (a) that there are physical and emotional satisfactions for the mother, either innate or capable of being readily cultivated, in caring for her baby; (b) that the dependency period of the mammalian infant, and more emphatically that of the human infant, is such that given abrogation of this function by the mother, unless an almost completely equivalent surrogate is provided, the infant cannot survive; and (c) that for some complex compound of psychological and possibly even also physiological reasons, which may or may not have culturally stereotyped bases, not all mothers automatically want to care for, fondle, and lovingly tend their newborn babies; and some may be helpless at going about it if they have had no experience with young babies.

We can, then, say that mothers' care of their children is necessary for social survival, and ordinarily satisfying to the mother, but that it is not absolutely and automatically provided for in the built-in makeup of every woman. The deep biological and psychological roots of maternal care must be nurtured and directed. Every culture must therefore provide an education in child-rearing, by example and character training, that will help the mother to want her biologically and socially dictated job and know how to go about it, and it must provide some sanctions and ideals by which to support her in the pursuit of this task. It does not, however, follow automatically that this must be true of *every* mother in a society; there must just be enough so that some, though not necessarily the largest possible, next generation will be provided for. Also, the pattern may be modified by providing substitute mothers for some categories, as in the upper class East European cultures of the recent past, where foster-mothers or "wet nurses" were so common. But with this limitation, the adjuration, "Mother, take good care of your children" ought to follow as a pretty universal agreed-upon principle; if any bio-social needs have an absolute structuring effect upon morality, surely this one must.

It is interesting therefore to notice that this principle does not appear writ large in every people's list of moral imperatives. This is not because it has no moral role, but because it is well enough rooted positively to be taken pretty much for granted. Our own decalogue found it necessary to adjure people to respect their parents, an important issue, no doubt, in a patriarchal authoritarian framework. (It is still, indeed, a problem in ours, although it is more likely to center around such issues as what kind of care to provide for aged dependent parents or questions of career and marriage choices as against helping at home, rather than simple matters of discipline and obedience.) But the decalogue culture did not, it seems, find it necessary to make an equivalent issue of principle of a mother's taking care of her child. That presumably needed no constant reiteration. Today the simple general statement would still not occur to most people if they were asked to make a summary of important moral principles. However, it is actually deeply operative, not only in relation to our judgments about violations, but also in many significant decisions that arise in the context of everyday living—questions of limitation of family size, of how much care a mother can delegate without feeling guilty about her performance of her role as a mother, of what is proper discipline, and more widely social questions such as whether children can properly be taken from parental custody, or whether one should prefer more advantages for one's own children instead of wider sharing of one's property for the benefit of really needy people at home or abroad. This indicates not only that the principle—"one ought to be a good mother"—is a genuine moral principle for us, but also that it is not a simple precept to interpret; we do not have built-in pointer-readings to tell us what it demands of us.

The matter becomes far more complicated when we look at it cross-culturally. The definition of a good mother, and of good child care, is ordinarily far more clearly indicated within most cultures than it is in our rapidly changing and sophisticated modern setting, but it varies enormously from one culture to another. A good mother may be expected to impose very severe disciplines, or to yield to the child's every mood and whim; she may be expected to feed him as much as possible, and a little more, or to teach him to curb his appetite, or limit it to some routine or timetable. The actual behavior of a "good mother" in one culture may horrify and shock the mother in another culture, equally concerned with child welfare. Whipping a child, weaning him by putting pepper on the breast, tying his hands to prevent masturbation, swaddling beyond the limits of any possible movement, even cutting off bits of his anatomy for some higher good, as in circumcision—all these are accepted practices, some our own, some other people's, which cannot but strike outsiders as refined bits of sadistic torture, though all are allegedly undertaken by their advocates as part of the good and normal practice of bringing up children.

Looking at such practices "contextually," from the point of view of the people who practise them, removes some of the contrast—but surely not all. Take, for example, the Plains Indian practice of pouring water into their children's noses to make them stop crying. Most Americans shudder at this; it strikes them as a wanton act of sheer cruelty. However, the Plains Indians are far from callous in their general attitude toward children. They treat their children with solicitude and affection, and indeed consider our practice of physically disciplining children—"spanking" them—as extremely offensive, seeing it not only as wanton cruelty, inflicting of pain on a young child by a large adult, but also as a blow to a child's pride and dignity. As they see their water treatment, by contrast, it is a brief precaution, a sharp clear method of handling children too young to be reasoned with in any way, used only because it is immediately effective in stopping them from crying. Living where an enemy war party might learn of the whereabouts of an encampment from a baby's crying, they must be sure of a child's absolute and automatic obedience in this respect; the alternative is the threat of destruction for all of them. Set in the context of love and pride in the child's accomplishment, such a training point is quite possibly less harmful to the child, less psychologically traumatic, than some of our "kindlier" techniques of humiliation, deprivation of affection, and measured punishment. This realization raises a significant point about evaluation. The fact that a particular pattern of behavior has been worked out by a given culture as a way of solving human needs does not necessarily mean that it is the best possible way of doing so, even under the other over-all social circumstances of that culture. Nor does it follow that because it is considered good in the context in which it occurs, there are not perhaps some very mixed motivations, as well as hidden psychological and social consequences, which an outside observer may perceive. It is precisely for the cultivation of such an outside-observer's perspective toward our own culture and its taken-for-granted value judgments and moral approvals and disapprovals that we need the anthropological laboratory most strongly in ethics. It is important to remember that the extent to which this common moral imperative—even with all these qualifications—actually does appear universally is an empirical question for research; it is not to be taken for granted as a logical necessity. A number of instances have appeared in anthropological literature which raise this factual question rather sharply about maternal care. One we can write off rather simply. The Alorese mother, we learn, provides what is comparatively a very inadequate kind of care for her babies. They are left at home from a very early age, while she goes off to work in the fields. We learn from Kardiner (1945, chs. 6-9) that this apparently has most traumatic lifelong consequences in their adequacy as people. We could raise questions about why the Alorese mother could not make the simple invention that so many other people do, faced with the same problem, and design a suitable carrying case for taking her infant along with her when she goes to work. But from the point of view of moral attitudes, we do know that the Alorese mother does not regard her neglectful behavior as ideal; she is concerned about the welfare of her child, and often spends long hours making it up to him for the previous day's neglect—a procedure which modern psychology may find as harmful as the neglect, but which at least leaves her innocent of the charge of being unconcerned about her child's well-being.

There are other instances which present us with more of a poser: notably, the Marquesan and Mundugumor mothers, both of whom have been described as indifferent, cold and rejecting (Linton, 1939; Mead, 1935, ch. 11). We know that there are some such mothers in our own society, but that is in contravention of the established code. But for the Marquesan and Mundugumor mothers these attitudes appear to be standardized. Mothers refuse to bear children, infanticide on a purely personal basis of not spoiling the mother's figure, is common—indeed the Mundugumor are reported to practise it sometimes out of spite against the husband's family line, which would claim the child if it were a girl—and when the children do live to be reared, the mothers are rejecting, harsh in handling the babies, quick to wean them, and so on.

Before we consider to what extent such data contradict a picture of a universal moral rule, we need to have the answers to a number of questions. For one thing, we need to know to what extent these patterns of behavior actually express or reflect moral attitudes. Are our accounts descriptions of prevalent but defiant practice, or standard and approved behavior? Practices cannot simply be equated with moral codes. Considerable contradiction between code and practice can be tolerated, as we well know from our own society,—though we do not as a matter of fact know how *much* contradiction, nor for how *long*, nor under *what* circumstances. So we need to know specifically by actual field inquiries pointed to such questions, whether these practices are justified or rationalized in any way, or are matters of no moral concern. What do the neighbors and the old people think of the rejecting and neglectful young mother? Are there any apparent social penalties, or other indications that she is disapproved, despite her temporary ascendance?

We might also ask what limits there are that operate to keep the practices within such bounds that some children are born and grow up. In the Marquesan picture it is very possible that we have class-differentiated attitudes, that the extreme picture may refer only to a particular segment rather than to the whole of the population. In Mundugumor, there is an apparent check on infanticide in the actual stake which the family of one of the parents has in the baby's survival. A woman's killing of her baby daughter will be checked by the careful surveillance of her husband's kinswomen present at the birth; their reasons, however, are reasons of their own interests, formulated in terms of the opposing rights of the different kin groups, not such more familiar moral considerations as the needs of the infant or the duties of motherhood, nor the wickedness of infanticide.

There is a further point to be considered. If given moral attitudes are part of the solution to universal biosocial needs, we must ask of any set of data which appears to contravene or limit the universal, how viable is this society in fact? Are these—to push our biological analogy to what may be a dangerous extent—moral mutations with a sickly complexion, destined to die out? There is certainly a striking impression that one cannot help deriving from the account available to us for the Mundugumor, that their cruelty and destructiveness were so great that, being a tiny group, they must surely have killed each other off if they had continued in the same way much longer.

We find, then, in our brief exploration, that mothers' care for their children, while it is an obvious minimal need, does not always take a very central conscious position of moral requiredness. It seems, rather, to be adequately supported in most cases by simple positive impulses prevalent in the normal interplay of family relationships under most conditions of character structure and general cultural values. Moral issues about it seem to rise more at stress points than as constant injunctions. We noted too that there were cases where goals of a different sort supervened; and that these require far more exploration to see to what extent, and under what limiting circumstances, such contraventions are really treated by the society as of no moral consequence, and if they are, to what extent such social forms are viable. It is by pushing forward in such key situations that we may be able to find out more fully how the biological and psychological needs of man actually serve as a foundation to generate or limit moral principles.

Chapter V

THE PROHIBITION AGAINST INCEST

Not all universals or near-universals are found by looking at the logic of the need-situation. There is at least one moral imperative whose ubiquity has long impressed observers directly; indeed, because of its many puzzling features and the wealth of ink poured out in analysis, one might almost better say, obsessed them. This is the prohibition against incest. Everywhere we find restrictions upon the mating of close relatives. And while we do not know that the restrictions everywhere involve the same kind of deep, dark revulsion which we recognize in our culture when we speak of the "horror of incest," we do know that their violation often brings grave penalties in its train. An incestuous couple may be killed, or driven forth from the community. Their offense may be seen as bringing a crescendo of ruin in its wake—disease, and deformed children, family tragedy of all sorts. Or incest may be viewed as a dangerous affliction which can be purified away only by degrading or tortuous ceremonies. Some people, questioned about incest, will express sheer disgust and disbelief at the possibility of such revolting acts: "Are we dogs, that we should do such things?" And violations of even the most superficial aspects of the incest tabu—like sitting on the same bench with one's sister—may be the occasions for vast ridicule and intense personal shame.

True, the definition of just *who* constitutes a close kinsman in this context varies a good deal. Even in Christendom there is a running debate about the propriety of the marriage of first cousins, and there are some sectarian differences about whether a sister-in-law is a prohibited mate or, as the Hebraic law holds, an ideal second mate. Among other peoples around the world there are all sorts of other variations. For example, a man may be permitted, or even required, to marry his first cousin if she is the daughter of his mother's brother, but may not even touch her if she is the daughter of his father's brother. Australian aborigines limit marriage to the members of one special quarter or even eighth of the tribal group, some of whom we would consider double first cousins, and others no kin at all; they shudder at the marriage of people one generation apart, but favor the marriage of great uncles to their own grand nieces! And so on and on and on, for various peoples and places.

But everywhere, behind all the variations, lies a common core: a ban on marriage and sex relations within the nuclear family. It is within this small unit that stringent incest tabus are to be found virtually everywhere. Mother-son mating is, so far as we know, universally disallowed; fathers may not marry their own daughters, and sexual contacts between them are ordinarily frowned upon, though intercourse is sometimes permitted or even required in special ritual contexts. Siblings too are normally forbidden to marry, or have sexual relations with each other. The only usual exception is that of offspring of families so noble that mixture with any other blood would be a pollution. Hawaii and Egypt and Peru all hit upon this device for maintaining the sacrosanct quality of the royal line—and the safety of the succession. But all of them limited this kind of marriage to the royal line; the marriage of ordinary brothers and sisters was banned, and its occurrence considered incestuous.

The small nuclear family is almost everywhere differentiated as a unit despite many variations in social structure, marriage patterns, and living arrangements. The picture may be obscured by peculiar forms of marriage, by frequent adoption, or by the enmeshing of the nuclear family in a wider kin group that lives and works together. But the small parent-child unit plays a significant role in relation to kinship organization, to the child's primary experiences, and the development of his social relationships. And it is this unit within which the common incest tabu prevails (cf. Murdock, 1949). The fact that exogamic restrictions take many different forms beyond this has tended to obscure the common core. But these varied extensions of the incest ban are themselves usually directly rooted in structural extensions of the primary group. They are extensions of primary incest barriers to further categories of people according to the logical canons of particular kinship systems. So, for example, in patrilineal societies distant relatives on the father's side are commonly barred from marriage because they are brothers and sisters by social definition. And where the family is embedded in a larger household group, it is often this widened "family" which is the exogamous group.

Though exogamic regulations tend to be direct extensions of nuclear family incest tabus, they are not to be identified with them. Neither their social significance nor their emotional meaning need be the same (cf. Seligman, 1950). Some of the confusion that has arisen over the study of incest regulations has come from the failure to differentiate different levels. Interestingly enough, the distinctions are quite clear in the differentiated attitudes toward incest violations which we find among many people. Among the Tallensi in West Africa (Fortes, 1949), for example, it is reported that the very thought of incest with one's mother is considered unbelievable. With one's sister it is impossible and ridiculous; no sane grown man could possibly be tempted to such ridiculous behavior. But a remote clan sister is in a different category altogether. Marriage with her is out of the question, by legal definition, but she is a deliciously attractive object of premarital attentions, which are all the more alluring because slightly illicit. It is quite usual for a girl to have a clan-mate as a lover; he may even be the one who later on acts for the family in arranging her marriage.

Similar distinctions, in varying forms, are reported from other parts of the world. Even in Australia, where breaches of the exogamic restrictions are considered so serious that offenders may be put to death, some technically "incestuous" matings are considered less disruptive than others. In these in-between cases the couple will merely suffer banishment for a time, and then be allowed to rejoin the community after a merely ceremonial or mock spearing. All of this indicates not that incest is a light matter in such social systems, but rather that extended exogamous bans are regarded differently from the regulations for very close kinsmen, which are often, though not universally, invested with strong affect. And it is quite likely that their causes and functions should be considered separately, too.

It has been suggested in the anthropological literature that the explanation of the ubiquitous incest tabu lies in the social advantage of exogamy. As the Dobuans so aptly put it, "If a man were to marry his sister, what would he do for a brother-in-law?" The whole structure of Dobuan economic duties and obligations is organized around marriage arrangements and the partnership of affinal kinsmen. Alorese comment points this up even more sharply; the reaction among the Alor to an actual case of brother-sister incest was, "From such a marriage you don't get any *mokos* (valuables)." Similar pictures could be outlined for many parts of the world. Certainly, there are social advantages to exogamy. Wide sharing of accumulated knowledge and skills, together with the organization of activities on an increasing scale of complexity, requires the interrelationship of a wide social group. Marriages between different kin groups are clearly an efficient way of organizing a wide nexus of crisscrossing affiliations, especially in a society organized along kin lines. No doubt exogamy has played an important part in human social progress, and its wide practice has roots in this usefulness (cf. Levi-Strauss, 1956).

But while considerations of this order throw light on the prevalence of complex exogamic regulations, they do not carry us very far into an understanding of the absolute prohibitions within the small family. True, avoiding inbreeding might have given small families too a social-survival advantage, by increasing the solidarity of wider groups and their participation in them; but this hardly seems sufficient to account for the strength of the attitudes toward incest within the family. It may be one factor, but can hardly be a total explanation of the wellnigh universal ban.

Nor does the popular view that rules against incest are based upon some realistic biological foundation—a kind of prescientific percipience about the harmful consequences of prolonged inbreeding—stand up well under scrutiny. It is true that many people formulate their arguments against incestuous marriages in terms of such consequences as the birth of deformed children. But then, incest may also be said to bring earthquakes, or, as among the Navaho, a kind of trembling called "moth sickness." Such folk-explanations and expectations can hardly be based on observation, though it is true that they may have deeper and more complex meanings than mere "tradition." In point of fact, no very obvious bad genetic consequences actually follow from the disregard of incest tabus. For one thing, in most populations the relative one is forbidden to marry may be no more closely related biologically than one who is designated a preferred mate. But in any case, in a small inbred population, the pool of gene variations is widely shared. A defective recessive in your own gene makeup will be shared by many other families, not just by your closest kinsmen; it might show up in any mating, not just in matings between siblings or cousins. Any small inbreeding population, whatever its rules about nuclear family incest, would be at much the same genetic disadvantage as isolated single families. They would perhaps be in even a worse way, since damaging recessive mutations would quickly spread throughout the population, rather than being confined to single families which would be neatly weeded out!

If incest tabus are not simple medical prescriptions nor to be fully explained as serving widened social-relationship needs, though that may have played some role, what other explanations can be adduced to explain their ubiquity, or strength and permanence? We are driven either to "instinct," some built-in human reaction against such matings, or to a very complex socio-psychological process rooted in common human experience. Obviously, there is no simple, direct instinctive revulsion against incest. Indeed, there seems rather to be a strong element of actual allure. The case records of any social welfare or policing agency, as well as the field records of many anthropologists, report the occurrence of incest, especially father-daughter, and sometimes brother-sister, when there are no strongly operative social sanctions against it. Dreams and infantile memories further suggest this. And myths and legends are often suffused with explicit or covert incestuous content. A standard Chiga riddle—and this is a culture with a strong incest ban—goes: "Which grass grows the sweetest?" and the answer is, "Your own sister's pubic hair." Folklore themes from many areas deal sympathetically with doomed incestuous lovers. Furthermore, many people do not share our view that brothers and sisters can be trusted together in situations which would be too tempting for other couples. Instead, we often find that their sexual distance is protected and guaranteed by the most rigorous rules of constant avoidance.

Incest tabus are, then, not based on simple automatic revulsion, some built-in disgust which makes such relations impossible, but are rather very complex phenomena, with roots in deep common human impulses and experiences, apparently including strongly ambivalent primary motivations. Just what these are, what they stem from, and how variable they are under different kinds of family-constellation situations, is the question which now needs careful cross-cultural examination, with the fullest battery of depth-psychological techniques, and great sophistication about varying patterns of social and emotional relationships. Such a field inquiry into what we may for convenient shorthand call the cultural variations and common bases in the oedipal drama and its resolution is barely in its infancy. There are many facets of inquiry which have been suggested. Malinowski, in one pioneering study (1927), questioning Freud's picture (1918) of the universality of the "Oedipus complex," suggested that the sibling tie is stronger in its allure than the parent-child attraction in Trobriand culture, as evidenced in their myths and other materials he collected. He traced this to such factors as the father's lack of frustrating authority, and to the full satisfaction of early attraction to the mother in prolonged breast-feeding. While his analysis is certainly over-simplified, it does suggest avenues of exploration in relation to social structure as well as early experience. Others have suggested paying more attention to the ways in which different cultures encourage different kinds of emotional climate both in infancy and later childhood (cf. Mead, 1949, ch. 5). Bettelheim's work (1954), though carried out in the context of our own culture, raises interesting questions about the primacy of castration threats by the father, so emphasized in orthodox Freudian accounts. He suggests that rejection of sexually-tinged ties to the mother comes rather from positive maturational needs of the child as he grows to maturity. This suggestion, if valid, provides a clue to a further possible function of incest tabus; for clearly the inbreeding family would be at a psychological and social disadvantage if it failed to promote growing up. In a vein more akin to Freud's dramatic picture of father-son rivalry in *Totem and Tabu* (1918) it is suggested that inbreeding families would also be at a disadvantage, because they would be disrupted by jealousies. Strict separation of oral and genital love objects, whether achieved from within the child or imposed by the father, avoids this (cf. LaBarre, 1954, p. 121 ff.) . Interesting light on the extent to which jealousy over a common love-object does actually disrupt family structure might be explored in the anthropological laboratory, in situations in which sons have access to their fathers' wives, though not their own mothers, or where a man may marry a woman and her daughter by another marriage.

It is clear that further data on this whole area are needed to resolve the factual picture of how much variation there is in the actual phenomenology of feelings with respect to the incest tabu, and to discover to what factors in human development, social structure, and character organization it is sytematically related. It would seem clear that light shed on this troubled corner is also importantly relevant to a critical area of ethics, the whole question of the relationship between impulse-satisfaction, impulse-postponement, and the social channelizing of drive expression. For it is in the resolution of the oedipal situation (to use Freudian terms) or in the whole early process of emotional development (to use more neutral terms) that ego-ideal and superego, or one's view of the self and its role, as well perhaps as the structure of conscience, have some of their major roots. The more complete understanding of the psychology and sociology of this area will throw light not only on the causes, function, and character of the incest tabu, but also on the whole problem of structuring desirable norms in the field of sex relations, where our moorings are most particularly cast adrift.

Chapter VI

CONTROL OF IN-GROUP AGGRESSION

WE HAVE now looked briefly at two common human moral concepts, binding requirements felt as important by all mankind. Mother-love, we found, was often not consciously felt to be a moral issue; because of its strongly positive social and emotional supports, it was simply taken for granted. However, we noted that problems may nonetheless arise over the abrogation of maternal duties, and when they do the moral issues are sharpened. On the other hand, we found that actual patterns of child care were extremely variable, and that there were some cultures where considerable emotional rejection, and neglect, were accepted, perhaps even stereotyped. This prompted the question for further inquiry as to how far a social order so constructed would actually be viable over any extended period of time. With respect to the ban on incest we found a more tangled skein. To unravel it will require far more information on how variations in the structure of the family, and in its emotional tone, are related to the complex ambivalences of growing up in human society.

We should like to turn now to another area which has caught anthropologists' attention as posing a more or less pan-human problem and generating some common moral reactions, though possibly of a more limited sort. This is the problem of controlling aggression within the community which lives and works together.

The very formulation of the question is a "problem" for "control" suggests that this field is conceptualized as quite different in its essential dynamics from that of mother-love. Principles regarding good child care are on the whole positive; they are over-determined by a convergence of social and personal motivations. Aggression seems to be in a different camp. Even if we rule out of serious consideration any Freudian "death instinct" as a common human source for aggressive impulses, there would appear to be enough unavoidable causes for anger, enough frustrations under any conceivable circumstances of human living, to generate some measure of aggression and hostility. If not absolutely a "given," aggression is at least an extremely prevalent and ready human reaction —though it may be varyingly expressed by a punch in the jaw, a thrust of the spear, or recourse to a witch-doctor's pointing stone. Certainly it is abundantly apparent that many forms of aggression, outside the immediate community or family, occur all over the world, and with full social approval. Wars and feuds are too much a part of our own experience for their widespread moral acceptability to need demonstration here, though we are perhaps always a little surprised that the enemy who may be killed on sight with impunity is sometimes a member of the next village, or a remote kinsman from a different lineage of the same clan.

Within the group, however, we, in common with most other people in the world, operate on a different basis. Killing one's brother or neighbor is almost everywhere regarded as wrong. Social relations are posited upon some measure of decent fellow-feeling, mutual trust and fulfillment of obligations. If these are violated or disturbed, and quarrels flare up, techniques are usually available to patch matters up. For quarrels to reach the point of violence is ordinarily a breach of norms of behavior, a breach which the participants themselves would categorize as wrong or bad. There is a considerable range of attitudes about just how much smooth harmony is desirable. Some cultures, as we shall see later on, insist on absolute peace and quiet, no tempers or abuse of any sort. Others accept and even approve bullying and bravado, boasting and shouting, even some brandishing of spears—but seldom their actual use. On the whole, a modicum of smooth in-group functioning is a condition of social living, and a shambles of uncontrolled fighting within the community hardly a possible social condition. How far, then, and under what conditions, does control of in-group aggression pose not-to-be-avoided tasks for human communities? Just how much in-group hostility and aggressivity can and do societies of different sorts tolerate? Are there any absolute rules such as disapproval of fratricide, any conditions under which societies can continue and survive while permitting the expression of aggression within the boundaries of the group which must live and work together? Does social control of in-group aggression always present a problem, or may the people who live and work together do so in peace and harmony through the cultivation of more positive moral attitudes, rather than formal checks and reins? Under what circumstances do we find the development of aggression minimized, or its expression successfully muted?

One thing at least seems clear. There is no such universal need for harmony as to result in a common absolute ban on all killing within the group. As a matter of fact, there is not even any one kind of killing which is universally ruled out as a heinous offense. Even fratricide and parricide are sometimes condoned. Of course, the frame of reference must be considered in interpreting the meaning of such acts. So, for example, when the Eskimo abandon their aged parents to die of starvation this is by no means callous murder. It is a bitterly regrettable necessity, which the old people accept and indeed, one is told, initiate and insist upon. It is not a wrong act, but a filial duty. Such behavior may also be further supported by a belief that people will continue after death in the same condition in which they die, so that it is obviously better to die of exposure while still relatively hale than to fade into decrepitude first. (To an outsider this also looks like a striking example of a dangerous aspect of man's moral character—his ability to mold his beliefs to salve his conscience.)

Other cases, however, do not have this self-explanatory color. Take, for example, such a report as Lowie (1925, p. 398) cites from Barton about the Ifugao: A man was murdered by his own sons because he refused to give them land to cultivate. The people with whom Barton discussed the case, instead of expressing condemnation, indignation, or any other appropriate "moral emotion" simply said something like—"Well, what else could they do? Wasn't the father denying them access to the land which he should rightfully have shared with them? Obviously they had no other recourse. Anyone can see that." Now it is true that land is an absolute necessity here which the sons had to have, and there was no mode of redress possible for them: no one else had any possible interest or concern in insisting that the father fulfill his obligations—or that the sons be brought to any kind of justice. Ifugao society functions through balance between separate and independent kin groups. Members swing their allegiance varyingly to different possible elder kinsmen as their immediate interest prompts them. Such decisions are based on the wealth of the leader and the strength of the group supporting him. Violence operates to maintain the relative prestige and strength of the different kin groups. It is not surprising that in such a system of anarchy and sheer power conflicts, violence should be an occasional resort among close kinsmen, too, if their interests conflict. And when it does occur, there is no one to take action or offense. If there is no one closer to the victim than to the offender, who can demand vengeance? No outsider has any stake in the case at all.

However, we need far more careful study of the moral implications of such situations. Do the Ifugao really make no moral issue of such occurrences, or is it simply that there is a different evaluation of their relative strength and importance? Perhaps killing one's father or brother is considered a wrong act—but only in the sense which has been called a *phase rule*: a do-only-with-regret rule (A. Edel, 1955, pp. 46 ff.). Certainly in many parallel cases in the anthropological literature where fratricides go unpunished, it is clear from comments and gossip, from the rituals of purification that are sometimes required, from efforts that are made to prevent brothers' quarrels from reaching the point of violence, that the acceptance of the act when it occurs by no means necessarily implies that it is taken as morally neutral.

In any case, it is clearly not enough to think of a common human social need for controlling in-group aggression. We may rather expect that different social systems will have quite different limiting effects in this aspect of the moral domain. They may, for example, have different thresholds of disruption. Take, for example, the situation which we find among the Chiga of Uganda (M. Edel, 1957, chs. 2, 6). This is a society where feuding and fighting are strongly valued masculine activities, where individual expression of hostile feelings is not disciplined, and men are expected to be quick to anger at an affront. Add to this that brothers are often suspicious and mistrustful of each other, and you have a situation in which fratricide, while not approved, does occur. The Chiga make a sharp distinction between cases in which a man has killed his own brother, or perhaps his father's own brother's son, and cases of merely technical fratricide, where the victim is a less closely related member of the kin group. In the former case, the act is deeply wrong. The man who has killed his brother may be put to death by his own father, though in practice he may take to his heels instead, and find safety in some other village, among affinal or uterine relatives or a pact friend. On the other hand, in the case where the victim is just a technical brother, the murder is more likely to be condoned. As fratricide it is wrong, but it can be reinterpreted to fit the pattern of out-group feuds. The community splits up into opposing groups, along lines dictated by closeness of kin ties with the murderer or the victim, and the killing is reckoned the killing of an outsider. Thus what, from a moral point of view, would have been a severe offense, is reinterpreted as "mere" homicide. If the two lineages thus split asunder were previously closely linked in peaceable social relations, some attempt will be made to reconcile them through payment of blood-money and a peacemaking ritual. The payment of blood-money does not indicate a disregard for human life, a simple quid pro quo in wealth for one's brother's life, but is, rather, a mechanism

to support and strengthen mediation and end further retaliatory bloodshed. (This is probably the general moral
meaning of this widespread institution.) However, as is
no doubt often the case elsewhere as well, the Chiga
mediators are not always successful, and a feud is on.

In this case, the community is split up by the act of
murder, but the society as a whole continues to function
with its principles intact, and the pattern of its normal
inter-personal and inter-group relations undisturbed, because the social structure is highly atomistic. Such cleav-
ages, for one or another reason, are an expected part of
the regular social order. In short, the Chiga social structure is one which can have a considerable tolerance for
in-group violence. Fratricide is not allowed to run ram-
pant; within some limits it is disapproved and con-
demned; but these limits are narrower than for many
other kinds of society.

The possibility of communities splitting apart, with
each segment continuing to function in the same way as
before, is one safety-valve which affects the extent to
which controls on aggression are absolutely needed for
social survival. In-group violence can also be permitted
if it is limited in its expression, channelized for example
into recognized terminal procedures, such as duelling. If
the causes are cumulative, there may even be regular and
accepted periodic conflict, which, as Gluckman has suggested (1956), may tend to have a self-limiting character: the actual conflict siphons off the hostilities and thus
permits the initial situation to continue without modifi-
cation. In short, in-group aggression in such a situation
may be necessary to the continuance of the existent social
forms.

We can see this in an interesting form in Bohannon's analysis (1958) of periodic religious uprisings among the Tiv in West Africa. Among the Tiv cannibalism is practised in a peculiarly West African form, which requires the murder by witchcraft and then the ceremonial eating of a victim who is a close own younger relative. By this outrageous act (they too consider it such) the cannibal augments the growth of strong power substance around his heart. Such substance also grows naturally; it alone is the source of the kind of strength which makes leadership possible. In such a theory, all the leaders of the community are obviously candidates for suspicion of being cannibals; one can never be sure that they have come by their power substance naturally. (They cannot be quite sure themselves either, because apparently the cannibalism occurs more in dream or fancy than in reality.) As Bohannan sees the system in operation, fear of the dangerous practitioners grows stronger over time until it finally reaches a boiling-point in some crisis such as an epidemic—clear evidence that the rate of witchcraft murders for cannibal purposes is increasing. At this point an open rebellion may occur in the form of an anti-witchcraft cult, which dares to put the older leaders to death and replace them with new ones. These may, of course, in turn themselves become suspect after a time.

The viable limit of tolerance for in-group aggression is clearly a function of other factors as well. The actual modes and weapons of aggression may affect the balance: there is surely a considerable difference between the effects of imaginery cannibalism and those of organized machine-gun fire in urban gang warfare. There are also factors in the material conditions of life and society—interdependence, density of population, organization of production—which enter in various ways. All of these bring home rather sharply the relevance of this concept of limits of tolerance of in-group aggression—of socially variable disruption thresholds—to our own situation. In the 17th century Thomas Hobbes suggested that the need for peace and social order was the primary requirement for human existence, so primary as to explain the whole system of moral rules in society—not just rules against killing, but proprietary relations and good faith and political obedience, and so on. There is much in our present integrated world to suggest that a similar logic may be not inapplicable on an international scale. That is, whereas Hobbes derived an ethics from the need to diminish in-group aggression, our contemporary world poses the problem of ruling out out-group aggression as well; or perhaps it may be described as the social need for the disappearance of the out-group. For certainly the total interdependence of the world today, and the massive character of our weapons of destruction, have changed our limits of tolerance for aggression. Violating the limits these new conditions set may mean extinction, or else jettisoning all men's other values in favor of service to permanent war machines.

We have been looking at societies in which there was some degree of tolerance for expression of in-group aggression. It is interesting and suggestive that in many of these cases aggressivity as such was a strongly positive masculine virtue. It has often been suggested that out-group aggression is an effective safety-valve, which helps to channelize and control aggression within the group. The data suggest that it may at least as often have the opposite effect. It would indeed seem obvious that in a society where taking scalps or heads, boasting of fighting or raiding, are the goals set for every man's ambition, recourse to violence is a ready reaction rather than a last resort, and so likely to be more rather than less of a problem within the community. There may be special solutions, as in such institutional patterns as the age-grade regiments of East Africa or the warrior societies of the Plains Indians, where emphasis on common action, common symbols, and the common purposes of the warriors all help to secure an outgroup direction of hostility. And it may be easier to achieve where the emphasis is not so much on individual glory as on the absolute social necessity of fighting for survival, or where bravery rather than aggression is the keynoted virtue. There is no doubt a possible difference between learning to be so brave that you can if necessary stand quietly while a fox gnaws your vitals, as in the classic Spartan story, and going along with papa at the age of six to stick a small spear into a bound captive, to learn how to do it with proper aim—and proper callousness—as in some parts of Melanesia. Contrasts in attitude show up very strikingly in the way quarreling children are handled; they may be separated, with or without homilies, or disregarded, or egged on. Distinctions may be drawn about *whom* to fight, or under what conditions. Erikson (1950, ch. 3) has suggested that one may want to plumb even earlier into the way aggressivity is channelled and developed, looking for some of the roots of its patterning in the very way the mother handles her son at the breast. In any case, this area would surely be a fruitful field for detailed cross-cultural study of the relations between moral patterns and character structure, showing some of the sources of the ease or difficulty with which people fulfill and pursue overt social goals and ideals.

This bloody picture of man-against-man which we

have been painting is, of course, not the whole story. Indeed, as we noted earlier, there is the opposite extreme—societies which totally condemn any in-group violence, and place an enormous premium on harmony and tranquillity within the group of kinsmen or tribesmen. The Pueblo Indians, for example, not only ruled out fighting, but eschewed any intemperate language or display of anger (cf. Benedict, 1934a; Brandt, 1954). When necessary, there was defensive fighting against outsiders, particularly against marauding raiders like the Apache, but within the village fighting or violence of any other sort was unthinkable. The extreme form which this abjuring of violence could reach is neatly highlighted by an historical episode among the Hopi, in which a rather serious quarrel about a point of principle split the community. Instead of having an angry conflict expressed in blows, the community settled its dispute by a kind of tug of war, after which the losing faction moved out to establish a separate, partially subordinate community of its own.

It is tempting to see the Pueblo attitudes against aggression in terms of very realistic needs which their total situation posed. The communities were tightly organized, set in an isolated desert environment, quite permanent, and subject to attack from without. While such factors may very well be significant partial explanations, whether we look at the data historically or functionally, they do not seem altogether adequate on a comparative basis. Certainly, other kinds of situations have brought about parallel results, among other American Indian groups. The hunting people of the Canadian woodlands, for example, whose community life is actually very minimal, have similar attitudes toward the expression of anger and hostility (Hallowell, 1955, ch. 15). They too are described as accommodating and peaceable, as abjuring all direct interpersonal aggression, yet their social order is one of considerable atomism and individual independence. Further exploration of such questions of the relations between whole social systems and moral attitudes, which have only begun to be raised, is clearly needed. We shall return to this kind of question in a later chapter.

It would be comforting to see these cases, whatever their causes, as neat examples of man's capacity to get along without hostility, even if only within narrow community bounds. The picture is, however, not quite so simple. We do not appear to be dealing in these cases with simple primary positive interpersonal attitudes, with the non-occurrence of feelings of hostility and aggression. It is rather that their manifestations are carefully suppressed. There is a deep fear of rage and anger, and of their destructive consequences. For the Canadian Woodland Indians evidence of suppression is pretty clear and near the surface, both in the projected form of witchcraft fears and witchcraft practice, and in intense suspiciousness about people's motivations (cf. Hallowell, 1955). And a similar picture, though a somewhat less intense one, has been painted also for the Pueblos, where beneath the cooperation and harmony, there is a good deal of malicious gossip, antagonistic clique behavior, and a prevalence of witchcraft fears and accusations (Eggan, 1943). Recent field work in Africa also documents comparable cases of a stress on interpersonal harmony within the community being sanctioned and overtly rationalized in terms of fear of malice and witchcraft, rather than loving brotherhood.

This then raises some very important questions for ethics. Is the muting of aggression always achieved only at a high psychological price? Does it rest primarily on fear rather than on in-group harmony as a positive experience? Do we find more positive pictures anywhere? For example, the Nuer of Northeast Africa (Evans-Pritchard, 1956) abjure quarrels within the close group, though they certainly do not share Pueblo attitudes toward compromise and placidity. They are a rather proud, warlike people, with communities that split up readily under the impact of quarrels; but they try to prevent this. Their attitude is that quarrels brought into the open and settled will avoid malice and continued bad feeling. This is a common African attitude, which the Nuer institutionalize. They take the opportunity of formal sacrificial occasions to permit the airing of any grievance that one man feels against another. The blood of the sacrifice then carries away all the bad feelings that have been aroused. It would be important to learn more about how effective such devices are. But it is at least suggestive that these people are reported to have far less fear of witchcraft and suspicion of hidden interpersonal malice, than is common among many of their neighbors. And what about the Arapesh, the New Guinea people described by Margaret Mead (1935), who so strongly stress positive values of in-group love and trust? Do they achieve their low level of aggression only at the cost of general inhibition, so that their low level of initiative and creativity must be chalked up as a part of the price? Or is this lack based on other failings?

If we grant that modern society has reached a point where sharp limits on aggression are necessary, we need more studies of cultures which do minimize aggression, of what prices they pay, and of how such prices can be controlled or lowered. But we also need to examine them to see what clues they may yield to a more positive facet of the problem, that of shifting the moral balance from control of in-group aggression to reducing its sources and causes. To what extent are the psychological preconditions for frictions of various sorts which are usually cited as pan-human, actually variable, at least in intensity and extent? Personality-culture studies are exploring many of these and their implications: looking to see the effect of variations in family structure, of many mothers and fathers, of differences in spacing of children and in who imposes what disciplines, and how and when, upon such things as the intensity of sibling rivalry and the chanelling of oedipal impulses and various measures of responsibility, anxiety, and so on (cf. Whiting and Child, 1953). Are such problems anywhere resolved so as to maximize adult freedom and harmony without jeopardizing individuality and creativity? Social psychology, too, points to areas that seem to be relevant. As Lewin, Lippett and White showed in their classic study (1939), some kinds of group structures appear to generate interpersonal friction and hostility, others to minimize it. Ruth Benedict (1939) suggested looking to the way frustrations are reinforced by humiliations or moderated by positive counterbalancing rewards. Others stress the economic roots of disharmony, suggesting a contrast between cooperatively-based economic orders and those—such as modern capitalist economy, with its competitive striving, built-in dissatisfactions, and opposing interests—which have an essential dynamic of potential conflict. We need a rich comparative study of the extent of conflict in different social wholes, and of the conditions—social, economic and psychological—which increase or limit it. This will help us to understand more fully what the positive roots for social harmony may be, and how far they can be achieved in a morality that will neither entail sacrifice of creativity nor increase projected hostility, and which will at the same time allow for such other values — freedom, let us say, and individuality, and material well-being — as are concomitantly sought in most of our ethical thinking.

Chapter VII

DISTRIBUTIVE JUSTICE

THERE IS no point in multiplying our illustrations indefinitely, but we should like to comment briefly on one other area of moral concern—the problem of distributive justice. Here too we have a genuine social need to be met: the obvious requirement that somehow a food-supply be produced, and used in such a manner that enough people will survive—and be motivated—to carry on the society. But clearly in this domain, instead of a simple set of moral principles—parallel to "Don't commit fratricide" or "Take good care of your children"—we have widely different sets of virtues and goals, ideals and standards, operating in terms of the different kinds of economic institutions which have grown up to fill this need. True, there are a few common denominators. Almost everywhere the small household shares a common purse, or a common stewpot—though even here there may be differences in the extent to which private disposition of goods may be permitted within it, or the width to which the family itself is extended as a cooperative unit. And almost everywhere there are some feelings of personal sympathy, help and reciprocity within socially defined limits, which enter at various points to color the moral qualities in this domain. These feelings can, however, be very peripheral. Centrally, we find a wide host of different principles operating, in response to what is after all a pretty complicated set of needs.

For obviously, the support of a total population cannot be guaranteed simply by there being a technology and work habits sufficient to meet the physical needs of the adults who do the immediately productive work. It means also—and this raises questions that are more often felt as directly moral—that the working adults must produce enough to provide not only for themselves, but for many others: the children, the temporarily ill, the aging; and in more complexly structured societies, enough also to release some people for military or administrative duties, or specialized pursuits, and to provide for all those entitled—according to that society's structure and canons—to the enjoyment of leisure, perhaps even of luxury. This requires a distributive framework, routes along which goods are distributed and obligations and burdens made to fall. We are accustomed to thinking of these in terms of economic institutions—markets and barter, taxes and gifts, patterns of property ownership and inheritance rights. But these are by no means merely mechanical chains of behavior, patterns or rules to be followed in order to obtain specific purely economic results. They are complex sets of human relationships, involving reciprocal obligations, motivations and sanctions. Moral ideas and ideals, virtues, goals and standards permeate this whole domain, but they do so in ways which sharply reflect the differences in actual social and economic institutions. Our own tradition, for example, has at various times included such directly moral or morally tinged notions as just price, the proper due of different stations in society, the virtues of good craftsmanship, thrift as a path to salvation, the demand for a fair day's wage for a fair day's labor, the right to the full produce of one's labor, the natural rights of private property tempered by the moral necessity for giving charity, ideals of wealth as a mark of fitness, and so on. Western philosophy has developed the general conception of formulae of social justice on the one hand and of social obligation and responsibility on the other, which partly express and partly idealize or criticize segments of prevailing distributive patterns. In this domain arise such slogans as "From each according to his ability, to each according to his work," or ideas of need as a basis for apportioning of goods, ideals of charity or conceptions of universal social security, and so forth, and some of these become implemented in actual social institutions.

In other societies too, the social demand for a distribution of food and other material necessities sufficient for survival requires not only distribution patterns but also related principles of justice and obligation. These attitudes are not necessarily formulated in sharply economic terms; the underlying need that is to be met may not be consciously paramount at all. Instead, the moral stress may fall upon some quite different aspect of the social system, which is part of the operative procedure by which the pattern of distribution is achieved. "Primitive communism" is by no means the general character of the system of distribution that we find in primitive societies. No society has been described in which the individual is in fact submerged entirely, or in which the communal rights are absolute. We do find widespread sharing and basic egalitarianism, but the framework of moral reference is seldom a simple mutual obligation in the sharing of all produce, though that may enter to some extent. Instead, we find a variety of rights and obligations, complex moral notions of right and proper economic behavior, of who may own what and why, who should enjoy what and why, and who must give what to whom and why.

Sometimes the problem of sharing goods so as to take care of the needy may be handled directly in terms of moral consciousness; we often find ideals of generosity, or duties of sharing and charity. However, such moral sentiments and principles cannot simply be read off directly as obvious expressions of common human sympathy. Instead, they are structured in quite different ways which relate also to realities in the social and economic framework. We, for example, certainly formulate taking care of the needy as a point of moral concern. Any appeal for an emergency need, such as a flood or famine, even in a remote part of the world, will usually bring immediate —though often short-lived—response. But on the whole, we take care of such feelings and such needs by "tithing" —by giving a limited share of our income, through taxes and contributions to organized charities—rather than, with Schweitzer or other dedicated souls, whose moral sensitivity we admire but do not feel constrained to imitate, by giving up our worldly goods. We do not neglect our own children to support starving children in distant parts of the world, and usually do not even drive an old Ford instead of a new Buick in order to give more to charity.

In earlier days, charity was a more immediate and personal concern, more directly tied to virtues, and more central. And so it is still, to many of the other peoples of the world. In some Plains Indian languages, for example, the possessive pronoun is not used with such words as "bread"; it is inconceivable to them that anyone should consider food something for his own private consuming. One may own other things—valuables such as horses, for example—but food is for sharing. To the Indian agent struggling with problems of distributing flour rations, there is only improvidence in the Indian habit of sharing the goods received among any of his kinsmen who choose to lay claim to his help. This would, however, seem supremely right and natural to most people in the world —the Chinese, for example, or the modern Greeks, as well as many primitives; indeed, our modern habit of sitting down to a full meal with only invited guests is widely regarded as impossible niggardliness and meanness. On the other hand, our concern for starving Navaho or Greek orphans toward whom we have no personal responsibility makes no sense at all to many of these same people. They find the obvious needs of kinsfolk and neighbors far more compelling, and those of outsiders far less of their concern.

The complexity of the social functions which the ideals of generosity may serve is neatly underlined by an interesting footnote to some of these attitudes. Among some of the Plains Indians, lavish gifts, such as a valuable horse, may be given away as a gesture in honor of some member of the family. Such gifts, like benefactions in general among East European Jewish groups, are not received with the expressions of gratitude we would expect. The donor's actions are taken to be self-rewarding. They gain him the esteem and approval of his fellows, or are counts of virtue in the eyes of God; the recipient—however needy—is simply the vehicle through whom he can perform such acts of grace. No special thanks are expected or forthcoming.

Obviously our attitudes and those of other people who react to needs differently and structure their giving differently are parts of different whole ways of solving the problem of distribution. We need a pan-human quality in our relatedness, to extend our feelings of reciprocal responsibilities and obligations to a wide world sphere, because we live in a widely interdependent world, and one in which kind hearts and door-to-door charity are hardly adequate to solve the realistic problems. Organized family welfare agencies, social insurance, lend-lease, and so on, are more efficient and reliable. They are compromises between felt needs and a whole host of traditional values and social institutional forms, reflecting not just sympathy for other people's needs, but the right of the individual to do what he likes with his own wealth (and indeed grab what he legally can), and involving not only social justice and morality, but problems of maintaining social stability as well. And we must see other people's patterns of sharing with their more limited circle of fellows as just as much of a complex compromise or balance of historical traditions, individual desires, moral rules and moral ideals, social needs and individual feelings of sympathy and compassion.

However, we must also note that neither generosity nor charity may have to arise to fill the breach of distributive inequalities and gaps. The problems may be settled through quite different institutional forms, and never become foci of moral concern at all. We can see this well illustrated in the very different ways in which the Eskimo and the Australian native tribes solve certain rather similar economic problems. In both cases we find people depending heavily upon big game, which with the techniques available to them provides a far from secure base, and one which can support only a limited population. It is essential that the occasional successful kill be widely shared, if the population is to survive. To the Eskimo, this consideration is a quite straightforward and practical one. The hunter has absolute ownership rights to his kill; that is regarded as right and proper. But he should also share it out of simple generosity with those of his neighbors who are needy—and in fact he does do this. He gets both the personal satisfaction of being the important man who has helped everyone out, and a considerable measure of social insurance. And to judge by the morals pointed in folk-tales and similar sources of moral comment, these are perfectly valid, explicit and clear parts of the total moral reckoning to him.

The Australian situation is quite different. Instead of the hunter's giving freely of his surplus, he divides the game he kills according to absolutely mandatory rules, fulfilling specific obligations to his various different kinsfolk; a particular share belongs by absolute right to his grandfather, his paternal uncle, his father and father-in-law, and so on. These are not gifts; they are their absolute due. In this way the elders are assured a comfortable share in the produce of the hunt, a share they might very well not get among the Eskimo in times of scarcity. There are legal and religious sanctions to support them in this comfortable position, which the hunter must respect, for the elders are the repositories of the most esoteric sacred lore—including the intricacies of the totemic ceremonies which are essential if the game is to multiply and be available at all. Sharing is accomplished—but this is not felt as the point of the moral obligation. That lies rather in the fulfillment of specific sets of kinship obligations.

Such a framework of kinship obligations is often paramount—though the exact patterning may be as varied as the many kinship systems in the world. Even when moral obligations between kinsmen are explicitly formulated in terms of help in times of need, they are often limited to particular categories of kinsmen. A Tallensi man, for example, would never turn to his clansman with whom he shares many ritual and legal obligations, for a gift to tide him over a time of famine; but he could ask freely of his maternal kinsman, not a member of his own clan, and expect to be helped (Fortes, 1945).

Religious obligations may be the moral center of consideration too. Among the Pueblo Indians, for example, the only purpose to which wealth accumulation could be put with any meaning, was to help finance a religious ceremony. In so doing, a man redistributed his entire surplus—giving help and support to the less fortunate in the community. But that was not the purpose of the undertaking; rather it was participation in the appropriate fashion in the religious rituals which was the good end desired. One could go on and on in this vein, exploring such varieties of goals displaced from obvious economic ends. Melanesian hunters in some areas must give away all the products of their hunting—not out of a streak of queer generosity, but because their eating of them is prohibited by a tabu bringing terrible consequences in its train. Political systems also may operate to bring about a balance. For example, the East African chief who receives surplus wealth in taxation, expends the bulk of it again through the community, through specific institutional channels: by bride-price payments which incidentally bind people to him as in-laws, by loans of cattle to young men who in return become his vassals, pledged to lend him military support, and by permanent open house. Here the focus of moral concern would not be charity or serving the needy, but rights and duties in relation to the chief.

It is important to note that these patterns of generosity, and of reciprocal redistributive techniques, function in a framework of general access to basic productive resources; this is the case in most primitive societies. Within such a framework, a society may even develop complex patterns of competitive wealth manipulation, as is, for example, often the case in Melanesia. When, however, the access to basic resources such as land is unequal, or other economic or political factors enter to disturb the reciprocal balance of rights and obligations, the problems that arise may be more complex ones. It has been suggested by contemporary sociologists as well as Marxist analysts that where exploitative rather than reciprocal relations prevail, some use of force is essential to the maintenance of a society. It is no doubt the case that there are limits of tolerance for predation and exploitation in primitive societies as well as our own, and these need empirical investigation. In this context, it would be rewarding to explore the roles which different ideologies play. Feudal ideals of contentment in one's station, the varying rationalizations of slave states, and other more modern concepts of justice, have their analogues in parallel situations in other parts of the world. We need to know what patterns these take, how they arise, and how far they serve to bolster social systems which would seem to the outsider to be rooted in inequalities. Any light on such problems would illuminate most fundamental questions about the relations between social systems and moralities.

Chapter VIII

A FEW REFLECTIONS IN MIDSTREAM

THE EXAMINATION of the four areas treated individually in Chapters IV through VII began, it will be recalled, in considering the search for invariants in a cross-cultural survey. That there is an enormous appeal in such a possibility is obvious; and it is particularly appealing in the contemporary scene, where changes are rapid, and the quest for mooring-points for our morals sometimes seems a desperate one. It is clear that we found few absolute rules and prescriptions, or even common specific goals, in the course of our search, even as responses to basic common human needs. Yet there is really little to deplore in this. There is far too much emphasis placed on uniformity as a standard for a pan-human morality. After all, an invariant "deep down in human nature" may represent only something that served its role in evolutionary development long ago, a kind of moral "appendix" we are stuck with, even though it gives rise to perennial troubles. An invariant that is accidental may mislead moral analysis: it might have happened that all men spoke the same language, but it would have been the need for communication, not the particular words or syntax, that had moral significance. On the other hand, an invariant that appears only under rare and specially cultivated but quite specific conditions—for example, if it turned out that certain kinds of societies with particular types of family structure or economic organization felt aggression to be an evil, and were able to implement this moral attitude—might prove of the greatest moral significance.

Nor again should we be led into the misleading assurance that there is a correlation between uniformities in the value or moral domain and peaceful agreement, or that differences must make for conflict. These follow from the content rather than the fact of uniformity or diversity. If men agree on the moral significance of intellectual activity, there is room for non-competitive truth-seeking; but if they agree on the moral significance of individual success in accumulating wealth and social eminence, then conflict is often a likely consequence. In parallel fashion, though differences may breed conflict, or concepts of heresy and righteous persecution, they are also sometimes compatible with mutual respect and each going his own way.

On the other hand, our brief exploratory survey has borne some fruits. We have seen a few concepts emerge which sharpen our tools for analysis and clarify the questions we must ask. The varying limits of tolerance for in-group aggression under different kinds of technological and social-structural conditions is an example of such a point. To explore the historical reasons for the development of the different social systems themselves is beyond the scope of the field of comparative ethics; but we do need to push on to see how close different societies come to the limit of tolerance, or to what extent and under what circumstances some wider concepts of sympathy and fellow-feeling also enter to color the moral view. We shall return to some of these questions later in our discussion of the moral community and moral feelings.

Or take another example, which leads to many important areas of exploration. We have seen that in some cases needs are met not by direct prescription, or by moral principles and ideals, in their own domain, but indirectly through cultural institutions which service some other set of needs, or operate in some other domain, and which in their turn generate, or are supported by quite different moral principles. So, for example, we saw that a stress on kinship and its moral claims might serve the need for adequate production and distribution of resources so well that there would be no need for making central virtues of thrift or charity, or thinking about an ideal of fair distribution. Obviously we cannot expect to find a simple atomistic relationship between particular moral rules and particular needs, certainly not individual biological needs. It is a whole culture which is man's adaptive way of meeting his needs, a.1d these needs form an orchestrated whole whose score is social as well as biological. It is the survival of the way of life, rather than of the lone individual in some unimaginable "state of nature" which is the problem people actually face; and it is their whole solution to this problem at a given time which morality is supporting—or perhaps, occasionally, working to change.

We have also noted that biological needs themselves must always be studied in this socio-cultural nexus; they have historical depth, and are sharpened and developed in the very process of culture growth (cf. Lee, 1948). The ways in which needs are met thus help to generate new needs, and past solutions help to determine the directions which new solutions are likely to take: culture has the kind of binding effect on problem-solution which the psychologist calls "set" in the individual. There are many simple examples of this kind in the concrete problems UN organizations faced in attempting to effect technological changes (cf. Mead, 1953). Even in the field of health and hygiene, where needs would seem to be obvious, and goals pan-human, the actual interrelations of moral principles, value commitments, and social institutions proved enormously complicated. To expect people to prefer tap-water to well-water because it is cleaner and easier to draw, assumes a whole host of shared values which simply are not shared by all cultures. It assumes that getting water from a well is purely instrumental to having it; that saving a little time is more desirable than taking time for friendly interchange and gossip, even courtship, for which village wells or fountains commonly afford opportunity. It assumes that having more water or cleaner water is obviously a common goal, forgetting that the extent to which we value cleanliness today is far from obvious to people who do not share our theories of disease. And it overlooks, too, other possible moral questions of a different sort that may relate to water-supply: economic dislocation of the water-carrier, or possible offense to a djin in the fountain, or the polluting effect of having people of different social classes or different religious affiliations drawing water from a common source. The possibilities are endless, and not all to be dismissed as trivial or incorrect as compared with our own "enlightened" views, especially when we take time to notice that the function cleanliness plays in our society today is itself far from the simple medical necessity which we like to think it. Rather, cleanliness plays a dominating role which sweeps aside many other considerations, particularly when applied to baby care and to the well-being of patients in hospitals.

Such lessons do not belie the importance of the need for water, or for avoiding its pollution. But they do remind us that even when central, needs are enmeshed in patterns of activity which have collateral ends, intrinsic joys, relational values of all sorts, over and beyond their need-satisfying character. And these too may enter into the moral picture as convictions, principles, goals, and ideals.

Obviously, not all needs are equally fruitful or powerful factors in generating moral ideals and principles, or in justifying them. This is not a simple question of their biological necessity, nor of the presence or absence of abundant resources for meeting them, though both enter. Certainly, sex-expression is a strong drive, though not a survival necessity for the individual; and in a simple physical sense, means for its satisfaction are readily available. There are almost everywhere roughly equal numbers of men and women, to say nothing of other Kinseyan outlets. Yet sex is nearly everywhere highly charged morally, for in addition to its high emotional potential, it is part of the most central nexus of human social interrelationships. The kinds of moral principles with which it is invested and intertwined may thus have their roots in quite different problems from the relatively simple ones of direct sexual satisfaction. Questions of child care, of property relations, of patterns of residence, as well as complex unconscious drives and identifications, may enter. To study these interrelationships therefore requires a very wide canvas, and at the same time very detailed analysis. In general, whether we are concerned with explaining wide-spread similarities, or probing for the roots of differences, it is obviously important to focus not just on the expressed point of the particular rule, be it chastity or exogamy or whatever, but on the whole system of values and goals, explicit or deeply concealed, which it is realistically helping to fulfill.

On the other hand, other biological necessities of a

more absolute sort may seldom enter the moral domain
at all. Breathing, for example, and the need for fresh air,
are ordinarily taken care of without our making a virtue
of breathing well, or striving for it as a goal. Santayana
(1905) suggested that the light of ideal goods is kindled
by the friction of material forces. And it is revealing that
today, when the availability of fresh air is not quite so
obvious, especially in our cities, it does generate dilemmas
which have moral implications. Questions of the control
of air-pollution by radioactivity, or of restraint of land-
lords' rights to continue using "old law" tenements with
inadequate window space, are not just simple legislative
problems. They raise profound questions of principle
about the priority of certain human rights over property
rights, and about how far national defense should be allowed to supersede the need for individual survival, and
so on. To understand the moral dilemmas that are generated, takes us into a whole survey not just of the need
for fresh air, but of all the values of our society, including
its conflicts, and also all our established habits of tackling
moral problems in terms of conscience, of absolute ideals,
of imperatives.

Obviously, then, there are whole fresh areas of questions which arise, and demand further investigation, both
with respect to the ways social and technological factors
enter in defining and structuring the challenge which different needs present, and also as to how different moral
systems operate as existent patterns through which fresh
challenges are mediated. We need to know more about
both of these. The former demands more knowledge from
sociology, psychology, history, as well as comparative anthropology. The latter carries us into an examination of

the structure and cultural relations of moral systems, to which we propose to turn.

We are not proposing a simple reduction of the complex whole of morality to a statement of biological, psychological, or even social needs; but rather that whether for descriptive analysis or for evaluation, the need-solution element be made explicit and realistic. Our data do not suggest any ground for assuming that a realistic morality must be somehow less moral, though its quality may be somewhat more rational, and it may be more open to reassessment and change. As we shall see later, there is room for many kinds of moral feelings, and a realistic analysis of consequences enters quite sharply into many peoples' moral calculations. That it is sometimes skewed by errors of fact, or falls short of the analysis the social scientist might give of its full function, is beside the point. Fuller understanding is a contemporary goal; we point only to the fact that the moralist need not be afraid of it, unless he has a rigid vested stake in some particular prescription.

We must also remember that the very idea of need-fulfillment has a value content. One can use biological survival as a measuring stick in a fairly neutral sense: a group which does not meet certain needs, unless it changes, may die out. The biologist does not have to enter into the moral problems of evaluating particular animal forms in noting that ones which cannot meet the challenge of competition for a particular ecological niche are wiped out. But an ethical assessment has to render explicit how far it is using life or health or avoiding such massive frustrations that it is impossible to achieve any values whatsoever, as ethical criteria, and whether they are taken as goods, or as necessary conditions of other goods. For men do not always give up everything for mere continued living, and indeed a Schopenhauerian could even interrupt to propose wholesale suicide for the species (cf. A. Edel 1955, ch. 5). As a matter of fact, moral attitudes to the fact of needs are themselves an interesting area of phenomenal investigation. Needs may be felt as outer driving forces and sources of energy, as basic constituents of the self,—or as enemies forcing compromises with the natural world. We must recognize that these varying views of needs may enter into the formulation of the very questions we ask as social scientists and philosophers, and so had better be explicated rather than left implicit, wherever possible.

The insights we have gleaned thus far are obviously just a beginning of comparative moral analysis. More questions have been asked than answered. There is need to go far beyond this. If whole cultures are the "experiments in living" that fulfill human needs and provide human joys, it is whole moralities, not piecemeal separate parts of them, which support those ways of life or act as a leaven within them. We need then to study whole moral configurations, not just itemized rules and principles. We need to study the relative balance of virtues, rules and ideals in a morality, and see how this whole configuration is related to the social order of which it is a part. But to describe the configuration of a morality it is not enough to describe the contents of its rules, virtues, ideals, and goals, and the way they are interrelated. We must also understand the sanctions that the morality uses to support them, the strength with which it insists upon them, the base upon which it rests them. This whole aspect of moral analysis presents so many facets for exploration, many of them familiar to philosophers but seldom isolated for comparative study, that it seems best to look at the various structural aspects of morality in some detail, before we turn back once more to the question of analyzing whole moral configurations.

Chapter IX

THE MORAL COMMUNITY AND THE PERSON

W<small>HEN WE TURN</small> to a specific analysis of the formal properties of moral systems, one of the most rewarding ways of looking at the comparative data is to see what bounds people draw around their "moral congregation." The point has frequently been made that our own universalistic morality is in sharp contrast to the morality of the primitive world, which is bounded by narrower limits. People draw varying boundaries for their moral communities, which define the limits of *who counts* morally. They also define in differing ways the community of those who *participate,* those on whom the moral obligations are binding, or for whom the moral ideals are relevant. And with this comes differential patterning of who is responsible and indeed of how responsibility is to be construed. These areas, while related and overlapping, are not necessarily identical. In our culture, for example, we chart them quite differently. We hold that infants and lunatics *count*; one has responsibilities towards them. But they do not *participate*; they are not held morally accountable. What is more, in many moral decisions we count in the well-being of future generations, as yet unborn. And we hold, in theory at least, that our major moral rules are applicable to our behavior toward all people, whether they themselves share our principles or not.

True, we need not behave in exactly the same way to strangers as to friends and relatives, but unless we can find some special extenuation, like national self-defense, we hold that even people of the most remote and alien corners of the world are human individuals, to be treated with respect and dignity—or at least not murdered or plundered with impunity and a good conscience. We also see the limits of participation in our moral community as potentially universal: on the whole, our tradition is to assume that given sufficient enlightenment all intelligent mature adults in any part of the world would share at least our most fundamental convictions. We are ready to make attempts to persuade them, if not to wear clothing or marry only one wife, at least to see the obvious rightness of the Golden Rule, or the importance of appointing the "best man" to a job rather than one's own neediest relative, or—perhaps the most important moral rule—to wash regularly!

Most societies of the world draw their lines rather differently, both with respect to participation and to counting. To most people the world over, for example, it is obvious that any morality is always the morality of a particular people. They expect people with different ways of life to have altogether different attitudes and values about rightness and wrongness and desirable ends of life, just as they have different forms of family organization or religious beliefs. There is no point in attempting to convert others to one's own views. These are rooted in one's own way of life, and have no relation to other people's. Moral principles are based on the practices of one's own ancestors, the dictates of one's own culture heroes, the tabus of one's own religion—not of other peoples'. Criticism or condemnation of others on moral grounds is clearly irrelevant. Naturally, if others' ways of making war impinge on one's own safety, such people will have to be opposed—disposed of in some way, not lectured to about virtue. And their attitudes toward sex, or whether a man shares his belongings with his neighbors, are interesting facts of their way of life, at about the same level as whether they wear red feathers or file their teeth. People may not like their neighbors' behavior, and may laugh at them or consider them less than fully human for their odd, or even disgusting, ways. But they do not need to *concern* themselves about the issue. It is not "all decent self-respecting people" who would be expected to behave in a particular way, but "all decent self-respecting Zuñi," or members of my village, or my clan.

The line of those toward whom one has moral obligations and moral concern—those who count—is also drawn rather sharply by many people, around the boundaries of the self-contained community: the village or the kin-group or the tribe. Head-hunters may undertake a raid on their neighbors to replenish the stock of names in the village, for new names must each be supported by a head. War may be undertaken entirely to give the young warriors in the group a chance to prove their manhood. No special provocation is needed; there is no problem of right or justice that can enter, for those killed are outsiders, beyond the pale of moral considerations. Nor is this lack of moral concern for outsiders just a matter of killing. Manus men (cf. Mead, 1937, ch. 7), who act with strict, indeed puritanical, propriety toward their own wives and other women of their own village, may capture a woman from another village, use and abuse her as a group prostitute with no moral blame from their peers, their consciences or, more importantly, their ancestral ghosts who are their moral mentors (though that is not to say it is with the approval of their wives). These outsiders may be individuals who speak the same language, and themselves share the same principles of action in general.

It is interesting and important to note that the definition of counting may be a variable one, which draws different lines for different situations. For the Chiga, for example, as we have already noted, the feud situation prevails; this means that there are many people whose cattle one may raid, whom one may kill with impunity, without such behavior being wrong; yet these people of different lineages and clans are in other contexts one's affinal relatives. One does not kill one's father-in-law who has come to a wedding feast, though at other times one will in fact join in a raid on his village.

As a matter of fact, however, there are often modifications of these limited applications of moral rules, which emerge when one looks below the surface description of formal regulations. Atomistic structures in which lineages are set up against each other, as among the Chiga, require in theory that a brother be supported in any act against outsiders; no question of the rights of outsiders, of responsibility toward them, is in theory morally relevant. Yet for the Chiga, at least, it is clear that some exceptions are made. There are conditions under which the primary duty to support one's brother gives way in face of a realization that he is in point of fact a nuisance because of habitual failure to pay debts or frequent thieving raids. In such a case a man's brothers may not support him, and they may even allow outsiders to assert their claims, permitting them to take his property or put him to death, without interfering to protect him (M. Edel,

1957, ch. 6). This is a kind of tentative or temporary extension of the boundaries of the group normally defined as setting the limits of responsibility; it is a contravention of the sharp priority of duties within the group as against any out-group considerations.

Illustrations of many such techniques of extension of the normal in-group occur in the anthropological literature. Very widely, where the moral essence is fulfillment of specific kin obligations, so that in a sense there is no meaning to non-kin morality, we find legal fictions introduced in order to fit outsiders into the pattern of kinship. In central Australia, for example, an outsider—other than a messenger—is subject to death for trespass. But if he has some bona fide reason other than hunting or trespass to be on another tribe's land, he may be dealt with as an accepted fellow-human. This can be accomplished by the simple device of finding some kinship slot into which he can fit. By custom these extensions have been worked into a web which interlocks virtually all Australian tribes, so that anyone can be fitted in somehow. Even if the outsider is a European, he can be set into the web of moral involvement: it is necessary only to adopt him. This kind of device is used by many peoples as a way of taking an outsider into the moral community, of recognizing him or accepting the fact that he counts. And in similar vein, many people, like the Chiga, establish moral ties with individuals of other kin groups by taking binding oaths of blood-brotherhood.

Just as limited moralities often include formal and informal techniques of extension, so, if we look at our own universality closely, we find many points at which it is less than absolute. By redefining the context as one of declared war, we may treat as outsiders people to whom we have previously sent food packages as anonymous friends; they now become subject to punitive raids and we may bomb their cities, bringing death to innocent civilians. The belief that all men are created free and equal was held for a long time side by side with slavery. Despite the Christian conception of the brotherhood of man, whole groups and classes of men have in practice been held beyond the pale: at one time serfs, at another landless peasantry (seen from above as "able-bodied rogues unwilling to work"), at a later time large masses of people huddled in over-crowded industrial cities (the "unfit" of Herbert Spencer, whom he saw as being thrust aside by the evolutionary process, or "the bungled and the botched" whom Nietzsche was ready to regard as the mere stepping stone for the race of super-men to come). Yet alongside this, there has been the growing positive ideal of all mankind as a single moral community in which every individual counts.

This ideal is by no means a simple one. It has several different components. There is the quantitative aspect that everyone is included, that no human being falls outside of the moral community or is utterly without some moral relations to the rest. There is the minimal content that is assigned to such relations—that no one is subject to wanton killing or attack, that everyone's well-being is to some extent in some way to be considered. There is what stands out as the qualitative aspect, that each man is regarded as a person, an individual possessing dignity or worthy of respect, and in principle capable of participation in the moral community.

Actually, any or all of these components may vary, and the widening of the moral community which each implies may in some sense be a distinct phenomenon. In the western tradition we tend to think that there is one "correct" morality which should apply to all members of the moral community; but obviously there could be instead a conception of pluralistic moralities with mutual respect. And there may be varied conceptions of *how much* each person counts; for example, we hold that each counts as one in certain common domains—each has one vote, each is equal before the law—but *not* in the sense that every man owes equal obligations to every other. There are certainly many contexts in which "Blood is thicker than water" is recognized as an acceptable moral maxim. It is possible for a strong kin morality to be formulated so as to be compatible with a universalist framework, provided that kinship does not become the defining mark of the total moral community. It is indeed conceivable that some of the areas of the world newly moving into global economic and political relationships may develop such a pattern.

If we raise the question of the similarity or difference between our own moral community and those of the primitive world, these various basic components of our universalism must be kept in mind independently. If we look merely at quantitative extent, the difference is one of degree. Boas wrote (1932, p. 227), "There is no evolution of moral ideas. All the vices that we know, lying, theft, murder, rape, are discountenanced in the life of a closed society." He suggested that progress in ethical conduct was simply "the recognition of larger groups which participate in the rights enjoyed by members of the closed society." Ginsberg, however (1957, ch. 7), takes issue with Boas on this point. He sees a qualitative difference. Looking at the "change in the conception of the human person himself" he sees a real difference in ethical awareness. He stresses the contrast between an abstract, universal, human meaning of goodness, which applies to any man by virtue of his humanness, and any concept, however wide, which remains rooted in common involvement in a specific network of relationships and obligations, which is the basis of most people's morality (cf. Read, 1955).

A parallel but distinct question is how changes from a closed in-group morality to a universalist morality could have come about. Surely, the latter kind of view will insist, not merely from expanding in-group brotherhood literally, for the essence of kin-morality is specific patterned obligations, rather than generalized ones. Redfield (1953, pp. 77 ff.) stresses the creativeness required in reaching from a kin-bound morality to a concept of pan-human brotherhood, taking a position parallel to Bergson's view (1935) of the creative intuition of prophets and saints, which moves out from a closed to an open morality. Redfield cites (pp. 130 ff.) a striking illustration of such a "moral mutation" on a modest scale in the case of a Plains Indian leader who was impelled to release a captive already bound for the customary torture. On the other hand, it is also true that there are common forms of sympathy, unstereotyped acts of consideration and compassion which reach beyond any limits of rigid reciprocal obligation, in many people's homely everyday behavior: the wife who feeds her co-wife's hungry children though she is not required to do so, or even the considerate, helpful treatment accorded anthropologists by most people all over the world, who surely have no prescribed duties toward them.

There is actually no real contradiction between these views. We can recognize the emergence of fresh ideals

in human consciousness under the impact of changing circumstances which reach an historical climax, and still see
the continuity of underlying problems, potentialities,
needs and feelings. Familiar historical examples show
the way in which the emergence of universalism has indeed been rooted in social realities and needs. The Stoic
ideal of the cosmopolitan individual came fast on the
heels of Alexander's conquest of Persia and the break-
down of Greek political localism. The Christian ideal of
the brotherhood of man gained strength among the op-
pressed — the "outs" of the Roman world. The post-
mediaeval universalism of the western world, whether in
its religious Protestant forms or its secular appeals to a
natural man, embodied a definite revolt against the hierarchical and fixed order of mediaeval society as well as
mediaeval thought.

All of these, however, do support the view that something more has happened than a widening of brotherhood
to include a larger group of brothers. Indeed, an examination of the historical conditions of the development of
western universalism suggests that despite all the differences in specific conditions, there was an essential common quality—a shift in the center of gravity which was
less a universalizing of in-group relations than a reformu-
lation of obligation in terms of an abstract and generalized
person. Even the ancient universalisms had this character. Stoicism stripped away all obligations to others as
secondary, leaving the maintenance of personal integrity
as the primary goal. Christianity gave each soul universal
importance by turning it away from the world, directly to
God. In more modern times the enthusiasm of a Kant
saw morality expressing universal legislation for rational
beings as such, wherever they be found (even if there be

other kinds of rational creatures on Saturn, he says!); the universality is achieved by reducing the full-bodied human to the thin strain of reason. In the 17th and 18th centuries, more and more the source of obligation was located in the self-assertion of the individual will—whether in the market, the state, or interpersonal relations.

The modern change in the conception of a person has been described in several ways from different points of approach. Legal historians see it as a shift from "status" to "contract." Economic historians see it as a reflection of the freer individual control of things in the new forms of production and exchange. Sociologists stress the replacement of a primary group embracing various functions within one framework by a set of separate associational relations. Anthropologists too stress the multiple relatedness of folk or primitive society, the deeper roots of the individual in his culture and in his social group, in simpler and more homogeneous societies. In any case, all note the emergence of a new basis for moral interdependence, one which is rooted less in the primary affective group, and more in structured institutional forms.

The question is thus sharply focussed on the other aspect of the definition of the moral community—what is the quality and character of participation? How is the individual seen in relation to the group? Is the tightly-knit structure of a kin-bound social system in which every aspect of a man's life is laid out for him in formal patterns of expected or correct behavior, in which choices are relatively minimal, one in which responsibility and the individual's moral role tend to disappear? Is there here a fusion of group and individual, so that the core of the responsible lone individual, which is so much stressed in our society, is absent, and the individual is instead blended into a wider total group responsibility?

That there is some meaning to in-group solidarity, to the "moral bonds" all too often referred to as a kind of self-evident base in family and small-group interrelations, is probably true enough. Social psychologists have noted that even in our society a group of people working closely together may develop strong bonds of sympathy, of awareness of common purpose, even common group rules and attitudes that are quite outside of culturally patterned commitments. These need not be explicitly understood and verbalized by the participants, and yet they may be quite effective. This is true not only of groups whose cohesiveness is generally recognized, like a small air-force cadre, but even of people whose joint participation is more limited, like a group working together in a particular job or on a particular shift in a large-scale industrial operation. If this can be so, the factor of spontaneous, deeply ingrained and easily generated mutual "moral bonds" in a community of people who live and work together for their entire lives might conceivably be far stronger. In practice, however, it would appear, as we have already noted elsewhere, that factors for friction are also generated; so that we cannot simply take for granted the common moral purposes nor any psychologically given common moral relatedness of any community. We need rather to explore it phenomenologically with great care: how do the individuals feel their commitments to other people? Are individuals subordinated in some significant way to the group? Or do we find that each is somehow forced to make his own decisions, and is somehow held accountable for them? Are there differences that depend on the structure of the group itself—its sources of authority, its goals?

Anthropologists have no simple answers to these questions; they have not been the focal center of research. But there is an accumulating body of relevant data on the actual interplay of forces within particular groups, the ways in which people make decisions, the felt phenomenal qualities as formulated in discourse, of conformity, obedience, or dedication, and the sanctions and justifications which people feel are relevant in their behavior. We shall explore some of these further in their own right later on. Here, however, we need only note that the felt strength of common commitment may lie in strong sympathy with living kinsmen, but it may also lie in a sense of dependence on common ancestors, or it may be given in the working out of the social situation, so that no felt alternatives press for claims. We need to know more about the varied conditions and qualities of reciprocal obligations, of communal goals and undertakings; but we can make at least one general point: in every case, in some minimal sense at least, it appears that the *individual* is functioning, not some mechanical robot enmeshed in a "cake of custom." The individual occasionally rebels, or fails to conform; and the individual, approaching *group* goals, is doing so not in some mystical subordination of self to group, but in a way which, while it includes some elements of symbolic identification, still gives scope to and needs the support of individual motivation and goals.

There are, of course, some totalitarian exceptions— just as there are in some contexts in our society. In some joint religious participation, in some forms of stringent military organization, the individual does give up decision making. Soldiers drop bombs without weighing the moral pros and cons. And certainly in many societies people automatically obey their fathers, or the priests, or the ghosts, or the laws, or otherwise place themselves in the hands of responsible authority. But rebellion is there as a threat, and occasional individual dissidence occurs, or yielding to temptation. This does not mean that there is no joint responsibility, no sharing of consequences, no mutual pressure to conformity. But when we look closely at various situations where there is such a common nexus, we find an important sense in which the individual is the active moral agent or participant: it is he who acts, moral duties devolve upon him, moral decisions are made by him.

Take, for example, the striking cases of what used to be known as "collective responsibility": this is the kind of case we find in vengeance feud situations where the vengeance of the victim's kinsmen is directed against the murderer's whole kin group. Legally, they share the responsibility; one of them may pay for the murder with his life. But this is no more a confusion of his person with that of the murderer than is that of a father with his son, when the former has to pay for a window the latter has broken. The father is legally responsible. But he will not castigate himself thereafter, and he may very well give his son a good spanking. So, too, brothers may in some cases exert pressure on their errant kinsman to stop getting the whole group into trouble; but in any case, they do not necessarily feel themselves guilty of the crime, nor do they all always participate as individuals in any fighting it precipitates.

Or take another kind of example which is of a fairly usual sort. An individual commits an offense, and the supernatural penalty that ensues acts upon his children or other members of his family, or spreads from him to other people with whom he associates. But if we probe the picture of the way the people themselves understand the happenings, we find that while the affliction affects the group, it is because of the wrong-doing of the particular man. It is he who must expiate it. There are often procedures of confession and sacramental purging which he must perform, though sometimes with the aid of his kinsmen. It would seem that the group-directed consequences (in so far as they are more than an explanation of the actual occurrence of epidemics, or the general scarcity of game in an area) are more of a sanctioning mechanism to enforce the individual's conformity than any evidence of moral identification.

It is also apparent that there may be a surprisingly individualized strain in the most group-oriented frameworks. Pueblo Indian culture, for example, can be described in very communal terms: everyone shares the same ends, peace for the village, religious participation smoothly carried out, successful work in harmony. There is no individual ambition, no competition or desire to outshine or excel or gain wealth at one's fellow's expense. Yet when Brandt (1954, p. 39 ff.) asked the Hopi what they most desired in life, they all answered in quite personal terms: they did not stress prosperity for the Pueblo, or peace and harmony, but rather successful achievement of *personal* long life, health, and good crops. There is a fusion here of individual and group interests, which work in harmony. The individual can identify himself with the group to a very great extent, without submerging himself in some mystic way in group goals.

However, if the joint participation in a small moral community does not mean purely automatic acceptance of group norms and some total identification with group ends, it does no doubt very often mean a close sensitivity to the feelings and attitudes of other members of the group. Ridicule and good esteem are opposite sides of a coin which can be of great value in a face-to-face group situation. But we cannot take these measures for granted. They may be institutionalized and underlined, and are in many societies; but there are also many situations in which the extent to which other people do in fact care about and attempt to influence each other's good and bad behavior is very slight. In spite of factors of proximity and inter-relatedness, people may avoid interfering with or criticizing each other's conduct and character. Perhaps it is sometimes *because* of the proximity, and its attendant danger of friction. In any case, we find that while some peoples have professional haranguers, or encourage certain categories of kinsmen to serve as "joking relatives," privileged to point a critical finger, or direct a moral rebuke, others would consider any such criticism or public comment as very unjustifiable interference. The Chiga will tolerate gross personal misbehavior on the part of a brother, and still continue to treat him as if nothing were amiss. The Pueblo Indians will gossip and comment about people's ritual observance and its concomitantly-required even temper, but will carefully avoid any interference in people's personal economic or sex concerns. There are standards in these matters too; but it is a man's own business whether he lives up to them. It is interesting that it is we, with our stress on independence and on the individual, who permit a degree of concern and interference that would certainly not be acceptable very widely. Particularly odd to most people is our view that it is the "disinterested spectator," non-kin, non-involved, who is most fit to pass critical moral judgments. And we should certainly find few places which share our missionary zeal, and our proneness to join societies for the prevention of cruelty to other people's children.

To understand this whole picture more fully, we really need to know a great deal more about how people conceive of and understand responsibility. This has been a key concept in our western philosophical tradition, and it has gone through a great many changes. Always at the center is the individual, with one life to live, and no chance to relive it differently in a hereafter (even purgatory is, after all, a purging of certain specific offenses, not a fresh new chance). But the view of what this person is, and what he is responsible for, extends with all sorts of gradations over a very wide range. He may somehow be responsible for far more than he could will, or could know, or do if he could know: as in the ancient view seen in the Oedipus story, of some kind of foredooming or overhanging curse. There is a similar implication in later theological ideas of predestined damnation, irrespective of what can possibly be done by a man, if grace is lacking. And some existentialists today hold a man responsible for anything which touches his life, no matter how little the extent of his actual power; for he could always choose death rather than let it go on with his tacit acquiescence. On the other hand, there are concepts that are tied to the idea of volition and motivation. The Sermon on the Mount makes a moral equation of lusting after a woman with committing adultery, and of unjustified anger with striking someone. Sometimes responsibility is narrowed down to hold only for what goes on within the spirit and for its attitudes. Thus St. Augustine in *The City of God* comforts the virgins ravished in the barbarian sack of Rome with the thought that as long as the will remains firm and unshaken, the sufferer is not at fault for what happens to her body: he attributes the shame that arises to the feeling "lest that act which could not be suffered without some sensual pleasure, should be believed to have been committed also with some assent of the will" (Book I, sec. 16). In a similar vein Kant places sole stress on the sense of duty as determining the morality of an act; consequences are regarded as wholly irrelevant morally. In the Utilitarian tradition, on the other hand, we find that it is precisely the consequences of acts that count morally; motives and intent are important as they imply dispositions toward certain kinds of actions.

These arguments are central and by no means out of date. Questions of responsibility in law often have a central moral core: for example, a criminal may be excused if he is out of his mind so as "not to know right from wrong." Changes in psychological and social understanding of personal volition are involved in the current shift of emphasis—still a moot legal problem—to a criterion of responsibility in terms of ability to control one's acts. Similar complex ethical and factual issues are intertwined in notions of responsibility, of punishment, of reclamation, in relation to treatment of juvenile delinquents. And questions of the individual's responsibility for action under "coercion" were sharply brought to the fore in the Nazi trials—how far down the chain of command was an individual responsible for outrages committed? From Aristotle's attempts to define "involuntary" to the most recent analyses of what is a legitimate moral excuse, philosophers have grappled with the task of sharpening judgments of responsibility.

We do not know nearly enough about this whole

legal-moral constellation in primitive societies, but we do know enough to see that there is considerable variety, and that many positions echo the controversies in our own philosophical tradition in a very interesting way, while a few strike entirely new notes. For example, there are many differences in the way volition and motivation enter. Pueblo Indians are concerned that a person's heart and thoughts be right, but they interpret this rather differently from the way we do: for, they say, love *is* the kind acts one does; acts rather than intentions count because it is *acts* which affect other people. In some cases, the question of attitude and intention may be wholly irrelevant; so in Bali we find that a moral breach like incest, or what we would consider a pure accident—like the birth of twins of opposite sex—have identical status, involving pollution and requiring ritual purification. Questions of intention and knowledge may enter even this kind of situation, as for example, when it is precisely cases of accidental incest with a kinsman so remote that the connection was not known in advance that may be purged away by a ritual act of cutting the kinship, as is the case in some parts of Africa.

All sorts of subtle shades and distinctions are drawn, sometimes quite as psychologically complex as St. Augustine's consolation of the virgins. Moral responsibility may be extended to dreams and wishes: a man may be guilty of making another man sick by having bad thoughts against him, though sometimes if the bad thoughts are justified the illness will be the sufferer's own responsibility for having provoked them. Acts performed in a dream may have such a reality status that a man may be responsible for adultery committed in a dream or for witchcraft he did without knowing about it. A man may be morally responsible for wrongs committed by others, if he precipitated the chain of acts of which they are the result. Responsibility may reach forward and backward in time, so that people pay penalties for offenses committed in previous incarnations. On the other hand, a man may be deemed perfectly innocent of the acts of which he is accused, if they were performed because he was possessed by a spirit or haunted by a ghost.

All these different views are not just differences about the ideas of responsibility; they reflect differences in the ideas of the self, of the nature of human nature, or causality. They are not just differences about how much *freedom* a man has, both with respect to his acts and to his intentions and motives—a controversial point with an enormously involved philosophical history—but also as to what he *is*. As Hallowell's pioneering work suggests (1955, ch. 4), there is rich variety in forms of self-awareness, in the limits of the self, and how it is related to the universe. Thus, thoughts may have effects without needing action; they may affect things only here and now, or at a distance and over time, so that consequences can follow a slowly-ripening course—perhaps be incubated like a disease. Redfield (1953, ch. 4) has explored the many different ways man relates himself to nature, whether as part of it, able to interact with it meaningfully, or by confronting it from without. Is it a moral universe, so that man approaches it with gratitude to the soil, and shame before the elements for his misdeeds? Does man cooperate by his rituals and his very attitudes in keeping the universe on its proper keel, or does he manipulate it coldly? Is his moral character part of it, influenced by it, and motivated by goals of satisfaction in it, or does his spirit somehow transcend it? We see happiness as a state of mind, a spirituality; it may overcome physical evils and can arise in defeating desire. Pueblo Indians have no such divided view of the person. Fulfillment of obviously desired worldly goals is good; it comes from right action—harmonious social action. If things go as they should, if circumstances are good, people will have the material base for happiness and will be happy—and that will come from men's having acted right. One's attitudes should therefore be confident and serene, and worry is a moral offense.

One can push beyond this to ask for clarification of the essential locus and degree of integration of the person, or the self. Just where is your you-ness located? Does it include your acts, your intentions, your thoughts? Does it reach out to the consequences of your thoughts? We tend to see our body parts as somehow peripheral: one can lose a leg without losing one's essential wholeness or quality as a person. To other people, any operation or loss of a part is a grave wound to the whole person and self. Even finger-nail parings, bodily excreta, clothing that has been worn, are essential parts of the person; what happens to them can still affect him. Are you continuous over time, though much of your body changes? Or are you somehow remote and detached from happenings, feeling no sense of responsibility for misdemeanors that are part of a past which has now gone by? It may sound very exotic to ask: if you have a werewolf soul which wanders about at night and commits terrible cannibal acts which you don't even known about, is it really you? And are you responsible? People do have such beliefs and they answer these questions varyingly. In some places we find that people assume responsibility and confess to the deeds, though they had no knowledge of them when they were committed. Others, however, see such souls as extraneous, intrusive; the victim of such an intrusion will be magically treated so as to be purged. Indeed, the question does not seem so exotic when we translate it into a perfectly real contemporary problem, the allocation of identity and responsibility in cases of split-personality.

There are very interesting insights into both responsibility and the self in different views of character and character training in educational theory. In our own tradition, children have been seen as evil or as innocent, to be developed or molded or unfolded or restrained. Such views are not simple psychological accounts; they embody values and ethical principles about responsibility, and in turn influence them. In any case, in most modern theory of whatever school, education is seen as deeply influencing the kind of person the child turns into. Similarly, in other cultures, educational theory—implicit, to be sure, rather than expounded in text-books—gives us a view of attitudes toward the malleability of the self. To some people a person is just what he happens to be born as. The Chiga, for example, have very little conception of education as formative. They do praise and blame people for their good and bad characteristics, but they certainly do not expect them to change. There is just one kind of character-trait that is handled differently: a husband may boast that he was lucky enough to beat the habit of witchcraft out of his wife by discovering it early. On the other hand, many American Indian peoples take a very positive view of character education. They see character as something that one can do something about. So people run ten miles before breakfast, or get children to roll naked in the snow, or plunge into icy rivers after a sweat-bath, all in the interest of developing bravery and

hardiness. In some areas a youth climbs a lonely mountain peak, rolling stones before him, and practices other
similar exercises, as semi-magical ways of developing valued traits of character which will come to him partly as
a resultant blessing from the gods.

Since the character and quality of human self-awareness is so variable, and so deeply operative in many phases
of ethical thinking, we have here a very important area
for further combined psychological, anthropological and
philosophical investigation. This may yield clues to the
way patterns of self-awareness are related to different
kinds of social orders, or goal orientations, or personality
syndromes. It will in any case help us to a fuller knowledge and more sophisticated level of analysis which we
need if we are to understand and re-evaluate our own
perspectives about the moral relations of the individual
and society, the role of creative individuality, and the
meaning of responsibility.

Chapter X

SYSTEM: ETHICAL CONCEPTS

A GREAT PART of any morality must be articulated in discourse. Since morality always includes processes of mutual guidance, it can hardly be altogether silent, even though many reactions and decisions may be submerged in emotional responses and automatic habits which are only partially verbalized. Analyses of moral terms, of types of moral assertion, and patterns of argument, teaching and justification are an important part of the study of any morality.

We may note many variations in degree of abstraction, coherence or codification, but we always find some order, expectedness and generalization in this realm, as in any sphere of human social behavior. Rules and appraisals, advice and teaching, however sporadic and ad hoc, are never limited just to indications in a particular situation. Even purely after-the-fact comment on children's behavior can hardly be limited to, "Johnny, I'll wallop you for breaking that window," without stating, or implying, "That *kind* of thing is *bad* (or wrong or dangerous)." Everywhere, then, we may expect to find some kinds of terms or linguistic devices that will bear the burden of moral communication, and some ways in which moral assertions, to some degree generalized, will be formulated and organized or systematized. In this chapter we shall concentrate on ethical terms and appraisive devices in communication. In the next, we shall go on to consider modes of generalizing and systematizing. Every culture has some terms that are used to evaluate, judge, express approval or disapproval (cf. Brandt, 1946). We are likely to forget in our own culture, because of the central role that "good" or "ought" have come to play in theoretical speculation, how rich is our vocabulary of appraisal—how many adjectives such as "fine," "contemptible," "admirable," "worthwhile," and how many nouns, as in "It's a gyp," "He's a cad," and so on, carry the weight of much of everyday moral judgment, even though a philosophical analysis may channel these words into our central concepts of "good" and "right."

On this lower level we can find rich examples from many cultures—no doubt from any. Appraisals may be implicit in the very use of trait-names or descriptions of actions or attitudes. When the Chiga say of a man, "He is generous as a mat," they do not mean to suggest that anyone can walk all over him, but rather to praise him for his welcoming hospitality. They have a whole set of terms for different kinds of anger, with very different evaluative implications. Simple anger, an immediate response to a slight or affront, is expected and normal; reference to it has no moral connotation. But "anger brooding in the heart," rather like our own terms "malice" and "spite," implies a negative evaluation; to say it of a man is virtually saying, "Avoid that man, he's evil." Such moral distinctions are sometimes indicated in the form of the language. So, for example, one can call a person a "witch." This term "witch," *omurogi*, is a simple noun from the word *roga*, to practise witchcraft. A witch is a person of evil character who habitually practises witchcraft. However, one would not use a parallel linguistic

form from the verb "to kill" to describe a man who had
killed; having committed a murder does not make a man
"a murderer." He is simply someone who happens to
have killed another man, and this is no special mark of
vice or virtue. This might be true of any man. Of
course, if he has killed many in appropriate feud contexts,
then he is "a brave one," and to be admired.

It is obvious that one must be careful not to read
one culture's evaluative connotations into another's concepts. The Hopi, for example, consider a term which
means literally "one who has a poor heart"—that is, is
humble, regards himself as of little account, even sometimes timid—as a term of praise (Brandt, 1954, p. 126).
Terms meaning argumentative, excitable, or just frank
or firm on a point of principle, carry a negative evaluation, as does to be worried. Such terms carry clear appraisive connotations for their users, because they touch on
very central virtue-constellations. For other peoples, who
value aggression or arrogant pride, they would have quite
contrary appraisive connotations.

Such examination of the contextual use of descriptive terms with evaluative connotations or associations can
give us interesting indications of the clustering of virtue
concepts. For example, the Chiga use the term "thief" to
include not only one who steals, but also anyone who is
mean, selfish or begrudging; while one term, highly derogatory, covers both dirty and lazy. Our own cultural
history presents comparable examples. Think of the combination of lazy and poor suggested in "shiftless," which
has to be understood in terms of the Puritan ethic. Even
more, can we really understand the meaning and role of
"ingratitude" in the mediaeval world without the view of
ordered hierarchical relations? Or the full impact of "im-

provident" in the 18th and 19th centuries without relation to the central role of prudence and the emphasis on saving in a commercially oriented world?

In other cultures too, to understand the morally evaluative element in an apparently simple descriptive term may lead us directly into important aspects of moral structure and belief. For example, among a great many people we get a peculiarly Erehwonian pattern of "illness" having some implication of moral wrong; it is a public indication that a moral misdemeanor has been committed, for this is held to be the cause of illness. And similarly, "being well off" may be part of the description of a good man. It implies having been careful and wise in husbanding one's resources, and having done nothing that would have involved costly rituals or payment of compensation money. This is the Navaho view, but it has a further twist: it does not hold for being too well off, for being very rich suggests the use of sorcery and also meanness in not helping one's needy relatives.

We have been dealing so far with terms descriptive of acts or traits or conditions, in which an evaluative element was also present. There are other terms in our culture's ethical vocabulary in which the emphasis falls more sharply on the evaluative element—describing or expressing the character of the appraisal—terms such as "admirable," "ridiculous," "disgusting." Investigating such terms for other languages is a complex task of both linguistic and cultural-context analysis. Brandt found a considerable vocabulary of such terms for the Hopi, some very comparable to terms we use, when roughly translated—"disgusting," for example, "admirable" and "object of contempt." There are many subtle distinctions in their meaning and application: father-daughter incest, for example,

Brandt's informants would not call "disgusting" or "abhorrent," but rather a "shameful act" (1954, p. 92). Obviously such exploration needs to be carried out more fully in the original language, rather than an interpreter's English.

Kluckhohn presents some such material summarized for the Navaho (1956a). His material suggests far more use of descriptive than evaluative formulations, and reminds us also that evaluative concepts may be expressed not in single words or phrases, but in more complex appraisive assertions. In many cultures we find such expressions in use as "That's behaving like a dog," or "I would be ashamed," or "People would laugh at you." The exact comparability of such terms and expressions is a matter for careful contextual exploration. They may focus upon the emotional reaction of the commentator, as at least the literal meaning of ours so often does. Or they may concentrate more on the total situation, or tell us more precisely something of the quality of the command, approval or interdiction, pointing to it as unthinkable, forbidden, tempting, incorrect, necessary, and so forth. Sometimes, far from being simple approval or disapproval statements, they may carry us to the heart of justification and sanction concepts. "Ridiculous" and "People will laugh at you" may be far from equivalent. When we dismiss a course of conduct as ridiculous, we are almost dismissing any moral significance—it is trivial or silly. But in some cultures "People will laugh at you" may carry a portentous institutionalized threat about major social reactions to an offense.

Insofar as such concepts can be carefully explicated and not merely roughly translated, they may be able to tell us a good deal about shades of distinction in negative or positive evaluation, about the stringency or merely preferential quality of prescriptions, and about the quality of the emotional reactions people feel in such contexts—indignation or shame or disgust or fear or remorse, and so on. They may help to pinpoint areas of differential selection of particular emotions—or cognitions—to do what Ruth Benedict somewhere aptly described as "the heavy work of morality."

We turn now from this whole lower or middle range of concepts in which there is a varying degree of fusion of descriptive and evaluative or appraisive elements to the upper range in which the ethical element—whether it be content or function—stands out centrally. These are, so to speak, the élite of our moral language—such terms as "right" and "wrong," "good" and "evil," "sin," "duty," "ought." In our culture they rise easily in thought and discourse to preside over moral discussion. They judge whether terms below have a truly ethical flavor, and they are the ones that moral philosophers spend tremendous energy analyzing. They are not, however, a closed group. Once in a while a term like "value" or "norm" or "desirable" may try to force its way in, and terms like "worthwhile" are constant hangers-on in the background. But if we have any doubts about the moral reference of the intruders, we go to the well-established set for explication: thus, for example, the ethical use of "desirable" is not just "usual or obvious object of desire," but must be interpreted rather as "ought to be desired" or "good that it be desired"; similarly, if we are uncertain whether "approval" connotes moral judgment, we distinguish a mere feeling of approval from "feeling that it was as it ought to be."

Unfortunately, the analysis of these fundamental ethical concepts is not an easy matter. Like many élites in the history of human affairs, they have traced their descent from the gods, denied their natural roots and turned their backs on their ancestral rise from the common folk. While some philosophers have stressed their functions— regarding them as terms elevated to carry out a marshalling role in the conflict of human wants and the crossings of human needs—other philosophers have been dazzled by their quality and called for an intuitive appreciation of their purity. What is more, if we look within the set, there are fashions in prominence. Different terms rise to the top in different periods. The ethical theories of the ancient world assumed that everything would fall into place in our moral life if we only knew the *good* that all men sought. In the mediaeval world, *sin* had a truly queenly role in any thinking about the moral structure. In modern moral philosophy since Kant the idea of the autonomy of the moral domain and the purity of the concept of *ought* has been central—even to say that something is "good" has at times been translated into saying that it is "as it ought to be" (Hartmann, 1932, ch. 18). Philosophers have studied the internal relations of ethical concepts with great eagerness and lined up in schools of devotion to the primacy of one or another over the rest. Thus G. E. Moore gives primacy to "good" (1903, chs. 1, 5), H. A. Prichard to the initial fact of "obligation" (1949), while W. D. Ross assigns them independent and coordinate roles (1930).

To pursue such analyses in other cultures is not a simple matter. Considering the difficulty in getting at the precise meaning of terms in ethical discourse in our own usage, despite the centuries of practice from Socrates to the modern analysts, it is not surprising that one may sometimes find it hard to ferret out with exactness the meaning of an ethical term in some other language and cultural situation. But it is also clear that such comparative inquiry may yield some very interesting clues. Let us take one example which has been analyzed in some detail—the Navaho term *bahadzid*. In his analysis of the Navaho ethical system, Ladd finds this the critical term (1957, ch. 13). Literally, this word means "for it there is reverence or fear"; the English word which appears to be closest to it in meaning is "dangerous," with the difference that for the Navaho the danger involved is often from a supernatural source. Like many terms in our own ethical discourse, the Navaho term includes a wide range of possible uses that are not specifically ethical: it applies, for example, to driving a car too fast. Some of the things *bahadzid* covers are purely ritual proscriptions. Others concern important interpersonal relations. But all are stringently enjoined—from avoiding things struck by lightning to proper observance of the mother-in-law avoidance regulations. Each of these has an automatic consequence—a particular form of illness peculiar to and consequent upon its violation. However, *bahadzid* does not cover all kinds of strong obligations and interdictions. There are many interpersonal obligations—parent-child and child-parent attitudes, the need to help your friends and relatives and so forth—about which the Navaho also feel strongly, whose violation is not *bahadzid*. They are required but not under threat of the same penalty. To neglect them may not make you or your family ill, but it will "put you into trouble" in various ways. There is involved in this "trouble" a whole complex set of ideas about mutual dependence, about how one man's behavior may influence another, even about the inconvenience and

danger of being thought a witch. Ladd's account of Navaho ethics stresses the continuum from *bahadzid* to these
other proscriptions and injunctions in their common emphasis on avoiding bad, painful or uncomfortable consequences. His analysis of *bahadzid* therefore carries us into
an examination of how it fits into the moral system, as
well as into religious beliefs, and psycho-social under-
standings, all of which are necessary to elucidating its
meaning.

We must note the fact that a good deal of other
material on Navaho has stressed not the *bahadzid* concept so much as a term meaning something like good,
"the path of beauty" or harmony. Ladd's claim is that
this term, for all its positive content and importance,
especially in religious observance, is nonetheless not as
central. He notes particularly that it is not to be equated
with anything like the Greek emphasis on the good and
on harmony. The Navaho do not seek the good, but
tend rather to assume it, providing one proceeds in a
normal course. They place their moral emphasis on the
avoidance of evil which will upset the balance or harmony of life. Certainly, Kluckhohn's analysis (1956a)
also suggests the prevalence of negative phrasing, though
he places more emphasis on a general term which means
"ugly," and applies to a whole range from filthy clothing to "repulsive behavior such as incest and witchcraft."

We shall not pursue other illustrations in comparable detail; but it is clear that they too would give us
pictures of wide ranges of difference in the application of
roughly similar terms, and also of significant difference
in basic emphases. Take, for example, the Hopi use of
ka-anta (Brandt, 1954, ch. 6), which means wrong, and
like our *wrong* contains the point of incorrectness, of the

sort which can apply also to solving an arithmetical problem—and is so used. The incorrectness aspect of the meaning of *ka-anta* appears to go much further than in our meaning of wrong. "A good head calculates knowledge" and a normally intelligent person applies his knowledge to following appropriate courses of conduct. For the Hopi as for the Navaho there is an unintelligent quality to wrong behavior. But the Hopi usage contains less of the absolute tabu quality of the Navaho wrong in *bahadzid,* though in many ways it too points to consequences.

It is interesting that the appraisive term which is perhaps most widely used in Hopi is simply *ka-hopi*—not-Hopi or unHopi. This is used of anyone whose general behavior is disapproved; it implies a violation of "the Hopi way" or the upsetting of its order.

Such comparative materials, from our own tradition and from other cultures, suggest that ethical concepts, while they may have achieved a high order of theoretical abstraction, still have rich cultural content, by reference to which they have to be understood. Just as the Navaho strain their moral injunctions through the concept of *dangerous,* the mediaeval world structured its moral content by means of the concept of *sin.* And it would be theoretical folly to try to understand the shades of feeling that entered into the sense of sin or the cognitions that were involved when a man confessed "peccavi," by extracting a pure concept of sin as some general idea of disobedience to authority or estrangement from ultimate reality. To leave out the religious reference, with its ideational and organizational structure and its relations to the historical life of the times and the cultural tensions and problems to which it was addressed, would be to empty it of a great part of its meaning. Thus any current non-religious use of "sin" can only be a psychological allegory based on this historical content. To speculate on a postulate system in which the term "sin" might be a primitive undefined term would be an interesting exercise, but any outcome would share the emptiness which a pure mathematics frankly acknowledges. It too would then require exploration of areas where it could be fruitfully applied or interpreted.

Such a lesson is pertinent to theoretical analysis of fundamental ethical concepts today. So, for example, there has been a century and a half of effort since Kant's day to purify *ought* of all content, whether natural or theological, psychological or cultural. To reverse the direction and seek a richer meaning by seeing the operative character of the concept in psychological, cultural and historical depth can prove much more fruitful. Instead of looking for the pure idea of obligation, we can examine where its phenomenal qualities rest on the structure of conscience, or how its bonds or ties are rooted in specific social and institutional relations, in the development of a self-assertive self and a contractual attitude to commitments, or an emphasis on instrumentality in the pursuit of aims, and so on. Unpacking these layers of accrued meaning has sometimes been pursued as if its purpose were to strip the container bare; it is no wonder then that it sometimes ends in just inscrutable intuitions or a vacuum that is filled by pure emotional expressions. We suggest it would be more helpful to examine and understand the contents. It is obvious that if we want to understand the different meaning of obligation in Japanese ethics, we have to explore its full cultural content in terms which include the idea of debt to the ancestors and the continuity of family living (cf. Benedict, 1946). Surely it would be equally obvious to a Japanese investigator that understanding ours imposes the same necessity of contextual interpretation. If we are to do our own investigating, we must learn to make our own cultural assumptions explicit.

Chapter XI

SYSTEM: ETHICAL GENERALIZATION

Having considered the prevalence and patterning of ethical terms, we have next to look at the ways they are used in moral utterance. How are moral statements formulated, organized and systematized? This is a tangled terrain, complex in our culture and barely entered into for primitive societies. It includes such problems as: What are the occasions and styles of moral utterance and the forms of moral discourse? How much generalization occurs? What patterns of organization are to be found, and how are they shaped for application? Is there a single or unique logic of moral discourse?

In our own culture, where we usually feel that we operate with a code and a system, we find in practice that we use many different forms and devices, and many different levels, in organizing our moral discourse, homely or formal. There are absolute rules of a specific sort cast in the form of commands: "Thou shalt not commit adultery," or "Thou shalt not covet thy neighbor's house." Moral injunctions may also be phrased as factual reports: "It is wrong to tell a lie," or "Honesty is the best policy." Sometimes we find very general points of principle set forth, like "Man owes some consideration to his fellow men," or "Cleanliness is next to godliness," or, once more in imperative form, "Do unto others as you would have them do unto you." We also find proverbs, metaphors and parables used to point moral lessons. "A stitch in time saves nine" or "Procrastination is the thief of time" really preach a whole ethic of care and prudence as virtues, while "Turn the other cheek," far from being a particular command about a particular kind of act, is a most general admonition about a whole set of attitudes and values. We also propose moral models—secular figures like Lincoln or religious ones like Jesus —to serve as the touchstone for reflection or pattern for emulation. Sometimes one of these forms may seem more appropriate than another, depending on whether the context is teaching the young, justifying a course of action pursued, thinking about one to be undertaken, criticizing deviant behavior, or sometimes even just reflecting on life and its ways. But all of these forms occur commonly in our moral discourse. And all are in some sense generalizations.

For other cultures, too, many different kinds and levels of generalization, and many different forms of moral utterance, occur. There may be some stylistic specialization: one culture may prefer pithy allegorical summations, another long proverbs with or without a stated moral. Still others may go in for a good deal of prosy moralizing, on the order of our copy-book maxims. And no doubt if these varying styles could be isolated for comparative study, in relation to the contexts of their use, we would find valuable clues for the study of the functioning of morality. There is not enough systematically gathered material for us to make any such attempt here; but it seems clear that there is wide variety on almost any point of form or organization that we may set up for study.

Let us look for example at an interesting list Paul

Radin has compiled of moral generalizations gleaned from direct translations of Winnebago texts (1927, p. 65 ff.):*

1. It is always good to be good.
2. What does life consist of but love?
3. Of what value is it to kill?
4. You ought to be of some help to your fellow men.
5. Do not abuse your wife; women are sacred.
6. If you cast off your dress for many people, they will be benefited by your deed.
7. For the good you do everyone will love you.
8. Never do any wrong to children.
9. It is not good to gamble.
10. If you see a helpless old man, help him if you have anything at all.
11. If you have a home of your own, see to it that whoever enters it obtains something to eat. Such food will be a source of death to you if withheld.
12. When you are recounting your war deeds on behalf of the departed soul, do not try to add to your honor by claiming more for yourself than you have actually accomplished. If you tell a falsehood then and exaggerate your achievements you will die beforehand. The telling of truth is sacred. Tell less than you did. The old men say it is wiser.
13. Be on friendly terms with everyone and then everyone will love you.
14. Marry only one person at a time.
15. Do not be haughty with your husband. Kindness will be returned to you and he will treat you in the same way in which you treat him.

---

*The greater part of this code comes from material originally published in *Crashing Thunder: the Autobiography of an American Indian,* edited by Paul Radin. Copyright, 1926, by D. Appleton and Company. It is reprinted here by permission of Appleton-Century-Crofts, Inc.

16. Do not imagine that you are taking your children's part if you just speak about loving them. Let them see it for themselves; let them know what love is by seeing you give away things to the poor.

17. Do not show your love for other people so that people notice it. Love them but let your love be different from that for your own.

18. As you travel along life's road, never harm anyone or cause anyone to feel sad. On the contrary, if at any time you meet a woman away from your village and you are both alone and no one can see you, do not frighten her or harm her.

19. If you meet anyone on the road, even if it is only a child, speak a cheering word before you pass on.

20. If your husband's people ever ask their own children for something when you are present, assume that they had asked it of you. If there is anything to be done, do not wait till you are asked to do it, but do it immediately.

21. Never think a home is yours until you have made one for yourself.

22. If you have put people in charge of your household, do not nevertheless act as though the home were still yours.

23. When visiting your husband's people, do not act as if you were far above them.

As Radin points out, these are far more than "mere proverbs and practical folk wisdom." They embody a wide variety of types of generalizing. Some are general statements about specific acts, such as gambling, but some refer to very general kinds of actions, such as helping your fellow-man. Some enjoin general virtues—truth-telling, kindness, friendliness—some concentrate on due performance of roles, and some even appear to suggest what feeling is appropriate. A number are highly general and abstract: certainly it would be hard to outdo "It is always good to be good." Some are stated as absolute, some as conditional imperatives. Others are more advisory in tone, and even interrogative.

In this Winnebago material we have a special slant coming from the source in written texts of a formal sort. No doubt moral comments would be pithier and more pungent if they were taken from protocols of actual critical remarks on others' moral peccadilloes. But the didactic tone of these statements reflects appropriately the basic role which these adages and others like them play in Winnebago usage. An important moral occasion, not only in Winnebago but in American Indian cultures generally, is the basic setting of prosy lectures by the grandfather at the evening fireside. Character training thus conducted is explicit and directed. This is well underlined in a comment quoted by Radin (1927, p. 81): "When the Indians have a child whom they love very much, they preach to him so that he may never become acquainted with the things that are not right, and that he may never do wrong. Then if, later in life, he does any wrong he will do so with the clear knowledge of the consequences of his action." Such character training includes pointing to models of good conduct, constant homilies and adjurations, and warnings for the future.

This list of moral adages and reflections, like our own Ten Commandments, goes beyond items of conduct to ideals and goals and principles of justification. But it is not an organized code, with a regular pattern and logical order. Nor does it claim to be exhaustive or to demarcate what is central and what is peripheral. The

Decalogue has often been considered to be all of these, providing a definitive, adequate, systematic account of all our major moral principles.

How much codification in this sense occurs among most peoples is something we do not now know. Certainly, it is not very common, though it may be that it does occur where there are formal initiation schools or other such contexts encouraging coherence and formalization, just as we sometimes find elaborately formulated theology or cosmology where there are specialized esoteric priesthoods to cultivate it. But sets of principles commonly referred to, explanations of some order of generality, easily adduced lists of appropriate behavior for different situations, these must all be fairly usual. If, using the term in the looser sense in which it is often employed and remembering that we will be dealing frequently with the implicit as well as the explicit, we may speak of such sets as "moral codes," then our present concern is with the qualitative properties and organizational modes to be found in moral codes.

In this area there are a number of topics that have been dealt with in ethical theory and also to some extent in cultural studies, without it being apparent that they were in large measure addressed to the same problems. When these trends are juxtaposed, new and fruitful areas of research clearly open up.

Let us look for one thing at the question of the appropriate form for ethical expression or assertion. This has been a topic intensely cultivated in contemporary ethical theory, and there has been considerable revision proposed of traditional positions. Traditional philosophical analyses of moral judgments tended to be *cognitivist*. They took moral judgments to be asserting or reporting moral facts, and therefore to be either true or false in their reports. Contemporary positivist analyses, influenced by the sharp separation of value and fact (itself a cultural emphasis in the theoretical world), have underscored instead the *expressive* elements in appraisive terms. They argue that "wrong" is not a descriptive property, capable of scientific verification, and propose instead a complete retranslation of moral assertions in expressive terms. For example, A. J. Ayer translates "Stealing is wrong" into "Stealing!!"—that is, into an utterance which simply gives vent to an emotion of horror (1936, ch. 6; cf. Stevenson, 1944). Bertrand Russell at one point argues that judgments of ultimate good are really optative in structure: you are simply saying, in effect, "Would that everybody desired this" (1935, ch. 9; cf. 1955, ch. 4). And many philosophers have followed the imperativistic line of translation, stoutly affirming that what seemed an indicative, like "Killing is wrong," is really a disguised imperative, "Thou shalt not kill," and so again has no relation to factual verification. At first there was some dispute about the translation to be preferred. Then these tendencies consolidated about what was common to them, as opposed to the older tradition, and began to compromise on a single term, such as "prescriptive." Moral judgment is compared to the judge's act of decision, or to the ceremonial utterance, "I do." "Prescriptive" signifies that the function of the utterance, set by the context of use, is to persuade, commend, exhort, or even to perform. The underlying assumption is that morality is really concerned with conduct in human life, and not with knowledge primarily, and attention has shifted from insistence on a preferred translation to the variety of contexts of prescription (cf. A. Edel, 1953, pp. 132 ff.).

This theoretical mellowing seems to us to have been all to the good; but the process is far from finished. For even if moral assertions are taken to be concerned with conduct, it does not follow that their function is necessarily limited to some kind of activist prompting. There are many ways in which a morality may be concerned with conduct. It may specialize in urging specific acts, or in cultivating general attitudes. It may incline towards commanding or advising. It may see the provision of knowledge as an effective way to reorient conduct, and gear its assertions to a situation of teaching and learning. It might even see influencing action not as a process of conditioning, but as one of awakening the mind by stimulation, and so lay stress in its judgments or expressions on raising questions.

We may, then, fruitfully look at the various theoretical analyses of the syntax of moral utterance as constituting a kind of model building, and use them as guides to see what an imperativistic systematization of morality would be like, or an optative one, a teaching and learning one, a feeling-expression one, and so on. And it is particularly illuminating to find that, to some extent, these alternative models can actually be found in the comparative laboratory. The Zuñi apparently look upon their morality as knowledge to be taught and learned like any other facts of the world. Moral decisions are matters for careful weighing and concern, with an attempt to figure out the "right" way, in the sense of correct. Mediaeval morality found no difficulty in looking upon every moral rule as a command; it was able even to assimilate laws of nature to commands, not by a logical confusion of the prescriptive and the descriptive, but because plants grew and stones fell only by God's will—for obviously they had no free will of their own. Certainly advisory or hortatory systems occur: that seems to be the essence of Navaho moral discourse. Items in the Winnebago list ("What does life consist of but love?") lead us to wonder whether one might not construct a model in which all judgments of ultimate value would be translated into interrogatives, rather than imperatives or optatives or indicatives—somewhat after the Socratic fashion, with a constant probing for the nature of man and life. And many refinements and perhaps whole new vistas may emerge when the linguistic analysis of different peoples' richly different conceptual perspectives reaches a level which can be brought to bear in this area.

The outcome of such correlation of philosophical and cultural studies is more than just to give model-building a freer scope. It also reminds us to view the models, whether they are drawn from our own history or from other cultures, as specific forms of ethical expression, to be understood in relation to their cultural context. This gives depth to their interpretation, and raises fresh questions rather sharply. What, for example, is the relation of imperativistic models to the source of commands? Who commands whom? Is it just parents ordering children, or is the whole social structure a highly authoritarian pecking order? And how is this supported by character training and personality development? Does the formal justificatory framework fall in line, perhaps with a power-ordered hierarchy of spirits as a source of moral commands? And what is the relation between these various aspects? Similarly, where attention turns to evaluation, it means that instead of pressing the question of which is the "correct" syntax of the moral language, we would have to ask which of the envisaged models best fits into the most accurate and fullest available picture of man and his needs and perennial aspirations.

Parallel lessons emerge if we look at a second question which has been raised about the organization of moral codes—the prominence of abstraction and universalization. It is evident that our culture has a fondness for the abstract and highly general. Our descriptive terms in moral judgment tend toward the more abstract: we mount the ladder from the relatively concrete "stealing" to the more general "honesty" and end up with an ideal of "personal integrity." Our moral laws, too, tend to be highly general, cut off from any particular reference to context or situation or role, and, as we noted in an earlier chapter, applicable to anyone simply as a person.

It is often claimed that most moralities throughout the world are more limited, more specific, and define what is moral differently for different people and different situations. But the use of sharply demarcated situational reference need not imply that there is no general ordering principle, any more than our frequent resort to principles should lead us to think that we do not have operative procedures and tacit assumptions about conditions for application. These, as we shall see, are to be found, though in the background. Conversely, it may be that in the more particularistic moralities, it is the ordering principles that are in the background. They exist, but are taken for granted, or are obscured by the fact that in actual practice particular applications rather than most highly general principles are likely to be stated. (After all, how often even in our culture will a man give as his reason for not cheating or telling a lie, that he believes in doing unto others as he would have them do unto him?)

Chinese morality has been depicted as highly situational (Hsu, 1953). It is full of rules written in terms of particular duties to be fulfilled in particular situations; the same behavior which is good in one context might be wrong at another time and place or toward other people. Yet this implies and indeed states quite formally a general duty to fulfill one's obligations, to play one's customary role appropriately. This kind of general principle has a different character and form from an explicitly universal one like our Golden Rule. And we might contrast their relative applicability and usefulness in different kinds of applied situations: the one, being set in terms of customary role, is less helpful in an unstructured or novel situation. The other can cope with novelty, but may get into difficulties if there are conflicting tendencies in the self. But certainly both principles are general and absolute in form.

Mediaeval morality had some of the same ambiguity. It dictated different codes of behavior for people of the different social orders. The same definition of a good man would hardly fit the knight and the serf. Yet both might be living by the principle of doing their duty to the station to which they belonged. In our day, too, we actually make important situation distinctions quite often. The demands of a war-time morality are different from those of a peace-time morality, home-morality is different from business ethics. Most people rearrange their moral priorities on such bases without feeling limited by the contradiction real absolutes would imply.

It is of course philosophically tempting to think of a sharp contrast between universalistic and particularistic. There is a traditional metaphysical conflict between realism and nominalism, the former assigning "ultimate reality" to the universal, the latter to the individual particular. But to yield to such a temptation would be to seek to clarify the difficult by reference to the more obscure! Perhaps we should read the philosophic lesson in reverse, and point out that underlying these metaphysical conflicts were different conceptions of language and its role, different analyses of the psychology of thinking, different estimates of the methods of knowledge, different directions in the orientation of life. So, too, when we find different stresses in the organization of moral codes we have to ask how far we are dealing merely with cultural or sub-cultural styles, how far with different conceptions of the nature and proper role of man, how far with assumptions about the complexity of the field and the possibility of systematic summary knowledge, how far with different value orientations or different social needs.

Take, for example, the conflict of legalism and antilegalism which stands out sharply in western religiousethical outlooks, both Judaic and Christian. The legalist stresses the touchstone of obedience to the letter of God's law as man's highest duty and his highest good. The anti-legalist stresses getting behind the letter of the law to the spirit underlying it, and relying on some general principle like the Golden Rule. The legalist trusts the adequacy of the code to cover the situations of life, the anti-legalist is more prone to stress the complexity of the particular. There are different estimates of the attitude of the individual in action. One side stresses obedience and conformity as in themselves good; the other feels that the letter kills but the spirit quickens. Sometimes in considering the legalism of orthodox western religions, one finds the merit of legalism as a structure argued on the basis of the weakness of the human will and the need for keeping it constantly in line. Questions of social need may also become explicit. This stands out more clearly in controversies over the legalistic attitude in the highly parallel field of law, and in other cultures as well as our own. For example, as Northrop points out (1952, pp. 11-12), the Chinese legalists attacking the Confucian view that, in settling disputes, resort to codes is morally evil, argued that advanced social organization, because of its complexity, demanded codification. In western law it is interesting to see how epochs of strict law lacking flexibility give rise to equity principles to serve as correctives, and how equity systems themselves develop to become simply other forms of law. Similarly, a revolt against moral legalism by a resort to underlying spirit may harden into a precise weighing of virtues and an inner regulation so rigorous that a legalism may appear to leave an inner freedom by comparison. So intricate is the dialectic of systematization modes!

If we turn now to the question of the kinds of organization or general unifying emphases that we find, a number of different directions may be discerned. In many moralities some type or aspect of content stands out as a focus of organization. This does not mean simply that one area of moral problems may bulk large, although this no doubt often happens. Ask young people in our society, for example, what they understand by morality, and the chances are that they will answer in terms of what is appropriate sexual behavior! It is rather that we sometimes find that the concepts and rules of an important region of content become the categories and principles for organizing many other areas as well. This can be seen clearly in a legal parallel. In the history of English law one is struck by the dominance in one era of the concept of property, so that any rights a man has at law will be conceived of as his property. In a later era, one finds the concept of contract used over a wider and wider area to organize the legal formulation of many social situations, and even the very structure of the state comes to be viewed as basically contractual among the members of the society. So too in moral codes, we may find pervasive goals or processes taking their place as the organizing principles of systematic moral thinking. In this fashion, the goal of pleasure takes on the organizing job in the hedonistic ethics, the goal of power in the Nietzschean outlook, or the process of compromising and harmonizing in many liberalist philosophies.

We find the same kind of thing, though around quite different principles, in other moralities. Social structure principles may for example serve as a major hub of moral organization. We can see this among the Tallensi, who, Fortes points out (1949) tend to "explain conduct that conforms to the norms by appealing to kinship." Indeed, "A gross breach of kinship duty is the prototype of the Tale notion of sin" (p. 13). Especially important here is the patterned distinction between different kinds of relatives, and the special quality of the relationship between those close patrilineal kinsmen who "sacrifice together." The Tallensi will use this relationship to explain why it is such a hideous offense for a man and his son to sleep with the same woman; for knowing of such a wrong committed by one against the other, how would they be able thereafter to participate in religious sacrifices in the proper spirit of harmonious good feeling which these require? Or a father-in-law drawing back in shocked refusal of a gift of meat from a sacrifice may explain that such a gift from his son-in-law is impossible, as it would mean sharing the sacrifice; this is wrong, for affinal relatives have too many occasions for quarrels over such matters as bride-price payments for a shared sacrifice to be proper. A special rule exists which calls it wrong for a father to press for bride-price payments while his daughter is pregnant (a rule frequently violated in anger, however). Here the argument runs that if he pressed for payment which was not forthcoming, a divorce might ensue. The child would thus be born in his home, and thus be deprived of the necessary protection of its own paternal ancestral spirits at the difficult time of birth. He should not involve his daughter and her child in this danger.

An underlying social structure principle served also in mediaeval morality, where the hierarchical structure of human social relationships, with their designated appropriate roles, was also the structure of the relationship between man and God, the general source of moral authority; and it is also part of the basic structure of Japanese morality (Benedict, 1946).

Sometimes the ordering principle appears to lie not so much in a point of structure as in a dominant value orientation, which lends a unity to diverse rules and principles. The idea of following the mean, of not going to extremes, has such a character in many moralities. The Winnebago, for example, emphasize through many of their moral statements the ideas of "moderation and proportion," and a good man tries to follow "the insistent admonition of the wise men and of the experienced elders that man learn the limits imposed by nature and above all that man learn the limitation to his own powers" (Radin, 1927, p. 91). In a parallel way, though in quite a different vein, an ideal of achievement and striving, or a conception of community, may run through a morality.

More specific and formalized touchstones may also be used, as highly general and all embracing as the Golden Rule in the thinking of some moralists in our culture. The Navaho, for example, as John Ladd has pointed out (1957), have a common principle by which to determine the right, the correct, or the good course of conduct, one which can be used not only to explain and unify existent rules of conduct, but even to reappraise them in new situations. The principle is that what counts are the consequences of an act, to the actor, in long-range terms. This gears the morality to looking for sources of trouble, which are to be avoided. Any course of conduct which will bring on illness, or the ill-will of your neighbors, is therefore bad.

No doubt a more careful examination of modes of organization will make more refined distinctions. These were just preliminary suggestions of the different kinds of directions in which we may fruitfully look for our data. Going on with such an inquiry, we should want to examine also possible differences in the way these different kinds of ordering principles function within moralities, both in stable situations and in times of stress and change. The way in which an ideal of character unifies a moral code may be different from the way in which an ideal of achievement accomplishes the task. Harmony may have a different character in a morality that is rising to dominance and in one that is defending itself against strong attacking forces. For questions of change particularly, the cultural-contextual analysis of historical materials might prove richly rewarding, providing a valuable supplement to the sometimes one dimensional data of traditional anthropological investigation.

A quite different direction of organization has been predominant in theoretical formulations in our own culture. This is based on logical properties, and is commonly called the "deductive model." The unity is sought not in basic content or goal or touchstone, but in formal organization and logical systematization. It is believed that once abstraction and generalization, such as our ethics abounds in, have been appropriately carried out, morality can function as a grandiose mathematical system or physical science. At the top are basic axioms or theoretical equations. Then come theorems or deductions, then applications, with particular cases following from the highly abstract general rules under stated sets of conditions. Sometimes it has even been held that every moral code is a partial step to a universal system that could be worked out through careful sifting and winnowing.

It is not only theoretical reflection that has used this model. Many a morality in our culture has carried on casuistry in the spirit of deduction from a closed system of "moral truths," which are authoritatively certified as correct starting points. There are many people even today who would insist that a code like the Decalogue contains all that one needs to guide one's life in any and every situation (if properly interpreted, of course!) with an assurance of completeness which contemporary logicians now reject even for arithmetic.

To what extent such a model describes our actual moral reasoning is a moot point in philosophical thinking. Aristotle asserted a long time ago that in ethics we should not expect more precision than the subject-matter would allow, and that to demand mathematical proof in morals would be as inept as to allow opinion in deducing a mathematical theorem (*Nicomachean Ethics*, Bk. I, ch. 3). Contemporary ethical theory has become even more critical of the deductive model (cf. Toulmin, 1950; Hare, 1952). Apart from the fact that belief in self-evident ethical axioms has suffered from the general critique of axioms in the development of alternative geometries, there is uneasiness about the view that systematization in all fields has to be construed as a one-way road toward greater deductive scope and rigor, and that a higher degree of such systematization is a sign of greater advance in civilization. Contemporary philosophers have begun to raise the question whether traditional concepts of systematization do not themselves reflect a particular metaphysics, such as the belief that the book of nature is written in the language of mathematics, so that the mind in developing a system is penetrating to an inherent natural structure of things. Such questioning points in the same direction as what have seemed to us the implications of work in the comparative laboratory—the hypothesis that different modes of organizing moral codes have taken shape in different cultures, and that these different modes of systematizing will be found to reflect culturally different needs and situations. Such a formulation does not sweep the deductive model aside; rather, it wants to see how that model itself has really functioned in the moralities that used or purported to use it.

What is more, once such inquiries are launched, contemporary reflections on the deductive model and its applications suggest a whole variety of problems for comparative study. For example—a question we have already discussed—to what extent have different moral codes reduced their highly specific situations to universal types of statements? If they have not done so explicitly, how far can we trace an underlying order implicit in their statements? We should ask specifically, how much of the field of their moral judgments is covered by such highly general principles? How consistent are their statements? To what extent are their generalizations so formulated that they can apply to new as well as to customary situations? What operative principles are there, explicit or implicit, for applying the code in practice? Are there subsidiary rules for structuring the situation of moral decision? For interpreting rules? For weighing or comparative judgment? For dealing with conflicts?

We can only touch briefly on a few of these questions here. But they will help us round out the picture of systematizing as itself not simply a formal but a culturally-rooted process, and to understand more clearly the basis of contemporary theoretical reactions to problems of systematization.

A central question in any serious reckoning with system is the question of consistency. In a purely logical sense, consistency is a relation of propositions; two propositions are inconsistent if the truth of either implies the falsity of the other.

This is not precisely what we mean when we speak of the consistency or inconsistency of moral principles. It might be wiser, to avoid confusion, to speak rather of compatibility and incompatibility. When we speak of two goals being inconsistent in a single morality, we do not usually mean that they could not be desired together, but that they could not be achieved together. And this might be, not because they could not imaginably exist together, but because man's psychological makeup, or the social conditions or cultural institutions were such, that to attempt to achieve both would bring disruption or frustration. And the same is the case for compatibility of ideals, virtues, and social forms.

It is quite apparent, for example, that many of our own general statements appear to be saying quite opposite things. Try putting into a syllogism the maxims, "All men are brothers," and "You should help your brother in need," and then add, "The Lord helps those that help themselves," and "Charity begins at home" (cf. Lynd 1939, pp. 60-63). To some extent such contrary maxims reflect actual contradictions in our morality. Conflicts of interest and of goals, whether in an individual or in society as a whole, may be very basic, and generate profound social and psychological problems. But as far as the statements themselves go, they are not as contradictory as they seem. They are, rather, incomplete statements. In practice they contain a great many implicit limitations, and situational differentiations. Our generalizations are far more "situational" than our preferred all-or-none universalized statements of them would suggest, though it is sometimes only when someone from an alien culture takes them literally that these limitations are called to our attention. Certainly we know that "Be generous" does not mean "Give away all your worldly goods." And indeed Hartshorne and May showed in their study of deceit (1928) that idiosyncratic limitations and judgments of relevance are a regular feature of much of our actual morality. The phenomenon is a familiar one. We all know that many students who would not dream of copying on an examination may be willing to supply information to classmates. Is taking an extra coin which you find in the telephone coin-return box a case of stealing, or failing to pay fare if a conductor overlooks you? And there are also conventional compartmentalizations which are quite familiar; some rules apply at home, others relate to business; one set may be for daily use, another for Sundays. Indeed, the conflicting sets of principles sometimes play a mutually supportive role. A Sunday morality may curb the guilt feelings that might otherwise be roused by exploitative practices or help mitigate their effects by encouraging charity.

Determining which rule is relevant to a particular situation actually involves structuring the way in which the situation is to be viewed. In the field of law, lawyers know that if you get the judge to see the case as falling into the pigeon-hole you have chosen, your case is half-won. Is loud-speaker advertising in a railroad station to be ruled out as an invasion of privacy or to be reckoned under a legitimate exercise of property rights? A sit-down strike can be disposed of far more quickly if it is ruled a case of running an inn without a license than by dealing with it under complex principles of labor law. Similarly in ethics, the structure of the situation as viewed may considerably limit the kinds of rules which are applicable. Kant's famous example (1879, pp. 431 ff.) of whether to tell a lie to save a man's life, if his enemy pursuers ask you which way he has gone, leaves only a simple set of alternatives—to tell the truth, to lie (which Kant rules out as wrong) or to refuse to answer irrespective of the cost. Ladd's Navaho informant, asked to resolve a comparable dilemma, saw the situation in very different terms as one of mediating a question in human relations, not of truth or falsehood. He thought in terms of dissuading the pursuer (1957, p. 378) !

To estimate the extent of consistency or inconsistency in any moral system requires this kind of analysis of the actual functioning of moral principles in contexts of application. Demarcation between areas of situations which have somewhat different conduct appropriate to them, is one way in which different rules or different virtues may operate together without creating special problems. Another is by fairly clear principles of relative weighting, which may or may not be explicit.

In our own morality, relative weightings are sometimes made explicit. We talk of "man's highest duty" or his "first duty" (these need not be the same duty: first duty may be to the family, highest to conscience or God or country), and we make frequent use of comparative expressions like "better" or "more important." Considering our general love for weighing and measuring, it is interesting to note that we have not carried this out very systematically in our moral thinking. True, the psychologist or the sociologist might expect anyone to arrange his moral preferences according to a five-point scale. But there is certainly nothing comparable today to the neat ordering of sins and virtues along a scale of relative distance from God which we find in Dante's picture of heaven and hell.

Whether they are uniform, consistent and explicit or not, weightings are present in many forms in different aspects of moral structures. There are differences in the degree of stringency of rules. There are some things that just must be done or must never be done. On the other hand, there are what have been called "prima facie rules" or "phase rules," rules that must enter into every reckoning in which they are relevant, but which may be outweighed. This is the actual character of many rules in our culture, although our statement of them is often cast in terms of all or none or never. There are rules that hold unless certain exceptional factors arise—there may be "mitigating circumstances"; there are things you should do but only if asked; things you should do at least some of (like charity). And there are many things that are good to do, in a moral sense, but are certainly not required of you. These may be weightings within a moral system, though sometimes one or another of these types may be the usual or preferred form in which moral rules in general are cast.

The same kinds of weightings can appear in relation to sanctions, to goals, to feelings, to virtues. There are things for which you will be punished, for which you will be blamed; you may be ridiculed, or merely looked at askance. There are acts that will arouse horror, others that will arouse fear, others anger or merely distaste. Goals may be arranged in various hierarchies—some that everyone must seek, others that one may choose among, and some that are merely lucky windfalls. Indeed, sometimes cultures with many similar moral principles may present quite different over-all pictures because they arrange these principles in different orders of preference and importance.

The several features we have been considering—formal or informal weighting, implicit or explicit understanding of the context to which a rule refers, patterns for structuring the way a situation is to be analyzed—can all be seen as applicative devices or operative procedures by which the general statements of a morality may be put into practice. They make decision smooth and automatic, or help it along if there is a problem. The nature of moral decision itself, however, and the kind of role it plays in morality, is also culturally variable. Individual moral decision looms very large in our view of morality.

This individual responsibility is rooted in practical problems of contemporary life, with its great complexity and constant change; and its importance, as well as its difficulty, is augmented by the generality of our statements and the inexplicitness of our applicative procedures. But it is also a function of the important role which we assign to the individual as a moral agent, and which is a central social and philosophical proposition of our culture.

Dewey (Dewey and Tufts, 1932, p. 174) has pointed out two quite distinct kinds of situations in which the individual may feel he has a moral problem. One is the temptation situation, and the other the genuine decision situation. Temptation situations no doubt occur everywhere in relation to morality. However strict the rules, we find that some people break them. Others face the same temptations and resist. We are not at this point exploring the sanctions that keep people in line. But it is interesting to see how often, faced with a temptation which would involve a moral transgression, the individual rephrases the situation and invokes a different principle as relevant. This is the familiar phenomenon of "rationalization," in its derogatory sense, although it is not easy to differentiate such solutions from more genuine moral decisions. Faced with the very homely question "Would you pass a red light late at night when there was no traffic and no policeman in sight?" students who answered "Yes" (in an ethics course pre-test given by one of the authors) gave quite different reasons. Some frankly admitted that though it was wrong, it was obviously safe to take a chance under the circumstances. Others, however, insisted they would do it in good conscience, because the traffic light should not have been kept on in such a time and place. We do not really know to what extent people in other cultures struggle with questions of temptation. But we do know that some at least are as quick as we at invoking extenuating reasons for aberrant courses of conduct. So, for example, it has been reported from several different parts of the world that a man choosing to make a marriage within ordinarily forbidden categories of kinship, has insisted that this particular marriage was ordered by a special dream or ghostly visitation.

Where the conditions of life are relatively stable and the moral principles have clearly stated or understood reference to most situations which ordinarily arise, there will obviously not be very many fundamental moral problem decisions for the individual to make. There may also be techniques within the culture by which moral dilemmas are removed from his personal concern. He may be enjoined to consult some specialist—priest or rabbi, oracle or diviner, or the old men of the community. Or he is expected to follow set procedures—prayer, fasting for four days in a lonely spot, listening to his conscience, reasoning out the implications of a situation—to find the correct solution. Our culture not only raises many moral problems and places many burdens of decision upon the individual, but also makes him decide what mode of decision to employ, and it does this in a framework which also emphasizes the deep responsibility of the individual for the choice he makes. No wonder that there is a tendency to seek for an "escape from freedom" whether in conventional conformity or a search for authoritarian guides.

While it is easy to see why the difficulties of life today lead many to look for the security of a closed moral system, it is also obvious that these very complexities make guiding generality rather than safe specificity not just a stylistic peculiarity of our system but an actual necessity. In a society in which people spend their daily lives in hosts of different contexts, where a tremendous number of alternative paths are open even to such uniform goals as making a living, where the multiform acts of production are far removed from the objects of consumption, so that people are busy doing things that may lead to diverse ends, where most interpersonal relations can take varying forms in accordance with the agreement of the participating individuals (within a framework that allows of wide variation in concrete detail), where paths and patterns change for the whole society within the several decades of an individual's lifetime, where the development of a single discovery like atomic energy or television or artificial insemination or a more rapid mode of communication may call for rethinking and restructuring material ways or institutional forms or traditional outlooks, we can hardly live by a set of highly specific rules. It is not surprising that a philosopher like John Dewey struck a responsive note when he attacked rigid moral systematization as unworkable in fact. Dewey (1929) stressed the uniqueness of the good in every situation and urged avoiding universal rules, since these could be a danger to intelligent appraisal of the full complexity and novel aspects of every concrete situation. His ethical theory invokes, instead, the use of principles as guides on the basis of past experience for the fresh analysis of the present case. He takes tools for use, not axioms for deduction, to constitute the appropriate ethical model. Existentialist philosophers, too, have stressed the uniqueness of present choice, arguing that to follow a rule itself is in effect to choose to line up with the past rather than to consider a change.

While the intensity of reaction against formal sys-

tematization in morality has its basis in the actual contemporary need for vast changes, such a basis does not
have to yield an evaluation that says all or none. One of
the advantages that accrues from a comparative study of
modes of systematization is that one is able to see this
question in a new perspective. If the form, degree and
type of systematization is itself to be evaluated in terms of
human needs, and the availability of alternative ways of
meeting them, then we are faced with a policy decision
in the light of values we hold. A complex morality can
use different models in different parts. It is just as in
the field of law, where one might decide separately which
branches can be strictly formalized and codified, and which
require a great deal of flexibility and so can be ordered
only by leading principles, allowing considerable leeway
for administrative application or judicial discretion. In
law, such policy judgments can be made because behind
law lies the normative field of morals and human values
generally. But in morals such policy judgments should
also be possible because behind any mode of systematization there is the whole moral pattern of virtues and goals
and ideals and feelings that are the subject of systematic
discourse, and behind the morality lie the human needs
to which the morality itself gives partial expression.

It may very well be that the modern world with its
rapidity of change has entrenched decision and challenge
as a primary category, so that a morality has to be geared
to a constant awareness of it, virtues and rules have to be
attuned to it, and any mode of systematization adhered
to only in a provisional and constantly on-its-mettle basis.
But we must also be careful to see whether there may not
be an element of moral pathology in overshadowing the
moral field with the ever-present ominous character of

decision. Here again the legal analogy may prove helpful. When the legal realists defined the law in terms of
what a court would act on—showing thereby the pivotal
role of creative judicial decision—their theoretical oppo-
nents complained that the stable part of the law never
gets to be tested, because it is so clear and established
that people act according to it, and it would be a waste
of time and money to take it to court. It was, they said,
as if one thought of health purely in terms of what is
restored when one is cured. On this type of approach,
the principles of an on-going system that is proving satisfactory in human life have as much claim to moral quality
as the crucial decisions in which they are tested—and not
necessarily rejected. A comparative study of systematization modes in the moralities of other cultures and in the
history of the western world, in relation to human needs,
may very well give us a clearer appreciation of the desirable relation of stability and change within the moral
framework. It can not only show us why we need more
general principles, but also help us to see how far operative and subsidiary principles may be rendered more explicit and more determinate without sacrificing necessary
flexibility.

Chapter XII

JUSTIFICATION

IN OUR CULTURE, ethical discussion does not stop with trying to systematize our morality. There remain the troublesome questions of "Why?" "Why should I turn off my radio?" "Because it's late and you're disturbing your neighbor." "But I want to play it loud." "Yes, but he has a right to his sleep." "Why should I respect his right rather than my own desire?" "Because he's a fellow human being." "But why should I worry about a fellow human being?" "Because"—and then anything from "Neighborliness is a good investment" or "Haven't you any sympathy?" or "It's the law" to "No man is an island" or "It's a religious duty."

This kind of pushing back along the "Whys" is commonly called *justification*. It has all the ambiguities and all the pitfalls of the question itself. "Why?" can send the inquirer, according to context or underlying perspective, to purpose, to explanation, to causal account, to a general background picture of what is going on. And so it can mean "Tell me more of your more basic reasons," or "Why this, rather than some conceivable alternative?" or even "Where does your morality fit into your whole philosophy of man and his world, and if you haven't an articulated whole philosophy, how about working one out?"

Of course, in ordinary discourse, giving reasons usually falls far short of a Socratic pushing back for ultimate meanings and assumptions. This is not an everyday practice of the "common man," nor does he find it very congenial when he is pushed to it. Still, from a wide knowledge of our own culture and tradition, we can push back from piece-meal statements and justifications, which people do give readily, to stopping-points in customary thinking at which most people would let the argument rest, and to the fundamental justifying perspectives which underlie these stopping-points. So, when a man says "My conscience won't let me do it" we know he is saying more than "I won't do it because my conscience would hurt," as he might say "I won't touch the hot stove because it will burn my hand." He is saying that his conscience tells him or reminds him that it is good to do or avoid the action he is discussing. And he is implying a whole system of relations between his conscience and religious precepts, or between his conscience and some possibility of direct moral insight into the good. And anyone who in a sophisticated vein does say "In the light of what I know about my own psychology, I must not do this; for, having been brought up as I was, if I do this I will suffer pangs," will probably readily admit that he is not at this point talking about or considering moral rightness at all, and that if the concept of morality does enter his scheme of thinking, it is on some quite different justificatory grounds.

The interpretation of the justificatory perspective which underlies a particular statement is not easy, as it may be a combination of many elements. For example, if one looks literally at statements of the Ten Commandments, one finds in the command to honor one's parents the conclusion "that thy days may be long upon the land

which the Lord thy God giveth thee." This sounds almost like an inducement, a justification in a kind of what-
do-we-get-out-of-it vein. But, knowing the context, and
having the whole code before us, we know that this is far
from the primary emphasis. The code includes very different justifications, related to a quite different theme.
So, for example, man should rest on the seventh day, because the Lord blessed it when He rested after the six
days of creation. In general, the basic principle underlying the whole code is the picture of God as authoritative
source and model of what is right. The stopping-point
on which the whole moral edifice rests is the principle
that it is the role and the whole duty of man to obey God.
This, together with the picture of God and His relation
to man, is the justificatory essence; the threats of punishment are not the meaning of evil but extra supportive
sanctions.

Many paths in traditional western morality lead to
such a religious account. Conceptual analysis of "wrong"
leads to the idea of "sin" and so to the notion of violating God's will. Descriptions of sanctions turn to heaven
and hell. Praise of specific virtues, such as charity or humility, is cast educationally in terms of biblical stories
and models. In fact, current lay statements insist that if
there is no religious basis, there is no morality; the re-
mark of one of Dostoievski's characters in *The Brothers
Karamazov* is a favorite in this regard—"If there is no
God, then anything goes!"

The full picture of our moral justifications is, of
course, much more complex. There are different religious
accounts with different moral potentials. One stresses
the element of duty and obedience and the individual
reward of life eternal, another the love of God and a

more spiritual kind of ultimate blessedness. In addition there have been, in the western tradition, competing this-worldly justification perspectives. The most familiar type is based on the view that men inherently desire happiness, and that moralities are to be justified (or criticized) according as they are productive of happiness. Other types substitute for happiness some account of goals arising in the evolutionary process, such as group-survival and the needs of group-solidarity, or some more general conception of group welfare.

All of these justification perspectives can be found in different and often conflicting ethical theories of the philosophers, if not always in our every-day views. And looked at in detail, they turn out to contain or to imply some account of man's nature, of human relationships, of the character of the surrounding world and man's relation to it, and some inventory of ultimate purposes. All of this constitutes a kind of "stage-setting," a more or less clearly structured arena in which moral qualities appear and moral processes occur, in which basic goals and orientations are provided. Such stage-settings, whether they are set up in terms of the drama of salvation or the struggle of the species to survive in an evolutionary unfolding, or the personal quest for happiness, or the maintenance of a universal harmony, have played a large role in our tradition in conscious attempts to justify moral ways.

When we look to the primitive societies that anthropologists have studied, we shall hardly expect to find systematic elaborations of ultimate bases carried very far. But we do find plenty of explanatory remarks and even explicit justifications presented in contexts of discussion or teaching or argument. We also find indications of the basic stage-settings in which the moralities are cast, ideas and beliefs about the nature of man, the sources of his satisfactions and the typical threats to his welfare, and his relations to a helpful or threatening, whimsical or just universe. These serve as a basis of justification without being necessarily underlined constantly in discourse.

It is clear from even the most limited kind of survey that there are at least three different basic avenues of justification which occur quite commonly. We may call them custom, religion, and human well-being. These different approaches may be found side by side in the same culture, sometimes jointly supportive of the same injunctions, sometimes directed to different parts of the morality. Often they can be distinguished analytically, even if in practice they are closely interwoven into one fabric. And within each of the approaches there are many sharply different formulations, with quite different implications.

The appeal to custom and tradition may be a very direct one: "Our fathers did so, and we must do so too," or "We just found it this way," or even just "This is our way of life." Such an appeal to tradition may involve a deep sense of reverence for the past; it may emphasize continuity with the ancestors in a way which is often deeply symbolized in religious practice or formulated in terms of religious justificatory motifs as well. "These are the ways ordained for us" by the gods or by our fore-fathers, or "This is the due return for what our fore-bears did for us," and so forth. This kind of view, very familiar in parts of our religious tradition, and still more strongly emphasized in many eastern world views, is found in many parts of the primitive world. But sometimes the reference to tradition may be more pragmatic than pietistic, more contemporary than past-oriented. To say, "We do it this way because the old men say it is wiser," is a justification in terms of the presumed lessons of experience as relevant for the present rather than pure reverence for the past. So, Sun Chief's return to the faith of his fathers, which we quoted in Chapter 3, made a specific point of its proven effectiveness in making life possible in his desert homeland, and Ladd gives a similar pragmatic interpretation of the moral rule of custom for the Navaho, suggesting that "we just used to do it that way" was not a sufficient moral reason for his informant (1957, pp. 268 ff.).

Custom need not always refer to ancient or long-established traditions. The customary may very often be not so much the traditional as the habitual. It is rooted in the satisfactions of the present, in the comfort and built-in acceptability of the habitual. Moral principles and attitudes may be just as much taken for granted as the use of one's mother tongue. It is in this sense that Fortes speaks of the values embedded in the basic social structure of the Tallensi as axioms in their moral system (1949, p. 18). They are quite conscious of this high valuation placed on their way of life as such; it is not merely unquestioned, but beyond any meaningful challenge. Such a valuation merges into a kind of aesthetic appreciative justification, as when the Tallensi say, "Is it not beautiful here?" referring not only to the barren hills of their homeland, but to the deep pleasures and satisfactions of their on-going way of life. A similar note is found in the poetic formulation of the Digger Indian quoted by Ruth Benedict (1934a, p. 21), who bemoaned the disruption of his people's traditional culture as the breaking of their "cup of life."

Although custom, no doubt, enters into all men's behavior, and often beyond their awareness of its binding effect, we should not take for granted that it always has a strong positive justificatory role. Not all men set profound store by their ways just because they have them. There are people who say of various aspects of their culture "You just do it any way you like." And although to the observer their realistic alternatives may seem very limited and in practice custom-bound, their own view of their lives is one of freedom. Custom can hardly play a justificatory role in such a perspective. Our culture, of course, goes much further; we often disvalue custom as such and approve of discarding "the shackles of the past" in favor of an ideal of progress. (However, as many commentators have noted, this attitude manages to coexist with a strong emphasis on conformity and conservatism in many aspects of our social order.) While the idea of progress is not a usual one in the primitive world, we do find in many cases, if not a ready welcome for change, at least a willingness to try out new ways.

The religious approach to justification also takes many forms. Respect for the elders and piety may be woven into a fabric of ancestor worship; gods may be actively concerned with men's current moral behavior— though interestingly enough, very often with only some of its aspects. They may appear as active agents, or be as much bound by some automatic cause and effect relationship as men. Emphasis may fall on penalties imposed, or goods which the gods provide as rewards for men's moral behavior. Religious sanctions and religious justifications form a tangled skein, as difficult to unravel as in some of the more fundamentalist views of hell-fire and salvation in the Christian tradition.

So, for example, among the Tallensi, to whose moral system we have already several times referred, the earth god and the ancestral spirits enter deeply into moral thinking (Fortes, 1945, esp. pp. 173 ff.). Warfare is bad because the earth abhors bloodshed; the stain of killing and the plagues it unleashes may follow a family for generations. The ancestors are deeply involved in man's performance of his obligations within his lineage. This is sometimes formulated as a sanction: "You'd better do these things or the ancestors will smite you with illness or poverty or sterility." But such references occur especially with relation to such reluctant figures as step-father. For the most part there is rather a simple avowal of man's deep indebtedness to the ancestors. One owes the ancestors obedience; their ends and yours are the same—the maintenance of the structure of human obligations and institutions. The needs imposed by correct performance of religious rituals are woven into the fabric of moral justifications too. A man's performance of his duties to his lineage-mates, his being just toward them and maintaining good relations with them, is also a moral requirement with a religious support, for they must sacrifice together in the proper spirit. Anything which would endanger their good relations would be a sacrilege and is ipso facto bad. The reference to religious justifications is thus set in a framework which includes an ultimate appeal to mundane human ends, both individual ones of health and well-being and general ones of maintaining the basic ongoing good life of proper social relations. There is specific appeal in Tallensi prayers "that undisturbed sleep may be slept," which implies the whole smooth functioning of the social system. Ideas and ideals of justice, and of the appropriateness of the fulfillment of reciprocal obligations to man as well as to the gods, are also part of Tallensi justificatory appeals. A son supports his father in his old age for all these reasons: because it is taken for granted as his duty; because he owes him a debt not only for the land with which he supplied him, but also for life itself ("Did he not beget me, and is not begetting hard?"); because he wishes his father to continue to perform the necessary sacrifices to the ancestors on his behalf; and also because the ancestors supporting the basic social order will probably punish him directly if he does not. Thus the ends of direct human well-being, of the maintenance of the social order, of the approval of the ancestors and the threat of their disapproval, are all parts of an interconnecting whole in which these various parts function in combination as ends, reasons and instruments.

Although religion suffuses so much of Tallensi justificatory thinking, it is thus obviously not the whole of it. The need for good relations among men and the satisfactions to be found in them are interwoven with it. And in some parts of their morality, particularly outside of the framework of the lineage, these considerations of human reciprocity and the need for someone to rely on are paramount and explicit. So, for example, the relations between uterine relatives are firm and friendly ones, with a high degree of dependability. The pervasive mutual security and interdependence within this relationship are explained in terms of mutual interest rather than of any kind of religious requirement.

There are plenty of other world views among primitive peoples where religion enters the framework of moral justification, though usually, as in this case, it is concerned not with the salvation of man's soul, or his life after death, but rather with very mundane goals. Certain distinctions need to be drawn. Explanation of an account of origins need not constitute a justification. Among many American Indian tribes, we find tales of the origin of particular injunctions or tabus which relate them to the adventures of a culture hero, who is both amoral, and unconcerned with the present behavior of man. He is simply a trickster figure, rather like Brer Fox, who established the features of the known universe almost by inadvertence. So there are rocks in the river because he happened to drop something there, and there are certain tabus because of some accident in his career. Although he is in some sense a spirit figure, he is accorded no worship, and such tales have no centrality in moral argument. They are explanations of how the rules came to be, but they are not formulated as justifications for them. On the other hand, where religion does enter the justificatory framework, the gods may be in no sense the authors of the regulations, but rather merely coparticipants with man. Thus, among the Pueblo Indians, the gods will come to dance in the plaza and bring the rain, when men have fulfilled their part of the religious obligations. And man's share includes not only the proper planting of prayer-sticks and the reciting of ritual, but also cooperation in the relevant community undertakings, and avoiding quarrels, or open expression of hostility. The gods did not ordain these rules; they, like men, must fulfill them. We should also note that there are large areas of Pueblo life where reference to such religious attitudes is irrelevant. Religious justification is not used in relation to sexual morality; here the justifications concern rather avoiding arousing anyone's jealousy or anger, or hurting anyone's feelings.

On the other hand, there are many primitive moral views in which religion plays no important justificatory role at all. So, for example among the Chiga, ancestral spirits are not concerned with the moral quality of their descendants' behavior. They are capricious and malicious beings, even less trustworthy than living men, who are basically untrustworthy; and if you make them offerings it is not because of piety and devotion, but sheer bribery. And if they smite you with illness, it is not because you have failed in any way in your duties to your fellow-men, but because they want more gifts. Clearly, the better the spirit, the less you will need to sacrifice to him. And the high god, who is essentially good, needs no sacrifice at all. He set the world on an even keel, and so it will remain if nothing disturbs it; he is too remote to be concerned with your good or bad behavior. Any troubles that befall you are due not to your malfeasance, but to the unprovoked malicious intervention either of your own ancestors or some other evil spirit or person.

This-worldly appeals may occur as moral justifications in their own right, without any religious implications. Other peoples are far less worried than we are about giving as an adequate reason for approving certain kinds of behavior that they provide human satisfactions or prevent human ills. To most people such human ends as long life, children, health or peace, or the good regard of one's fellows with all its advantages of reciprocal fulfillment of obligations, are unquestioned purposes and adequate reasons, which clearly need no further probing. Even so strict a moral rule as incest may, as we noted earlier, be justified by the argument that if a man married his sister he would deprive himself of a brother-in-law who was a necessary work-partner; or that it would cause hard feelings within the family. "Quarreling spoils the family" is not just an empty aphorism, but a profound appeal to the needs of social relatedness as primary, and "then people will like you" is not an appeal to hypocrisy, but an obviously adequate reason for espousing a set of virtues.

Such an approach seems pushed to the extreme in the Navaho view, which, as Ladd found it, under some Socratic probing, constantly pushes back to prudential considerations. There is no idea, as we noted earlier, of intrinsic right or wrong, nor is religion or tribal tradition an essential moral argument. Moral principles are simply weighed in terms of their consequences. Some acts are absolutely wrong, for they have built-in automatically dangerous consequences, such as various forms of illness. These tabus appear to have no significant religious ideology. The penalty follows in a directly causal way, like electric shock from touching a live wire, and contains the same possibility of sheer "taking a chance" which no wise man would do but a fool might get away with. When a wrong act has taken place and the consequences occur—a long time interval may elapse before they do—then the harm can be undone by a ceremony, a "sing" which both cures and purges. Sensible men have themselves sung over from time to time anyway, just to play safe, for actions that are unintentional and even unwitting can be as dangerous as known and purposeful evil-doing. This complicates the moral quality of the Navaho view for us —but not for the Navaho. For them, the world is full of dangers, and the wise man treads a careful path among them. If prudence dictates performing certain kinds of social behavior, and avoiding other kinds, then these acts are respectively right or wrong. If the consequences are built-in, and certain, so much the better; the good or correct course is clear. If they depend on other people's reactions the reasoning is the same, but the judgment is not always so obvious or predictable, and may need more weighing. In any case, actions which will "put you into trouble," will cause you to quarrel and alienate people, are bad actions; drunkenness, for example, can be very bad. On the other hand, if a man gets drunk quietly at home, it is not bad. Actions which provoke other people's malice—too much wealth, or stinginess, or trying to be too much of a big-shot—are unwise and wrong. Men in a family should help each other because an outfit must stick together; you may need your relatives' support some day as they need yours now. And in general it is dangerous to provoke other men's anger.

The strongly individualistic prudentialism of the Navaho has a number of obvious roots in their social order. Navaho social structure has been called "familistic individualism"; there are no forms of political authority and no compelling social sanctions of a formal sort. Interdependence is primarily a matter of family relationships. Even religion is individually oriented. Many attend a "sing," but it is given by the individual who finances it, paying the singer to perform the ritual on his behalf. It is scarcely remarkable in this framework that the Navaho moralist finds that his strongest appeal is to self-interest. This is still further emphasized by the special role of the Navaho moralist, who is almost a public official. He is called upon to give general lectures about behavior at such functions as weddings—which might lend themselves to merely pious sentiments—but he is also expected to harangue people who seem to be wandering from the not so very straight and narrow path of common decency and industry, to be "getting into trouble." If he is to appeal to the miscreant he must be persuasive, and there is no body of common ends to appeal to which are likely to move him. However, the argument from prudence and personal advantage cuts deeper than this. Ladd's informant, who was such a moralist, accepted this framework of argument as the only one which made sense. Indeed, when pressed he was ready to admit that if it were certain that no one would know or be angered, a course of action like stinginess or even stealing "might be OK." This judgment appears to be confirmed by the many others who have worked with the Navaho (cf. Albert, 1956; Kluckhohn, 1956b). They sometimes see more interest in positive good than Ladd found in his informant's basic formulations; but in any case it is calculated individual good. Furthermore, there is apparently a readiness to reappraise even fundamental rules. Mother-in-law avoidance is being questioned, for example, in the light of the observation that its violation by whites, and some "modern" Navaho, does not bring the predicted blindness. Even conservative Navaho are considering abandoning the tabu as a kind of error.

This congruence of the prudentialist principles of Navaho justification with their rather anarchic social system is a very obvious one. In the other justificatory schemes to which we have referred, similar relationships can be discerned. Pueblo morality, for example, is more stringent, its emphasis on conformity very strong, especially in those areas of behavior having to do with religious observances which bring the rain. The interweaving of religious ideology, and the appeal to the accepted way of life and its standards, fits this picture of a highly integrated community structure, though it is noticeable that

the individual's conformity to the group is apparently
seen in terms of this also being part of his own best self-
interest. And for the Tallensi, we saw religious justifications also used in a situation which emphasized group
harmony and cohesion; while not organized in a tight political framework, Tallensi life does demand a considerable degree of patterned cooperation and organization.
A very neat contrast is provided by the far more prudential non-religious Chiga morality; their cultural forms stem
from many of the same traditional roots, but their social
structure is far less tightly organized even within the
lineage, and their mode of life demands far less group
cohesion.

It would be valuable to pursue this kind of question
in a thorough study of comparative justificatory perspectives, and to see how far such congruence really goes. We
need to look for the relations of justification not only to
social structure, but also to economic needs, religious beliefs and general goals and ideals. We need to look for
historical factors, whether of diffusion or tradition, as well
as to the contexts in which justificatory statements occur.
How do different kinds of justifications function when
there is an emphasis on individual achievement, for example, or where there is some class differentiation, such as
we do find in parts of the "primitive" world? We know
from our own ethical tradition that the relations of justification to the rest of morality, and to social needs, is
not a simple one. Different perspectives may be supportive of approximately the same picture of men's actual
duties, although they may differ in the account of his
underlying good, and in the types of feeling and sanctions associated with the moral content. In this sense, a
Puritan morality and a Benthamite utilitarian morality

share a large sub-set of virtues; but within the utilitarian justifying perspective itself, just as within the religious justifying perspective, there are important value disagreements. The actual variety of justifications in our complex society may sometimes betoken not a serious conflict, but rather that different groups and different interests respond to different appeals in support of the same moral pattern. On the other hand, there are suggestive indications of the varying roles different justifications have played in relation to changing social needs. Differences may take the form of reinterpretation within a broad common framework. So, within Christianity, Protestant theology emerged to contrast itself with Catholic, with significant differential moral involvement; or again, in liberal social theory, an individualistic morality which was associated with a developing economic individualism in remaking the mode of life in the western world, passed from a natural rights justification of fundamental liberties to a utilitarian justification in terms of general welfare, and in some areas to a biological evolutionary survival-of-the-fittest type. Changing modes of justification, changing moralities, and changing social life thus present a complex interactive process.

This suggests that it might be very rewarding to undertake a study of comparative justificatory perspectives in situations of change. Do different kinds of justifications arise where there is a significant shift in power and property relations? Do different kinds of justifications actually serve to facilitate or to inhibit change, or to help reintegrate moralities in a framework of new institutions and goals? Such data might be difficult to gather, but would obviously throw important light on the kinds of functions justifications perform. Even if in some cases justifications turned out to be essentially epiphenomenal, we should have to understand why men need such appeasing elaborations to keep psychological morale in tune.

In the western tradition, the study of justifications has been too bound up with struggles over what is the "truth" of morality to focus dispassionately on such a search for multiple modes of functioning and varying social-psychological roles. And when the study becomes conscious of the fact that different justifications are not merely alternative hypotheses, but modes of thought having psychological and cultural and social and historical interrelations in the lives of men, it tends to go to the opposite extreme of an anti-theoretical reaction. Many have looked in a disparaging way upon all ideals and generalizations and principles as a kind of intellectual froth of rationalization, instead of recognizing that the inevitable correlate of multiple functions—intellectual and practical—is multiple justification.

One of the striking features of justificatory thinking in ethical theory today is the fact that it seems no longer content with probing behind obvious justifications in the hope of finding theoretically satisfying stopping-points. Earlier philosophical theology probed behind justification by God's will to ask whether something is good because God wills it or whether God wills it because it is good—in short, whether the good is arbitrarily dependent on divine will, or objective and compelling. Similarly, philosophers probed behind conceptions of evolutionary trends expanding the length and breadth of life to ask what was the good of life itself. But contemporary theory criticizes even the very conception of theoretically satisfactory stopping-points. Logical questions are raised as to whether *any* factual picture of the world and of what man is can really serve to justify any morality, since it is always possible to raise the question of the goodness of that world and that kind of constitution which the picture ascribes to man.   And if the justification perspective embodies some practical social or cultural purposes, it is again possible to raise the problem of evaluating those purposes themselves.   Thus justification has no inherent bounds in the movement of thought; at best there is a kind of dialectic in which it is now bound and now jumps its bounds.   This inherent *restlessness* has loomed large in quite different philosophical schools recently and in quite different formulations.   In a naturalistic Deweyan conception (1922, esp. Pt. IV, sec. 1) it is seen as a factual picture of human life—the endless succession of problems that require constant reassessment of older principles. In the religious language of a Reinhold Niebuhr (1943, ch. 1) it is seen as an inherent human power of self-transcendence, which is relied upon to establish that man cannot be reduced to a natural phenomenon.   In G. E. Moore (1903, ch. 1) it is given an analytic formulation: "good" is indefinable, whether in terms of natural concepts such as happiness or metaphysical concepts such as divine will, because you can always say of any content you assign to it in definition, "Is *that* really good?"—in short, because another push-back is always possible.   Perhaps the fact that we are dealing with a common characteristic of restlessness is not always recognized because in one it is a push-on, in the second a push-up, in the third a push-back!

Perhaps this elevation of restlessness in justification theory to a central position may itself provide a clue to the particular needs that justification theory has been trying to serve in our time.   It may be that, as in previous historical transitions of large proportions, a shift in the mode of justification is mediating a shift from one morality to another. In this case the intensified restlessness would be a mark of the tension points in the process of change. But much more may be involved: it is also possible that a strong moral component is beginning to center about the fact of change itself, that morality is becoming increasingly geared to a world in which change is a part of the normal living process, and that change embraces standards of evaluation as well as the content evaluated.

Such a view of justification theory and its functions does not, as suggested above, preclude or eliminate the problem of comparative evaluation of different justification perspectives so much as render it more complex. Certainly, questions of factual truth arise in dealing with their stage-settings, although these are sometimes enmeshed rather tightly with methodological and metaphysical claims. Factual claims about what causes disease or what witchcraft can actually accomplish are perhaps more easily assessed than claims about what will make men happy, or about the properties of supernatural beings. Such inquiries merge with the general philosophical issue of the range of application for scientific investigation. Again, comparative evaluation of justifying perspectives may be carried out in terms of such further criteria as consistency and comprehensiveness for the purpose for which justification perspectives operate, or in terms of an evaluation of the kind of orientation different perspectives provide for human life. Of course in all such evaluations embodying value-criteria the tendency to press on to further justification will be the more evident the more self-consciously and overtly value assumptions are held. On the whole, in philosophical discussion of this problem of the limits of justification three different possibilities are envisaged. One is to stop in ultimate intuitive first principles. This is the traditional rationalistic view of axioms that has suffered a serious defeat in contemporary philosophical analysis. A second is to regard the initial stopping-points as the arbitrary postulates of the person or culture. This is the approach taken in the relativistic views of morality. A third is to treat these alternatives as arising only in a formalized system of justification and to recognize that the whole system is being developed and used to further certain human purposes, so that, in a different sense from justification within the system, the bases of the system itself may be evaluated in terms of the way it furthers those purposes. No matter how much is incorporated into the system there will still be the matrix of life in which it operates and so of purposes not included in the system. In this sense, concepts of *vindication* (Feigl, 1950), or of continuous *instrumental appraisal* (Dewey, 1939), or of a growing *valuational base* (A. Edel, 1955, ch. 9) have been suggested to push still further the limits of justification. On this third view, the stopping-points at any time will achieve a lasting stability only if they reflect basic human purposes, perennial problems and dominant instrumentalities, and the correctness of embedded knowledge.

Chapter XIII

SANCTIONS AND MORAL FEELINGS

Aɴᴏᴛʜᴇʀ ᴀʀᴇᴀ of moral structure that looms large in any survey of morality is that of sanctions, those motivations and pressures which operate to help maintain conformity. In our own popular morality threats of punishment are impressive, whether fires of hell, anguish of conscience or public disgrace. And on the other hand, positive rewards are stressed too—peace of mind, eternal life, or the subtle appeal of praise and prestige. Other societies play up different penalties from ours. Ridicule may be publicly institutionalized, and fear of illness is frequently involved. Positive sanctions, the esteem and approval of one's fellows, participation in ongoing activities, reciprocal favors, are obvious motivations or rewards in many situations, though not always looked into or documented in those terms by the investigator, and these too will have culturally specific forms.

The term "sanctions" itself covers a rather wide gamut, and some of its meanings need careful discrimination. It carries us on the one hand into the macroscopic-social or public procedures of reward and punishment, on the other into the microscopic or deeper-level layers of motivation to ask what internal stimuli or play of feelings operate effectively in guiding paths of choice.

Take, for example, a rule such as "Thou shalt not steal." In our culture, this is an important moral rule, justified differently in different perspectives, but upheld by all. It is a divine edict, as well as a basic principle of our kind of economic and social life. As such, it is, not surprisingly, sanctioned in many different ways. For some, the moral rule is enforced by fear of arrest and jail, for others by the shame and disgrace that being caught would entail. Such motivations may be reinforced by job-loss threats. The principle is supported by a whole set of different sanctions as well. There are religious penalties of damnation, promptings of conscience, concern over the effect the loss would have on the person stolen from (there is a widespread sympathy in our culture for the Robin Hood type of banditry which takes from the selfish rich); and, for many people, feelings about the wrongness of stealing are so built in that even when they are given the opportunity, the temptation to steal does not seriously arise. Most of these sanctions have an inner-motivational as well as an outer-institutional aspect, and it is not always possible to differentiate very sharply between these. Clearly, religious sanctions have both aspects. Even external physical force, if it operates to move people, must have an internal-motivational foothold in the fear it engenders. Only the deepest pangs of conscience and internal shame appear to operate almost entirely within the individual without reference to other people's knowledge or reaction or any external penalties. While these feelings are in a sense purely internal, the educational procedures by which they are established may have an identifiable institutional form. For most people, all these different sanctions operate to some extent together, with differences in their relative weight.

We sometimes find certain sanctions referred to in

both philosophical and anthropological literature as "moral sanctions" as though this were a specific description. Such usage is not wholly uniform. Sometimes the term is intended to refer to an allegedly unique type of feeling, such as the sense of duty as distinguished from ordinary feelings of fear and sympathy and shame. Sometimes, on the other hand, moral sanctions are contrasted with legal or religious or physical sanctions; in Bentham, for example (1823, ch. 3, sec. 9), the reference is to the informal reactions of others (as in his own quaint illustration of the man who withholds assistance from another in a fire because he does not like his moral character). Anthropologists commonly use the term to suggest that actions are supported by interpersonal feelings and attitudes, or are so embedded in ongoing institutional forms that no special resort to formal punitive threats at any level is required.

Here we shall not attempt to differentiate a particular type of sanction as distinctively moral for all cultures, but shall deal rather with the whole field of sanctions insofar as they are used to support morality. Sanctions, very often the same sanctions, may support other areas of behavior than morality. There may be sanctions of ridicule for lapses of manners, legal penalties for filing one's income tax late, damages to be paid for accidental breakage or injury; the wrath of the gods often descends for the accidental violation of some purely ritual prescription. We must therefore distinguish, in any descriptive account, where particular sanctions operate to support the morality, or where their application is irrelevant to it or even, as may sometimes be the case, against it, as when coercion is used to force a man to act against his principles. We may note, too, that a morality may embody a moral evaluation of sanctions themselves. We certainly discriminate some sanctions as morally approved from others which are morally disapproved. To avoid stealing for fear of imprisonment is not a morally good reason in our culture. To help another with a clear eye on reciprocal benefits may be customary but it is looked on askance; we prefer sense of duty, religious feelings or sympathy. In a peculiar moral paradox, we use the death penalty as a support for the rule "Thou shalt not kill." In a comparative survey, however, we cannot rule out any set of sanctions, whether in terms of their institutional form or their motivational footholds, as outside the field of our concern. For even a sanction that is negatively evaluated in a culture may in fact be operative as a support for the morality.

There are also complex interweavings of sanctions with justifications which need careful consideration. Refined theory may draw sharp distinctions between justificatory assumptions about the moral, identifying tests for what is moral, and supportive sanctions for the morality. Jeremy Bentham, for example (1823, ch. 1, 3), taking all motivation to lie in the pursuit of pleasure and the avoidance of pain, finds his ultimate justification in the greatest sum of pleasure attainable, his tests in pleasure-bestowing and pain-avoiding properties, his sanctions in the many forms in which men anticipate pleasures or pains from nature, from others, from supernatural beings. One can distinguish the justification, the test of the moral, and the sanctions, but the same content is woven through them all. On the other hand, Joseph Butler, presenting a religious ethical theory (1726), finds his ultimate justification in divine will, and his tests for the moral in the clear and authoritative voice of conscience. When he points to the support given by the cool reflective voice of one's self-love, this coincidence is fortunate and provides a helpful supportive sanction, but it is not an integral part of the justification. In exactly the same way, "Honesty is the best policy," at least in its heyday, was not intended to supplant a religious justification with an appeal to selfishness, but only to supplement it.

We need to use the same analytic differentiation for other cultures, whether they make the distinctions sharply or not. We may then find, as among the Navaho, that the sanctions are deeply woven into the very fabric of justification. For the Sudanese Nuer, on the other hand, we find differentiated formulations (Evans-Pritchard, 1956). When they say, "We do it because it is the will of God," or "This action is good because it will cause good feelings between people," they are talking in the language of justification; when they say of the same acts, "If you do this, God will smite you," or "If you don't support your kinsman, he may retaliate," they are talking in the language of sanctions. They sometimes identify an act as wrong because God punishes it; an illness may thus serve both as sanction and mark of the immoral.

In a comparative survey, we find several different kinds of sanctions widely used to support morality. Among these a very prevalent one is the effect of other people's opinion or attitudes, whether in the form of subtle pressures or outright force, of negative fears or positive desires for approval or rewards. This provides not a simple set, but a whole family of moral sanctions, with different motivational appeals, different institutional formalizations, different degrees and kinds of overt recognition. Most obvious and direct is the simple withdrawal of reciprocal support. Other people will refuse to support you and fulfill their obligations toward you if you have failed to behave as you should toward them. Such considerations are an explicit part of many people's moral reckonings, and are underlined in education in terms which range from "If you do that, people won't like you" to far more specifically calculated consequences. Other considerations may outweigh the reciprocal balance in theory: in some cultures, one's duty to a kinsman should be fulfilled irrespective of his possible remissness; or, in the Trobriands, although exchange of products between communities is vital, direct calculations of return are morally shady and should not be given primary weight. But in all such cases, people who do not keep up their moral credit rating may nonetheless be discriminated against in subtle ways which are perfectly apparent in operation even though they are not underlined.

Sanctions of public opinion are by no means always informal; they may be highly institutionalized. One group of such formal public opinion sanctions plays up the ridicule-shame end of the gamut of relevant feelings. There is, for example, the well-known Eskimo drum-match, which is a licensed occasion for making up scurrilous songs about someone and singing them publicly. Among the Eskimo this takes the form of a contest in which the wittiness of the accusation rather than its accuracy may move into the spotlight. In the excitement of the competition, hard feelings are sometimes purged—though occasionally they are exacerbated instead. In any case, the occasion serves to publicize private errors in an atmosphere of ridicule. In other parts of the world, public songs of ridicule may become such powerful weapons that the individual who is their victim is virtually forced to leave the community for a while until the ridicule and shame blow over. Another form of licensed public ridicule which occurs widely is that of the hurling of insults by a designated "joking relative," usually a cross-cousin. He is allowed to tread on very touchy ground, and make capital of any deviation on your part, while you are expected to accept the teasing with a shrug. When it does hit home, though, everyone knows it; and this is a clearly acknowledged consideration, an explicit public pressure device in many cultures. Of course its effectiveness as a moral sanction will depend on the developed sensitivity of the individuals in that culture to ridicule and shame. If this character foothold is lacking, such a sanction cannot be employed to any effect.

The force of public opinion, the effect of other people's attitudes, may take other institutional forms. There may be fear of actual retaliation, whether in open forceful redress, or more often in some less direct but equally threatening recourse to sorcery. Among the Chiga, for example, the sorcerer is virtually a licensed practitioner, as legal as a police officer, who directs his magic on behalf of an aggrieved individual against the person who has wronged him. While this device is not always used to support morality and justice—in some places a sorcerer may let his power fly without special concern for the rights of a case—the point is however often specifically made of this recourse being used only where it is deserved. A sorcerer will send his magic to bring back a runaway wife, perhaps, or in retaliation against a thief, but not to do some man malicious mischief. Indeed, sometimes, especially where the recourse to sorcery does not involve a professional, but is employed directly by the injured man himself, the belief may be held that only the guilty will be vulnerable. Where such beliefs are prevalent, it is obvious that erring individuals may anticipate the reprisal, and fear of such action is an acknowledged deterrent to wrong-doing.

The injured person may take his revenge in other formal ways, which have effective force in the moral domain. In Africa, particularly, public curses are developed as such a weapon. They call down not ridicule, or shame, but direct and sometimes very serious injuries— illness, or death, destruction of property, infertility. Such curses, calling down precise penalties, are operative until revoked: and revocation requires not merely forgiveness, but expensive gifts and ceremonial expiation. Different African peoples differ in the extent to which they elaborate the moral implications of this institutional form. Among the Chiga a father's curse makes the recipient an outcast, cut off from any share in his proper inheritance. What is more, it is contagious, and will spread to anyone who helps him in any way. This threat is an effective weapon in maintaining sons' obedience to their fathers. But there is no guarantee that a wicked father will not use it unjustly. There are other African communities, however, where such curses are effective only if deserved; they have to be mediated through the ancestors or the gods, who will not implement them if they are unprovoked. In such thinking, the person who sets a wrong in motion is responsible for the whole long chain of its unhappy consequences, which may be very remote and unforeseen; and he may be called to account for them to his neighbors as well as to the gods. A beautifully symbolic expression of this whole point of view is embodied in the beliefs of one Nyassaland tribe (Wilson, 1951), who stress the idea that "the breath of man"—adverse attitudes, hostile feelings engendered by wrongs and grievances—can be an active source of harm and danger, just as powerful as explicit curses, even if never actually voiced by the aggrieved parties. It therefore behooves everyone to be extremely sensitive to other people's possible reactions to his behavior, and particularly to commit no actions which might be considered hostile, offensive, or unjust.

Sensitivity to other people's reactions may be made capital of in other ways too. There are devices which merely assure that moral violations will be given publicity, though not in contexts of threats or ridicule. So, for example, as we noted earlier, the Nuer in Africa expect wronged persons to express their grievances publicly on ceremonial occasions. The idea is that hard feelings that have been engendered may be purged and social harmony and good will thus be fostered. But the practice is also a far from subtle public sanctioning device. Other widely used publicity devices, also helpful as moral sanctions though sometimes cast in other terms, are public confession and public accusation by diviner or medium. These are tied to the idea that moral wrongs bring specific consequences in their train automatically (this is in itself a sanction of no mean effect). When afflictions befall an individual or the community, someone's moral behavior is at fault. Health, the availability of animals for hunting, or whatever else has undergone a decline, will be restored only after the guilty person has been discovered and has made proper amends. Sometimes confession is all the amends required; sometimes great sacrifices and penalties may be necessary. The force of such a sanction is brought home very tellingly in an account by Hallowell of a Salteaux woman who broke down when her child was very ill, and publicly told with deep emotion of her husband's having forced indecent forms of sex relations upon her (1955 p. 273). Margaret Mead has raised the interesting question of the great moral consequences the introduction of penicillin may have upon cultures where moral sanctions are built not just around the fact of illness, but around the public diagnosis of its moral cause. Again, we must point to the fact that the emotional implications of such public devices may vary. The appeal may be to guilt as well as to fear of shame and disgrace. Both may be purged with ceremonial restitution; indeed, redress rather than shame may be the specific effect aimed at. But certainly the degree to which such devices are elaborated in many parts of the world suggests that there is, if not a single common base, then at least a family of possible reactions which they appeal to.

Forceful redress or open retaliation is, of course, an ultimate sanction in some cases, in our morality and in many others. We have formal, legal punitive machinery which may be invoked to retaliate, to remove the offender from the scene so he cannot repeat his offense, to deter and to reform—even, in some theories, not as a sanction at all, but as a sheer expression of abhorrence at the offense. Authoritative physical coercions are seen clearly as moral instruments in their use in education, whether they be administered through spankings or more refined deprivations and penalties. In less politically organized societies, retaliatory measures may be taken directly by the injured party or his relatives rather than by a police force, but in so far as they have common support—overt or in the form of non-interference—they are at least quasi-legal in form. Such legal and quasi-legal sanctions may range from fines to flogging, from cutting off the ear of an adulterer to death or expulsion from the community. Of course, we have to be sure in the particular culture that what appears to be a sanction really is felt as one. For example, the possibility of a retaliatory vengeance raid need not operate as a sanction for a moral ban on murder; on the contrary, it may be seen as a risk well worth taking for an action which—provided it be directed far enough outside the kin group—is rather one to be proud of. Again, the role of force may be quite external to moral considerations when it is used to impose the will of one class or group upon another, or when it takes the form of coercion to make people act against their moral principles. But it is none the less a technique which up to now has certainly been widely used in some areas of morality, though it may be only as an extra supportive sanction rather than as the primary consideration.

We may note too from our own moral experience that the mere existence of the possibility of the resort to force does not determine that it will be exercised, nor where. Legal sanctions are certainly not used for the whole area of morality, but only for limited parts of it, even where their possibility is neatly institutionalized. The whole question of the conditions under which different types of sanctions are employed for different aspects of morality is an important part of the social-functional study of morality. Just as the content of moral rules varies in a complex but intelligible way with the kinds of social institutions of which they are part, so too does their stringency and the kinds of sanctions which are attached to their violation. Look for example at the way sanctions against adultery have changed in our culture as the structure of the family and the position of women has changed in recent generations. While adultery is still on the statute books as a penal offense, it is no longer so enforced.

What about religious sanctions? These loom very

large in our morality, but, as we saw in the last chapter, the relation of religion to morality is a complex rather than a simple one, and this is true for sanctions as well as for justification. Gods may play a central role in the pattern of sanctions. Manus ancestral spirits, conveniently living in the rafters where they can watch everything that goes on, Tallensi ancestors, Nuer gods, and many others, take a very active concern in man's moral life, awarding benefits and smiting with afflictions, in return for good or bad behavior. They are a constant living presence, as fully a part of people's moral reckoning as the Hebraic and Christian God, though the effects of their judgments are likely to be felt here and now rather than in a life to come hereafter. But in many other cases, the gods neither decree nor support the moral principles of the society; they smite for their own ends and purposes, or they do man's bidding in response to cajolery, flattery or bribery. The relationship of man to his gods is a very complexly varying one in different world views, and this is bound to be reflected in the great variations in the ways in which they enter—and fail to enter—the field of moral sanctions. Indirectly, of course, religion may enter in other ways: joint participation in religious ceremonies may strengthen men's bonds of common purpose, and the withdrawal of religious services may be a threat as sharp as any other threat of withdrawal of social support. But on the whole, religion does not play as comprehensive a role in relation to moral sanctions as would be suggested by our own cultural experience.

Automatic penalties associated with moral offenses do often occur. Indeed, the theme of illness, like that of witchcraft, runs widely through many moralities. Somehow the widespread prevalence of afflictions, the lot of man everywhere, is very frequently seen as resulting from man's own behavior. Sometimes the offenses are religious; but sometimes they are not. In any case the moral offense may bring on its own penalty without involving the gods in any way. Illness may follow from breaking a moral rule in a kind of automatic and immediate fashion, like syphilis from visiting a brothel. These are the wages of sin, with or without a religious perspective. Indeed, as we noted earlier for the Navaho, the very belief that consequences are automatic and direct may make it possible to put presumed cause and effect relationships to the test, and so to question the validity of particular moral rules when they do not lead to the anticipated ills. The association of illness and other afflictions with human moral offenses is sometimes taken to be evidence of a deeply moral view of the universe. However, no overall concept of "immanent justice" need be explicitly involved. It would seem advisable in each case to probe for the specific phenomenological picture rather than to assume it is of one pattern. This would also be true of the problem of exploring the implications of the moral role of witchcraft fears and witchcraft accusations, where complicating factors of projective hostilities and guilt mechanisms certainly enter.

    In any study of sanctions, whether on a comparative basis or within a culture, it is largely the negative sanctions which attract attention—the "or elses" which serve as ultimate threats to compel conformity or penalize the ones who have strayed. But in any morality there are strong positive sanctions as well. There are positive feelings paralleling the negative ones—pride and satisfaction, sympathy and mutual interests, may play as much of a role as fear, guilt and shame; and there are positive rewards as well as punishments. Strong among these is a kind of sanctioning effect which the actual on-going social situation may be seen to have. The pursuit of goals with their clear determination of suitable, socially acceptable courses of action, the intermeshing of cues and habits in normal everyday social relations, the structural forms of the social institutions through which one satisfies one's needs, determine the course of one's normal conduct in ways which may carry for the normal individual in the ordinary pursuit of his life no conspicuous awareness of alternatives, and no conscious reflection in terms of sanctioning threats. The very need to participate, to be part of ongoing life, to follow the usual course in relation to one's elders, one's relatives, one's children, one's community, in order to have a plot of ground to cultivate, companions to hunt with, partners to trade with, rituals performed, dances to enjoy, a bride-price paid for one—these are more positive than the almost unimaginable threat of their withdrawal, of working out a scheme of life in which one's community participation would not be a part. It is only in extreme or marginal cases that we see the phenomenological picture emerge in terms of negatives, of do-it-or-elses. Whether the question be taking a job to make a living in our culture, living with your father-in-law and obeying him in a bride-service culture, respecting your father's authority in patriarchal society, accepting the validity of conservative ways in the Pueblos, paying your debts to a trading partner in a Melanesian society—all of these normally operate through socially and institutionally built-in positive motivation, in which threats of punishment, or withdrawal of reciprocity, or shame and disgrace, need not be an issue in most people's thinking at all. And when the individual thus pursues his own goals by following the course society expects of him, and for which at the same time it rewards him, and achieves the ends of harmonious social functioning, one does not have the problem of "reconciling the conflict of the individual and the group," which has loomed so large in our own individualistically-oriented thinking. This does not mean that the individual functioning in a positively oriented social situation has no frustrations, bafflements and disappointments. It implies only that these may be so well compensated by reciprocal rewards and satisfactions that special added compulsions or threats are not needed.

This whole aspect of moral sanctions is likely to pass unnoticed except under very detailed analysis; it is like the balancing, but submerged, portion of an iceberg. Very often it is only when forces of change impinge upon the on-going institutional forms, in the face of conflicting patterns of economy or political and familial control, that the importance of the submerged portion may be revealed. As the neatly articulated balance of reciprocal forces is upset, mutual benefits no longer work out the same way, alternative paths are opened up to the satisfaction of individual needs, and new needs arise. With the disturbance of power relations, the homilies of the elders, though sometimes more sharply formulated than ever, are suddenly empty words, stripped of effective force or compensating rewards. At such points we may find violence and conflict, ruthlessness, disruption of marriage patterns and family relations—a total moral upheaval (cf. Collins, 1952, and Linton, 1939, ch. 7). As the positive sanctions of rewards and goals, habit, and joint participation lose their effectiveness, we find that even the negative ones become attenuated and ineffective, incapable of doing the job themselves.

Whether we look at the positive, satisfying or the negative, threatening aspect of morality, we must still recognize that basically studying sanctions involves more than just surveying institutional forms. It includes investigating the psychological emotional footholds which the various sanctions have within men. Negative sanctions have their roots in a host of negative emotions—fear, guilt, shame, and so on; positive ones may be seen in terms of pride, and goal-seeking, sympathy, and so on. And the sanctioning effect of on-going social institutions which we have just been pointing to also has its psychological bases in a whole family of psychological considerations—habit, the many-faceted process which the psychologists call "internalization," the very character of man as a creature of socially-developed and socially-fulfilled needs. Character structure as well as cognitively recognized values, convictions and beliefs, and habit-reinforced attitudes, work together in the field of moral reactions. And insofar as there are different components, or at least emphases, in the normal personality and character structure of individuals in different cultures, it seems evident that the feelings which are involved in morality should be differently standardized. In some cultures, as in our own, guilt feelings, and their compound cousins of remorse, and anxiety, are very important in the moral field. In others— and this Ruth Benedict and others have pointed out as perhaps true of Japan—shame may loom larger. But guilt and shame have many different senses, as psychologists have been pointing out. There is shame at being found out, and shame which operates entirely within the person, shame at failure to live up to some image of the self. And this will have different essential qualities if it is an image of worldly achievement, or of character.

There may even be guilt at being ashamed, shame at feeling guilty, all sorts of wheels within wheels (Piers, 1953, Pt. I, 7). Different aspects of these may be characteristic emotional responses of different people, or characteristic emotional developments of different cultures, and varyingly called upon to do the "heavy work of morality." There is a whole brood of other recoil reactions that can be called upon, as horror or shock, disgust and indignation, which may support morality and implement institutionalized sanctions. Fear itself may be parent to a whole family of emotions utilized in negative moral reactions—whether it be fear of consequences from others, from nature, from the gods, or even from one's own internal censures. And again, there are various ranges of positive feelings which may be involved or invoked: respect and awe, which are themselves in some ways akin to fear; sympathy and a sense of community or common purpose; even love and compassion, or persistent attraction, or aspiration. In many shades and combinations, such feelings may enter the moral domain in different settings, though their passports may not always be considered equally valid, or the jobs to which they are assigned have equally high social standing.

Anthropologists have been calling attention for some time to the wide range of differences in the developmental paths which different cultures standardize in their child-rearing techniques (cf. Honigmann, 1954, ch. 10). These lay the groundwork for differences in available emotional armaments. Although some, like Róheim (1950), stress the similar experiences which lie behind the diversity, there is little question that the resulting total personality differences as between "typical" individuals in different cultures are at least of the order of difference we find between individuals in our own culture. What are here accidental differences in the impact of circumstances on the child's development at various stages, can be stereotyped differences in different cultures. Pursuing such lines of inquiry, Kardiner (1945), for example, has pointed to the role of maternal neglect in the apparent failure of the Alorese to develop any character-structure equivalent of our super-ego. Indeed, analysts working with some of the Alorese Rorschach protocols find their whole ego-development weak, and this checks with the observations that their everyday handling of reality has little persistent carry-through and goal orientation. There is clearly little emotional base—neither guilt nor shame, nor any wide range of pride or even fear—for Alorese morality to root itself in.

In a somewhat different but even more strongly morally-oriented vein, Mead (1950) has pointed to differences to be looked for in the structure of conscience, of guilt and anxiety feelings, and in reactions of shame, where there are variations in another important aspect of socialization: the extent to which the parent punishes the child himself—physically or by withdrawal of love—or delegates such punishment to a more external agency to which both parent and child are subject. Both Pueblo Indians and Balinese, for example, use bogeymen, and share the child's fear at least externally, though with enormously different overall emotional impact. Other differences in child-rearing, with strong characterological implications which relate to possible reactions in the moral field, include treating children as highly responsible, or indulging them until they "understand"; revulsions of disgust at an infant's inevitable faecal soiling or very unaffected acceptance; relegating child-care to age-mates, or siblings who may treat them as scapegoats or toys, and so on. Such differences might well affect the development and patterning of shame and guilt reactions, of responsibility, of ego-ideals, and goal-orientations, as well as sensitivity to ridicule, fear of aggressive tendencies or need to exercise them, tolerance of frustration, feelings of sympathy and warmth, and so on, all of which are related to the emotional footholds with which sanctions must operate (cf. Whiting and Child, 1953). All this, of course, is over and beyond—or perhaps we should say below—the explicit parental verbal adjurations, which instill explicit attitudes to sanctions: reiterated "People won't like you" or "You'll disgrace the family" or "Wonderful, wonderful, we are proud of you" or "God will punish you" and so on, which in some cases may boomerang in rebellions or reaction formations of an opposite sort, but which normally do help to set a child's moral sights, in an emotionally tinged context, from the beginning.

All this is merely saying that the groundwork of theory is there for understanding how different emotional reactions may be standardized differently in different moralities, and utilized differently in the field of sanctions. It is not, of course, doing the actual job of analysis and mapping on a wide comparative canvas. This still needs to be done. And in doing this job, it will be important to bear in mind all the distinctions which this theoretical approach implies—the distinction between obvious conscious reactions and those revealed by deeper psychological inquiry; the difference between institutional forms like the occurrence of a joking-relationship with its privileged jibes, and the particular kinds of reactions whether of fear or shame or guilt or some combination of these, which this provokes. We could also push such an inquiry eventually into an examination of the distinction between the occurrence of a particular set of responses in the character structure and their utilization in morality. For example, we may find that Róheim (1950, ch. 8) is right in claiming that despite the frequent insistence of observers that the Navaho are a "shame culture," their dreams reveal that there are deep oedipal guilt feelings. Instead of this being a simple contradiction, it may suggest the complexity of the problem we face, in seeing how and if possible why Navaho morality is oriented in a direction which relegates such guilt feelings to the dream-life and other projective areas, and does not use it as a reliable sanctioning force in morality. Does the answer lie in the highly amorphous, non-authoritarian structure of Navaho society? Such investigation of social correlations is necessary in this field, although hardly possible before the terms of our descriptive survey are more sharply refined.

The problem of complexity and possible variety is perhaps more sharply underlined when we look at the somewhat higher-level jobs that are sometimes assigned to feelings in the western theoretical and cultural tradition. We need not go into those outlooks in which feelings are given the supreme post of defining the moral as such. Once in a while, it is true, there have been ethical theories that actually argue that morality is basically a matter of feeling and that there are certain feelings which are the "moral feelings" par excellence. Westermarck's *Ethical Relativity* (1932) presents such a thesis. The moral emotions are a particular set of retributive feelings—indignation and gratitude of a special sort—and all discourse of morality is ultimately analyzable into statements about or expressions of the comings and goings and linkages of these feelings. Interestingly enough, in the most influential of such theories, that of Adam Smith (1759), it was not guilt or shame but sympathy that won the top post: every moral concept, including duty and obligation, was analyzed as some pattern of sympathetic responses, often highly complicated.

On the whole, the most common central job assigned to the feelings with respect to morality is not that of being completely definitory, nor being merely supportive —whether as motives in goal-seeking, grounds for satisfying responses, or bases for negative ones—but as fusing cognitive functions with triggering or sanctioning, and acting as *moral indices*. This type of role for feelings is familiar to us in the conception of *conscience*. Conscience both tells us when we are going wrong and lashes us when we have done so; and what is more, if we are versed in its ways we both recognize and respect and even fear its authority. However, the analysis of conscience has never been an easy matter. Even psychoanalytic theory gives it different causal explanations: Freud (1933, ch. 3) roots it in the way in which oedipal guilt finds resolution in identification with the authoritarian father figure; Fromm (1947, pp. 141-172) distinguishes the authoritarian conscience from a humanistic one, pointing to differences in both character-structure and social-institutional forms to account for them. And recent sociological and psychological analysis has pointed to a shift in the very quality of conscience in our society, from a deeply inward feeling to one built far more, both descriptively and causally, of components which are sensitive to other people's responses (Riesman, 1950). It would seem, insofar then as one can say at all "look to your conscience to determine what is right," one is referring not to a simple feeling but to a complex function or job carried out by a dynamic system of forces in the individual. Whether this task can be done with equal effectiveness by varying parts of the range of emotional responses, remains a question for investigation. And perhaps the winner in such a contest might not be the familiar authoritarian Puritan conscience after all. For this is an instrument that can be blunted and distorted by neurotic anxieties and guilt-feelings, even to the extent of interfering with normal expressions of positive values—as for example in the all too frequent cases where guilt feelings interfere with morally approved sexual expression within the marriage relationship. It may be that some member of the love and sympathy family, orienting man's thinking in positive terms of fellow-feeling, could serve the purpose of moral index better.

Reflection on the history of ethical theory points to the same conclusion as we see emerging from the scientific materials even in their unsettled state today. Just as there has been considerable effort to develop a pure concept of "ought," so there has been a persistent attempt to discover the existence of a pure moral feeling or quasi-feeling which would be *sui generis,* distinct from the passions and self-love and affection and sympathy of the natural world. The hope has been that if one stripped off the husk of collateral and confused emotion, the purely moral reaction would be left clean and shining to act as an unerring indication of right and wrong. This affective side of the moral consciousness or the moral reaction or the moral attitude is sometimes spoken of as a feeling of obligation or a sense of duty. There can be no doubt that there is such a feeling. But that it has the sought-for simplicity is doubtful, for considerations exactly parallel to those that arose in our examination of conscience.

Even in the purely theoretical field one is struck by the wide variety of descriptions of the reaction. One philosopher feels it as a command, another as a contract-commitment, another as a debt. Bergson, for example (1935, ch. 1), distinguishes two senses of obligation—the aspirative and the instinctive—and warns against their confusion: the instinctive is compared to a habit, an accumulated exertion of pressure, a "must because you must," whereas in saints and sages obligation is not a pressure or a propulsive force but an appeal or an attraction. Some accounts appear to be embodying a definite model. For example, Kant, although he sought to remove all traces of empirical content, associates his *ought* and the unique feeling of awe or respect that goes with it, with a legalistic model that becomes explicit when he defines conscience as "the consciousness of an *inner tribunal* in man (before which 'his thoughts accuse or else excuse one another')" (Abbott translation, p. 209 ff.).

A more theoretical consideration is the serious controversial issue about the role of the cognitive aspect of any feeling-situation. Are the feelings to be regarded as in some sense specific discoverable reactions which may be oriented to different objects by a kind of cognitive association? Or are they in some sense constituted in part by the kind of object they are directed toward? In the one direction lies a theory of pure feelings, in the other a kind of field theory in which the phenomenal elements are indispensable in the actual description of the feeling. But if the very analysis of attitudes and feelings involves terms descriptive of human purposes and the cognitive field, then their moral meaning may very well depend on these constituents. A feeling could then serve as a moral index only within some wider theory of its development, purposes, roles, and relations; and its role would be in turn subject to critical evaluation.

On this hypothesis, what is spoken of as an obligation feeling or sense of duty may best be regarded as a deeply and many-rooted or diversely-rooted psychological-cultural product. The variety probably centers around two major types of common feeling-clusters—one stemming from the character of internalization as a process and involving something of the shame-guilt group; the other stemming from the simple common sympathy bonds that are developed by the facts of associated living. Specialization of a morality along either of these lines seems possible as a matter of emphasis. But it would also be both interesting and important to know how far moral feeling could take a predominantly goal-oriented line, and how far, if at all, it could really develop in a purely prudential or expediency way. In any case, we may suspect that we will not be dealing with pure feelings, but with a compound of familiar affective materials fused in varying proportions with selected phenomenal qualities and structured in different rational configurations.

Chapter XIV

MORAL CONFIGURATIONS

W<small>E HAVE</small> been surveying the kinds of items that
enter the content and the structure of different moralities, exploring their variety, meaning, and function. A
great many distinctions, both sweeping and subtle,
emerged in the exploration of these various, and varying,
areas of moral concern. Together, these inquiries and the
distinctions that emerged provide us with a set of coordinates for the multi-dimensional description of moralities. We know that, for any morality we wish to understand in depth, we must know not only the content of its
moral rules, the virtues it approves and the kind of behavior it deplores, the goals or ideals it cherishes, but we
must also map its position along many other, more purely
structural, axes. We must note whether its injunctions
are imperative, or mildly advisory; what kinds of terms it
uses for moral appraisals; whether it stresses ideals, or
models, or rules. Do many of life's aims and goals come
into the morality, or does conscious moral emphasis play
only a limited cultural role? Are its formulations abstract
and generalized, or highly specific, and differentiated according to kinship or other relationships or situations?
Is it concerned primarily with individual behavior and
individual responsibility, or are there conscious reflections
about group goals or "social policy"? Are its sanctions
rooted in automatic retributions, human or divine? Is

moral education verbalized and explicit? Are there strong
emotional commitments in the moral field? Are moral
decisions often necessary, and how are they mediated—
through officials, or objective techniques, or reckoning of
consequences in human relations? Does public pressure
play a large role? Does it take the form of punishment,
or ridicule, of compulsion or advice? And so on and on
and on.

Such a mapping gives us more than a mere itemiza-
tion of separate elements; it also gives us a way of looking
at the whole configuration of a morality, of seeing its
various emphases and salient features, in short of drawing
its *moral profile,* and assessing the qualities of coherence
and unity it may possess. Suppose we conceive of this
moral profile as rather literally mapped in a series of
vertical rectangular blocks, like a bar graph, with each
bar representing one of the traits we have been discussing. One might then make "size" comparisons of the
parts of the morality. These would, in effect, be judgments of the prominence, salience, predominance of various items in the total area. Thus in one morality virtues may loom large, specific rules small; in another we
may have the reverse. One goes in for distant "high"
ideals, the other for practical "low" ones. And some
moralities would have to be represented in a kind of double focus, for their sanctions, justifications, and systematization are different for different parts of the code.

The outline of the profile is not the only distinguishing aspect of whole-morality properties which we need to
note. For many moralities there are also pervasive modalities, qualities which appear to suffuse the morality
as a whole, or many significant parts of it. Stringency
is perhaps the most obvious example of such a modal

characteristic. It may appear in different ways in different areas of the moral profile—in sternly imperativistic injunctions, rigidity of conscience, a deep feeling of moral commitment, or in heavily enforced punitive sanctions. It may appear in absolute definition of situations for the application of particular rules or fixed interpretations and techniques for resolving moral dilemmas, or the justificatory base may stress the threat of terrible dangers or the urgency of need areas. And stringency may be different in its effect if it appears in some of these ways rather than others, or in more rather than fewer. We might obviously see other properties or qualities in the same way: an ideal of love, a virtue of kindness, a wide concept of the moral community, together or separately might give a morality more or less of a pervasive humanistic stamp. Similarly for other sets of properties some of which have been used to describe whole cultures, or their value systems: a morality may have a negative quality in many different aspects or ways, it may be activist or passive, individual or social, and so on, with respect to virtues, justifications, the role of moral feelings, the form of rules, and so on.

Without pressing the conceptual model of visual representation too far, we can see how such qualities too could be represented graphically: we could think of such suffusing properties as a kind of color wash applied to the whole or major portions of our graph. The different areas showing the color would indicate the spread of the property, differing shades of color its varying intensity. That is, instead of simply characterizing a morality as stringent, or negative, and so on, we should say in each case, how stringent, and in respect to what. This would make possible a far sharper characterization of a particular morality; there is surely a difference between stringency expressed in character structure and conscience, and stringency mediated through imperative rules enforced by punitive sanctions, though both might go with clearly demarcated rules and virtues. Their relations to patterns of justification might be quite different, though both would serve to assure a close toeing of the moral-requiredness line. Each of these in turn can be studied for its relation with the social structure and ecological base, and so on.

Qualities of wholeness, of meaningful integration, appear in moralities in other respects than the adjectival ones we have been discussing. A goal-orientation of a particular sort, an emphasis on community needs, on resignation or passivity, may be so strong that it not merely colors but appears to dominate the morality. Such integrational properties (we shall not go so far as to toy with the idea of representing them visually—perhaps as vectors?) may not always be easy to describe or discover, but in some moralities at least their impact is so pervasive as to impress itself forcibly on the analyst. The virtues fall into definite constellations, dominant goals are related to them in a clearly verbalized or highly practical fashion, the structure corresponds in its way of organizing sanctions; the verbalized justifications, the modalities of positive or negative emphasis, stringency-qualities and so on, are all intelligibly congruent.

Models of such highly coherent whole-morality configurations can be found both in the speculative workshop of the philosopher and in the practical laboratory of the anthropologist. Thus, it is quite clear that Ruth Benedict's well-known analysis of Zuñi culture (1934a) in terms of its Apollonian emphasis is in point of fact actually an analysis of its moral ideals and approved value-orientations, and one that appears quite intelligibly related to the socio-economic base of the culture. The outcome is clearly a moral configuration in the sense we have considered. We shall not attempt to chart it here in relation to all our proposed dimensions, but just note some of its more striking features. Pueblo morality, it is clear (cf. Goldman, 1956; Brandt, 1954), stresses the virtues of cooperation, hard work and thrift, the value of conformity, of careful fulfillment of patterned common obligations, and the muting of aggression. Not from any striving for personal ambition—which has no structural meaning in this framework—but from pride in his good reputation as a member of a good family, playing his role well, can a man take any personal satisfaction. However, individual conformity is formulated not as subordination of individual to group goals, but as a kind of self-fulfillment; for the ends of each man's work, his economic and religious performance, and his proper moral character, guarantee his own well-being. Men and gods must work together to give the feasts, perform the rituals, all in the proper spirit of cooperation, without violence or bad temper, so that the rains will fall and the corn will grow. There is strong social pressure for conformity, which is developed through strong childhood training, in which the gods (visible as masked dancers) are invoked to threaten lazy, disobedient children; it is also enforced through a highly authoritarian social structure, a council of religious leaders which can invoke strong penalties. These, however, will be called into play only against offenses which violate basic principles. The lazy, shiftless individual or family will be left to its own devices, scorned and criticized, but not penalized; the council's concern is with keeping the strong and able in line, with muting aggression, individualism, ambition. Patterns of cooperation are built in early; Pueblo children have long baffled American-trained teachers, who cannot "motivate" them with more stars or higher marks than their neighbors, achievements which would only be sources of acute shame to the children.

In the Pueblo moral structure, religious rules and procedures are absolute, but moral injunctions and rules are not phrased as imperatives; emphasis is on the general pattern of cooperation, compromise, walking well in traditional ways. Raising one's voice in anger, injuring someone directly and causing trouble, are clearly seen as threatening, and are strongly abjured. Doing reciprocal favors in return for favors conferred is necessary to self-respect and community respect. But in the whole field of sex, the individual's behavior can remain his own concern since no threat to the community is involved.

There are too many disputes in current anthropological literature about the precise character of Pueblo moral convictions—the extent of fear of community disfavor as against internalized guilt, the source of the suppressed hostilities which express themselves in antagonistic cliques, gossip, and accusations of witchcraft—for us to push this analysis further now (cf. Eggan, 1943). There may be some shades of difference in interpreting the exact quality of the Pueblo moral system, but that it is a coherent whole in which even the exceptions, the areas removed from central moral concern, can be understood in relation to the whole, is sufficiently apparent.

We cannot assume that such unity of pattern must be present in any morality. Certainly there is more apparent hodge-podge of particular elements, less obvious relatedness between the kinds of sanctions and where they fall, and the stressed goals of society, in many moralities. However, we must also remember that the first impression of a hodge-podge is not real disproof of underlying pattern, though the organizing point may lie not in the obvious features of the moral content but in the role and function which the morality plays in the culture. A witch-doctor's poke may present a miscellany of items with no apparent similarity, but it is far from a random grab-bag. The snakes' vertebrae and owls' eyes, the collection of dried herbs, may be unified by the theory on which they operate—classical "imitative magic," or some special individually acquired dream revelation of the sorcerer; and there is unity in the purposes they serve and in the ways they are put to use. So too the unity of a morality may lie not in principles of ethical structure, but in what we might call "external" integrational factors—factors of psychological coherence, or social-historical factors, such as the needs posed by military conquest, or feudalism, or slavery, or a patriarchal lineage system; or factors in the ecological base, such as scarcity or abundance of resources, large or small, compact or diffused communities, and so on.

Certainly if we look back at the Zuñi system, its very coherence makes better sense if we view it from this perspective. The needs of a small compact community attempting to make its living by agriculture in the midst of a semi-desert, harassed by marauding enemies, can account for highly stringent devotion to community ways. The stress on peaceableness of disposition, on muting of hostility, has a wide American Indian base: as we noted earlier, we cannot simply ascribe it to the needs of tight community organization, for it occurs among other groups where the community is very nearly anarchic; but certainly the important role it plays in the Pueblos, and the various ways in which social pressure is used to support and enforce it, the muting of some elements—individualism or ambition—which might interfere with it and with the ordered social structure, all these can be seen as gaining their centrality from their importance in the over-all situation. The emphasis on conformity and treading the measured path of a known way of life also gains some of its strength from the emotional factor of safety it conveys against a realistically difficult background. And one could probably also relate some of the very features which do not fit the overall stringency picture to elements in their social system—ease of divorce, for example, with the fact that a woman has a permanent home irrespective of marital changes.

Models of configurations can also be extracted from philosophies of history. Sometimes these bear chiefly on one special area of the morality. For example, Comte's picture of the development of civilization along the lines of intellectual stages from theological to metaphysical to positivistic, suggests different patterns of justification, irrespective of the question of order of development. And Nietzsche's historical speculations yield contrasting virtue-constellations of the mass-type and the heroic-type of man. Spencer and Marx provide more full-scale models: Spencer the "military" and "industrial" types, and Marx such socio-historical configurations as "feudal morality," "bourgeois morality," or even in more specific detail, "petit-bourgeois morality," each bound, as it were, with an economic cement.

The philosophies of history and civilization have often emphasized these external unifying or configuration-endowing properties or relations. Sometimes they do this by ascribing to some aspect of a culture—the economics or politics or religion or technology or type of mentality—a determining role in binding the culture into a unified pattern. Sometimes they do it by offering a theory of historical development for mankind as a whole; the unity at any time is then to be found in the place occupied in that developmental scheme by the society and the contribution made to it by the different aspects of the culture. Marx illustrates well both these procedures. The mode of production and its economic relations are given a primary place in shaping the whole character of a society, and the coherence of the morality is found in the way it is geared to and furthers productive activity and the specific aims of economic classes dominant at the given time. On the other hand, since successive classes are seen as widening productive power and increasing the scope of human freedom and control, a pattern is proposed for understanding the direction of change in moralities.

Different schools of ethics may themselves act as valuable sources for possible models. We can speak in a meaningful way of a Stoic ethics, a Platonic ethics, a Kantian ethics, a Utilitarian ethics, and so on; while in part these are conflicting *theories,* in part they also represent pictures of existent though sometimes opposing *moralities,* or sometimes proposed configurations for a broadly common morality. This approach must not be misunderstood: it is not attempting to override whatever real issues of fact or logic or metaphysics may be involved in the controversies of schools. It is simply an "extractive" process, emphasizing the moral component in ethical theories, and useful because the theory has usually succeeded in making more explicit the configuration of the various items.

In this way we can readily delineate a Stoic ethic (cf. Epictetus) . It has a distinctive set of austere virtues and a general end of peace of mind construed as a kind of "apathy" or dominating independence of spirit through resignation, in which will is detached from ordinary aims and human relations. It makes an explicit assumption of a universal moral community in which every man is an individual member. Its concept of the good becomes the maintenance of virtue and the avoidance of vice. Its systematization of morality is in terms of role, with each role having its ready duties. Its underlying justification scheme assumes that man is part of the universal rational order (in the classical pantheistic form, the divine world fire is at the core of each man's being). It utilizes internal sanctions of pride and shame fused into a kind of proud humility. It is no misnomer to see it as adding up to a "stoical" moral configuration, for all its elements point in this configurational direction. The universalism releases you from the local bonds that might enmesh your spirit and makes your individual self the focal point; the pantheism assures you that the will of God is *in* the world, so that there is good reason for whatever happens to you. Accepting it with humility and resignation is at the same time the recognition of victory over yourself —for the role you are playing has no other hold upon you than that of an assignment to be satisfactorily fulfilled, and this means to show your virtue in its exercise. And so on.

Compare with this the model to be extracted from a Plato's *Republic*. The virtues are the familiar Greek set of wisdom, courage, self-control or temperance, and justice. The duties and assigned tasks come from a fitness-determined status in the community—broadly categorized as production or meeting the material needs, safeguarding the social order and protecting the community, and determining fundamental policy. The goals of men are similarly threefold—bodily satisfaction, honor, intellectual pursuits. The governing ideal is harmony of functions both within the community and within the individual, under the dominance of the leading interest. The moral community is on the whole limited to the actual community. Systematization is along the lines of function, resting on a twofold theory of justification. One line of justification is a human-nature theory in which every man is composed of rational, spirited, and appetitive parts; Plato compares a human being to a man, lion, and dragon bound in one, with justice consisting in the ability of the man and the lion to keep the dragon in check. (The political analogue is explicit—the rulers and their executive helpers have to keep the mass of men in check.) The second line of justification is metaphysical and ultimately theological: a belief in an eternal reality that can be grasped by the mind, in doing which lies man's ultimate satisfaction; and a doctrine of the immortal soul's being tested in a succession of afterlives. The sanctions in the Platonic model are internal, with strong esteem and shame components, built in by education—but with reliance on coercion as unavoidable. The permeating element would seem to be total order hierarchically organized to secure an intellectual release as an individual salvation for the endowed few.

We have had occasion to touch on the Hobbesian survival model, and in some contexts on the Benthamite calculative prudential type. There are a great many others to be found in the ethical tradition—rigorist Kantian universalist-rational types, with a strong built-in guilt component; familial types with a common sense of shared central purpose; fixed human nature types, with concepts of healthy growth and expression; evolutionary types with a model of group survival, growth and adjustment; ascetic types and cynical types; and so on. We cannot, of course, even begin to list them all here. But it is worth stressing that since they are all elaborated in a reflective way, there is usually a clear sense of the integrating properties, and the result is a coherent moral configuration.

The construction of moral configuration models probably cannot proceed fruitfully by sheer speculative synthesis, as if one were to work out all the possible combinations of each of the different items in the several areas, one at a time from each area. But some freedom in speculation and construction is desirable. Once one has a configuration, one might speculate on the changes that would occur by varying any of its component items—somewhat as the non-Euclidean geometer varies an item in his initial axiom set. And it may prove to be worth following hunches about possible goings-together of items whose relations are suggested by varying leads in psychological or ethical materials—somewhat as Morris has done in working out alternative "paths of life" as whole syndromes (1956, ch. 1).

The models extracted from ethical theories are not to be reckoned among the purely speculative possibilities. For although they embody some creative and imaginative elements, they are rooted in the problems and needs of particular times and places. Analyzing each in terms of its historical context might provide important insights into determining conditions of both causality and relevance. For example, the Hobbesian model can be discerned in at

least three widely separated historical contexts. One is
the ancient Greek moderate sophist view of the social contract, exemplified in the position considered by Plato in
Book II of his *Republic* as a thesis he is setting out to dis-
prove: this is the view that morality is a kind of treaty of
peace between the inherently predatory interests of different men, to maintain a minimum of peace and order,
since the dangers of being the victim of aggression over-
weigh the possible advantages of aggression. The second
is Hobbes' own presentation in the turbulent era of the
17th century. The third is in our own day, in the current discussions not of private morality, but of national
morality in the international scene: the views that power
is the legitimate and only tenable national goal, and compromise to avoid disastrous war and losses the only justification of international morality. Similarly, there are
suggestive contrasts if we compare ancient Epicurean prudentialism in an insecure or contracting social situation
with the Benthamite prudentialism in the expanding ac-
quisitive situation of the English industrial revolution.
Studies, where possible, of consecutive changes in a moral
configuration rather than on a comparative but widely
spaced scene, might catch factors that shape morality in
their very operation. For example, the changing character of the Stoic ethical model from its cosmopolitan revolu-
tionary temper in its earlier career to its stress on the
inner psychological battle of the individual against himself in its typical late Roman forms might prove a very
revealing case study for the consideration of the altera-
tion of items and shifts in item emphasis. In the modern
era, studies such as Tawney's of the transformation of
religious modes of justification with the growth of an ac-
quisitive society throw light on the possible forms of inter-

relation of modes of justification and of changing economic forms, as well as on the Puritan-ethic configuration we shall consider shortly. Such studies raise complex methodological questions, but they are no different from, and no more tangled than those in other fields—looking for "culture-patterns" as a whole, or for significant "value-configurations" and their psychological and historical correlations, or for that matter trying to find more specific models of "explanation" in the social sciences and history that will fit what investigators generally deal with when they offer explanations in these fields.

Thus far we have been stressing the search for configurational properties of particular moralities. By placing some emphasis on the independent analysis of different features and aspects of the morality, we have found that it is possible to look at the relationships between the various parts of the moral structure and content, and between aspects of the morality and the social needs, traditions and beliefs, and historically-developed structure of the whole culture. But if the intelligible relationships which we discover, the meaningful interpretations, are to have more than intuitive descriptive value, we must move more explicitly toward a comparative approach as well. The linkages which we discern have to be more formally stated, and their recurrence noted in other cultures; the explanatory roots, historical, social, psychological, on which they appear to rest, have to be more sharply formulated as hypotheses, so that the comparative field can be surveyed for their support.

So, for example, we can look for possible repetitions of whole-morality configurations. Can we find Zuni-type moralities, or Platonic-type moralities, repeating all or some significant parts of the patterns we have outlined? And we can try to discover under what similarities of circumstance these similarities in moral patterns occur. If we find high goal orientation and considerable rigidity and stringency in Zuñi, associated with tight community organization and strong pressure of realistic external dangers, we can look to see to what extent these go together in other societies which have such pressures and needs. Or we might note the dominating Zuñi emphasis on non-aggression, and see what similarities and differences we find in other societies which share it, and what differences are to be found when, as among the Navaho, it occurs in a setting where community sanctions are not so strong, and community organization is far less compact.

We can proceed to make comparative studies of this sort between different moralities, and parts of moralities, whether in different parts of the world, or with common historical roots. We can ask innumerable interesting questions, such as: Does rule-emphasis or virtue-emphasis go more commonly with strong ridicule sanctions? Do strongly internalized obligation feelings tend to pervade moralities with strong goal-orientations; and are there some goals with which this characteristic is particularly congruent? Is prudentialism a special feature of anarchic minimally-structured community situations? Can we find any special set of correlates for the use of witchcraft fears in morality? Is individualism uniquely tied to a commercial emphasis in society? Is absolutism in moral justification linked in any way to the acceptance of repression in the structure of society? Are there any emergent forms of moral structure which appear in complex socio-economic systems? And so on.

Obviously in such inquiries we are not looking for

simple sets of one-to-one correlations between different parts of the morality, nor do we hope to find that character types, environmental influences, or particular kinds of social structure or historical changes will yield uniquely corresponding configurations in morality, any more than they yield simple correlates in any other part of the field of social relationships and ideologies. We can hope only to confirm the significance of discovered tentative relationships, and gain a fuller insight into the partial causes and conditions which operate in this complex field of multiple interacting factors.

It is, of course, tempting to reflect on how convenient it would be to put our data into a kind of statistical hopper, and settle our questions by tabulation and multiple-factor correlation. But the state of our knowledge in this field hardly permits of such a resolution in the foreseeable future. Analysis of the meaningful units in the moral field is not refined enough, nor do we have the massive quantities of comparable data any statistical approach requires. There are, of course, also innumerable methodological handicaps and pitfalls in handling anthropological data statistically, which are familiar enough from other problem areas. We cannot, for example, simply count heads; and if we count cultures, what shall be our unit? Shall three historically-related occurrences count for one, or for three? What if the tribes in question have some political unity? Ought we to separate for statistical treatment large and small societies, areas of widespread communication and those of narrow isolation, and so on? We need not review all these dilemmas here (cf. Whiting, 1954). But even if these difficulties force us to rely on comparisons of a limited number of case studies on a kind of clinical approach rather than a statistical one, this does not put our inquiries into a unique or hopelessly handicapped position: it only reminds us that we must operate in depth and make our particular studies careful and searching. Exploring repetitive syndromes that do occur, noting concomitant changes in various parts of a moral pattern that take place under conditions of cultural change, analyzing differences to be found within somewhat similar patterns—all these procedures will give us a more systematic view of the meaning and function of morality, and the complex interacting factors which help to determine its many varying forms.

We can see how such an approach can be utilized by looking briefly in an exploratory way at a repetitive configuration that has already been pointed to in the anthropological literature. It is a syndrome which includes similarities in virtue constellations, stringency qualities, strong direct religious sanctions, individual responsibility inwardly structured, and strong goal-orientation in terms of competitive wealth manipulation. All of this is to be found in the "Puritan-morality" complex which has been so often described and analyzed in our own culture, both for the early development of western commercial society, and more recently in the questions psychologists and sociologists have been raising about its transformation—a current shift alleged to be taking place from this "inner-direction" to "other-direction," along with a shift from individualism to team-work, from thrift to installment buying, and from "guilt" to "shame" as motivating sanction. The earlier relation of the Puritan syndrome to the rise of the striving middle class, building capitalist enterprise on accumulation and calculated investment, with its relentless drive, its sense of proving its worth to itself, its stern virtues of thrift and sobriety and justice, its transformation of the religious justification from an ordered hierarchy to an open individual communion, has been richly documented in the sociological and historical studies of Max Weber, R. H. Tawney, and others. This requires no recapitulation here, nor does its relation to the general social shift from the stability of the earlier feudal society to the commercial-industrial society with its vertical mobility and competitive status-striving, and its general reorientation of social and political institutions.

In at least two different parts of the world, very similar configurations have been noted. One is that of the Manus of the Admiralty Islands in New Guinea, the other the Yurok of California.

The Manus (Mead, 1937, ch. 7) are a trading people, who lived until recent decades in houses built up over a lagoon, depending for their livelihood on fishing. They exchanged their fish for other foods, for raw materials and for various manufactured products, with tribes who lived ashore on the islands. Food for the village, and for necessary trade with the inland neighbors, was pretty well guaranteed by the sea; but Manus men worked much harder than that at their fishing, and the women at the netting and weaving that was their share of the work effort. For the goal was not simply to have enough to eat, but rather to amass a surplus great enough to use in the elaborate financial transactions which accompanied all major life activities—marriage and childbirth and death. These occasions all required huge ceremonial exchanges of food, strings of dogs' teeth, woven mats—between families who were related by marriage. Everyone was involved in these affairs at some time in his life. The young men particularly had to work, to pay for their marriages; but this was done on the installment plan. Their marriages

were financed for them by older men, and then they had
to pay them back over time, at a considerable rate of interest. Theoretically, it was a man's father who arranged
to pay for his marriage, but in practice the financing was
done by "big men" who undertook financial manipulations on a widely-ramifying scale. This activity yielded
prestige, and power over the younger men, who worked
for them in repayment, and sometimes became their permanent satellites.

Status in Manus had come to depend on position in
the financial hierarchy, on being involved on a large scale
in wealth exchanges, rather than on hereditary family
position, which was an underlying archaic strand in
Manus culture. Economic activities dominated Manus life,
with other interests all subordinated, or disvalued to the
extent of explicit condemnation. Sex pleasures, for example, did not mix with this life goal: sexual activities
were strongly regulated, and kept within very puritanical
bounds, except for the occasional quite extra-legal flings
we noted earlier, when the men captured a girl from
some other village. Sex prudery, and very strict moral
principles about not even flirting with one's neighbors'
wives, were stressed in moral training and were basic attitudes here; so was hard work, attention to financial problems, thrift, regard for property rights, scrupulous repayment of debts. These were the virtues stressed, and they
were built deeply into Manus character. Youngsters, Margaret Mead tells us, were extremely scrupulous about returning even scraps of paper they found, and never dam-
aged anyone else's property. The whole weight of conscience, and an unusual degree of religious concern with
individual morality and fulfilling obligations were evident here. Ancestors' ghosts watched one's every mis-

step, and punished it; all illnesses, as well as other mishaps, were blamed on some moral misdeed, which was dug up and publicised by the diviner consulted for diagnosis of the illness.

Here we have then a syndrome richly parallel to the Puritan picture of our culture: vertical mobility, competitive wealth manipulation, a clustering of virtues around hard work and thrift, with puritanical sex attitudes amounting almost to Victorian prudery, close supervision by religious beings deeply concerned about correct moral performance, individual responsibility and individual reward combined with publicity for moral misdemeanors, reminiscent of the thunderings of the Puritan divines, though needing no threats of hell-fire and brimstone, nor even public shame, since the penalty of illness was conveniently here-and-now and already at work to promote guilt-feelings and repentance. There is thus much in the structural pattern as well as the content which is highly similar to our own Puritan past. The precise relation between justifications, sanctions and goals may be a little different here from the relationship in some forms of Protestant Christianity. There is, of course, a very real distinction between "Be good that you may be wealthy" and "Be good, and if this is a sign of your living in God's grace, your worldly success will also show it." But there is enough difference—and confusion—between different sects in our own tradition to mute the significance of this distinction. "Worship God that you may be rewarded" —and sometimes directly with business success—is often enough the theme of sermons; and, on the other hand, Manus moral concerns cut much deeper than a merely prudential calculation of success.

Many parallel highlights have been pointed out in the

analysis of the Yurok of California by Goldschmidt (1951) and Erikson (1950, ch. 4). We shall not attempt a description here, but the significant points there too seem to be wealth manipulation and competitive vertical mobility —not quite so sharply divorced from hereditary status— linked to much the same set of virtues of work and abstemiousness and careful regard for property. There is a similar divorce of sex and wealth, though here sex activity is not abjured—it is simply required that it be put into a separate department, women being polluting. And there is here too a high level of religious activity oriented to wealth getting, and requiring the strict practice of virtues in order to achieve it. A man must stay slender by working hard and not indulging himself, in order to be able to take a daily sweat bath in the ritual sweatlodge with its tiny circular exit, so narrow a man could barely wriggle through it; its regular use is a required religious activity, necessary for anyone who wants the blessing of wealth. Precise institutional forms are certainly quite different in all their details, but the basic syndrome reappears: individual responsibility, strong personal concern with fulfillment of moral requirements, internalized goads of conscience supported by religious sanctions, all geared to wealth as a goal, are stressed to make a very parallel kind of configuration.

We have thus a group of moral items that tend to cluster together, and the question "Why?" naturally arises. An explanation may be attempted either in terms of intra-moral integration properties, or by reference to some general psychological or social theory or pattern of historical development. The cultures themselves, as seen in their modes of justification, tend to follow the first path. Common to all three is the idea of success with wealth as the content or mark of the success itself. It is true that at one time in our cultural history wealth was evidence of the fact that one was among the elect, whereas in more recent times there was more likely to be justification proposed in terms of a moral type—that is, sacrificing enjoyment to carry the burden of the ideal of progress. But in any case, success and wealth, though understandable as human motives, do not constitute a sufficient explanation. They do not explain why other cultures have different stresses, nor why these particular features have gravitated together as they do. Hence explanatory theory has sometimes looked to psychological accounts of character development, since particular traits loom so large in the syndrome, and sometimes to social and historical generalization about wealth-gathering and wealth-manipulation.

One interesting suggestion that has been made is that we have here a characterological type which follows a specific route of psychological development, and which may become standardized in some cultures. This was described by Freud and his followers as the "anal character structure" (cf. Fenichel, 1945, pp. 278 ff.), because its predominant traits—of frugality, orderliness, obstinacy—were believed to take their specific form in part as reaction-formations against anal-erotic activities, and in part as sublimations of them. Erikson has pointed to the very open alimentary symbolism of the Yurok mythology and rituals: climaxed by squeezing through the narrow opening of the sweatlodge. One cannot but note also that Mead's account (1956) of the changing situation in Manus today indicates that there was a special concern with latrines when the new village was built on land, and that men and women line up at their respective ends of the village for regular morning toilet-going! There has, of course, been considerable controversy over the concept of an anal character structure, and over the part played by cultural factors in its development. We shall not press the special relationship which has been suggested between faeces and wealth-manipulation. But there does certainly seem to be wide agreement that not merely the nuclear traits but the wider type—grudging, avoiding sexual pleasures, restrictive, "tight" in exactly the slang sense, as well as more generally rigid, highly moralistic and critical of both self and neighbors—has some sort of characterological coherence. Whatever explanation the psychology of personality will eventually offer for this character structure will obviously be relevant to the analysis of the moral syndrome.

It is equally clear, however, that any authenticated characterological type will not explain the whole syndrome. For one thing, while it may explain why these moral features arise and function well in relation to an emphasis on wealth manipulation, it does not explain the wealth-getting economic organization itself. The trading pattern by which Manus lives has considerable historical depth. It is a widespread Melanesian way of life; its roots are in the realities of getting a living, though it is elaborated in terms of social meaning and symbols. Similarly, wealth acquisition in our own culture in the whole of post-feudal times was strongly realistic, both in relation to the gains for the individual, and for the restructuring of society as a whole. Clearly we cannot explain these economic factors as a consquence of an anal character structure. Nor do we suggest that anal character structure must arise whenever this economic pattern is present. Take, for example, Alor, to which we had occasion to refer earlier in this book. In Alor, as in Manus, "big men" support the great feasts which must be given at major life-crises, and expect returns at interest for wealth accommodatingly loaned out. But Alor certainly has no Puritan character structure, nor Puritan morality. Here people bluster, instead of paying their debts. Big men especially are prone to cheat, and get away with it. Death feasts are postponed, houses go to pieces; the wealth surplus is largely "on paper," so to speak. And as we noted earlier, field reports suggest that "the Alorese have no conscience." The why of the contrast we do not touch upon here. How much of it lies in character structure, in the factor of relative maternal neglect Kardiner has pointed to, how much is due to the conflicting cultural emphasis on vengeance and head-hunting (also rather disorganized in its structure in Alor), or what other factors may be involved, we do not know. But certainly the contrast between the highly efficient wealth-producing dynamism of Manus society and the bickering confusion and inefficiency of Alor is very striking, and it emphasizes the way in which the moral syndrome we noted for Manus, though not necessarily a consequence of this kind of economic system, is highly congruent with it, and highly effective in implementing it.

We are not suggesting, either, that this moral emphasis and character pattern are the only efficient ways of organizing a competitive wealth-getting economy. The very contrast between the Puritan syndrome and the "might-makes-right" power morality of the "robber barons" in our own history, is reflected also in the primitive world. The Ifugao (cf. Goldman, 1937, ch. 5) have a way of life in which wealth and power are equated, and in which a kind of Nietzschean morality appears to dominate the picture. Conflicts are open and obvious, duties and obligations are binding only in so far as they can be enforced; all offenses can be compounded by payment, but only after mediation in which relative strength in wealth and numbers of the conflicting groups is a formal part of the considerations. And numbers depends on wealth, for a man gives his allegiance to the wealthy relative who is his strongest available patron, from whom he can rent land and borrow rice and animals at a high rate of interest. We cannot examine the Ifugao moral configuration in detail here, but it is highly suggestive that it appears to be functioning in a context of emerging class-differentiation, with land in wealth as a fixed property right, giving genuine economic power over the disappropriated. There are certainly nowhere in Manus society people who are dependent on others for their basic livelihood, and this is a point of substantial economic difference in the entire life pattern.

Attention to the possible historical roots and changing economic and political systems in which major moral differences may have their essential explanation, however tentatively developed here as a hypothesis, is at least a reminder of the general need to look at any morality in a way which includes the possibility of development, change, emergence, rather than as in a permanent static equilibrium. To probe for the economic or historical conditions which make major social shifts possible is a project beyond the scope of ethical inquiry, but it can and must look into some types of historical questions: the ways moralities themselves change, how they become consolidated into new patterns under changing circumstances, and even the way and the extent to which ideological factors in morality—whether justifications, evaluations, or actual moral rules—enter in some contributory way into the directing of change that takes place. It is true that data on processes of change are hard to come by, but there is surely a great deal to be learned from research on the modern scene, where rapid transitions are in process, and also from reconstructions of the sort anthropologists have learned to work with, which are based on cultural comparisons within one area. Such comparisons within an area would be fruitful even if they yielded no actual clues to time sequence, for by holding some factors of common tradition if not constant, then at least relatively stable, they enable us to look more sharply at the differences which occur, in single features or complex sets. So, for example, it would no doubt be particularly revealing to compare Manus with the other Melanesian cultures which share its trading base, just as we suggested comparing Zuni with other American Indian cultures, and as we might very well compare the segmentary lineage cultures from Africa—the Nuer, the Tallensi, and the Chiga— whose contrasting moralities we have had occasion to note in previous chapters.

We have come a long way with our initial proposal to investigate one syndrome, that of the combination between vertical-mobility and wealth-getting, with a kind of Puritan conscience and emphasis on work and abstemiousness. We would probably get equally far were we to work out from any other repetitive syndrome we may find, even if its scope is a little less impressive. So, for example, we might look into what we might call a Spartan moral configuration, a common clustering of virtues and character emphases among cultures in various societies in different parts of the world who live their lives girded for war, and vaunt its glories. As in the Spartan system depicted

in "Plutarch's "Life of Lycurgus," pride, bravery and stoical fortitude are central virtues. There is a glorification
of the individual combined with his subordination to common goals. This is secured through the building of group
morale in various forms, such as age-grade regiments and
warrior societies. Other ties and allegiances and virtues
are minimized. Hardness and spare living are emphasized
and there is either impersonality in sex—often conducted
with groups of girls living in warrior huts in Africa, with
no thought of marriage and its distracting emotions and
responsibilities—or abstemiousness, as when Plains Indian warriors count it a boast to father children ten years
apart. Children are often reared, at least for part of their
youth, in age groups, away from the softening influences
of home, and steeled to bear pain as well as to inflict it.
In such societies, guilt anxieties may not be important
features of the conscience pattern, nor can fear of physical
pain be a major sanctioning base. But shame and ridicule,
both explicit and deeply internalized, are powerful moral
weapons. Tales of suicide in the face of public shame, or
of suicide squads sworn to go ahead no matter what, occur
repeatedly from these cultures; and required roles must
be played out to the limit, in an exacting way. Plains
Indians make an accommodation for this which reveals its strength: the man who cannot play a man's role
well may take over the woman's role, and live his life as a
transvestite. The role-related character of morality in
such cultures is often symbolized in the sharply different
character and performance demanded of people in different age positions: elders, for example, as leaders in peace
and advisors in council, must give up their aggression and
fierceness. The role of priests and religion as fostering
the goals of war achievement in various ways, also enters

this pattern, which stresses goal rather than rule.

Here again, a fuller explanation would plunge us into an examination of the personality roots of character structure congruent with such an orientation, and into the historical causes of the development of this way of life. Certainly, it is not as geared to class-preservation in other areas as it is in Sparta. And we should find it fruitful to compare different Plains Indian moralities, where the fundamental social organization and economic bases differed; comparing the Omaha, for example, with their significant wealth differences, and a more egalitarian group like the Cheyenne; or seeing what moral differences there are between some of these Plains people and the Iroquois, whose warfare went along with strongly integrated cooperative communities, and large-scale political organization. Shifting moral patterns as conquest takes over as a goal could also be investigated for Africa, where it was a strikingly recurrent phenomenon. And here too, variations within areas of shared traditions could be pursued. And so on.

It is clear from our discussion of moral configurations that this branch of inquiry is characterized today by a comparative wealth of insights and a comparative dearth of really detailed studies. But the study of morality cannot proceed with confidence on only a few samples or on impressionistic accounts. The ideal here would be a moral map of the globe, in historical depth as well as spatial spread. Such a map has to be worked on in the same spirit in which science charts the detail of the globe in a geophysical year, or in which the varieties of insects or sea-inhabitants are being mapped. There is, however, an even greater need for haste. Some phases of our world are likely to remain constant for a reasonable while. But the existent moral consciousness in many parts of the world is undergoing rapid change, and we had better take its measure while we can.

Chapter XV

EVALUATION

W<small>E</small> NOTED at the very outset of our work the strong philosophical tendency to insist on the autonomy of the normative, reflected in the contemporary world in many such slogans as that science gives us means, but cannot give us ends; or that from an account of what *is* we can never derive what *ought to be,* or that science is *descriptive* whereas ethics is *prescriptive,* and so on. Such views, we noted, have often been used to preclude any attempt at relating science to ethics. We have taken the very different position that they have a great deal to say to each other, and that there is a considerable area that philosophy and the sciences of man must plow together.

In this book, we have attempted some studies and proposed others which we believe show that this approach is potentially an extremely fruitful one, that ethics can be wedded to science, and that the data and perspective of anthropology in particular have very definite philosophical implications in the field of ethics.

For one thing, we saw throughout as a constant lesson that the path for evaluation is opened rather than closed by each wider description and each deeper explanation. Men's actions and desires and character in any society are subject to evaluation in that society in terms of its moral conceptions—the moral rules and prescribed goals, the virtues and vices, the ideals of achievement and ap-

propriate institutional functioning. But we saw that
these can in turn be assessed for the way in which they
satisfy the biological and social needs of men. These
needs in turn are not wholly biological or even psychological "givens." There is always a complex interplay of cultural institutions, needs and satisfactions, goals and standards. For that matter, the very description of a morality
is rarely that of a fully-set pattern of stable ways, like the
rigid habits of "crabbed old-age." There are usually some
areas of a striving that knows not quite what it wants, that
has a sense of problems to be solved, ways to be fashioned,
or perhaps pressing evils to be battled. A comparative survey may very well exhibit the variety that such points—
whether conscious reaching forward of ideals or mere
budding-points of possible growth—can take in different
kinds of cultures. Evaluation in practice as well as in
theory finds us always in the midst of things, never at a
sheer beginning or a sheer ending.

The same perspective opened out of our examination
of moral structure. We saw that one can always raise the
question whether the boundaries of the moral community
should be extended, whether the criteria of responsibility
should be altered. The very evidence we presented to
show that moral concepts have deep cultural roots and
that modes of systematization are in part instruments of
organization reflecting cultural patterns and problems, by
its raising the issue of alternative modes raised thereby
the issue of their suitability, either in general or for a particular culture. The diversity of modes of justification
raises questions about the comparative truth of underlying assumptions, views of human nature and of the human
predicament, as well as about the assessment of the general orientations which different justification modes may

entail. To realize the wide variety of patterns in which sanctions and human feelings are woven, is again, of itself to call for evaluation in any given culture, or for mankind in general. Think back, for example, to our discussion of conscience. As long as it was regarded as a faculty given to man, then the most that could be sought were its verdicts. Evaluation would be limited to straining one's inner ear to catch the fine shades of the voice within. Once the full scope of conscience as an office is realized, evaluation becomes a task of the widest educational— psychological and cultural—scope. We can ask what sort of conscience has been typical in our society, what conditions have made it such, what its sensitivity or rigidity or blunt- ness has been, how it might be improved, what other human mechanisms or abilities can be brought within the scope of moral decision, whether they can largely replace the previous occupant of the office of conscience and take over the job, what path of reconstruction would be desir- able.

The general effect of deeper study is thus to under- stand the grounds and occasions and conditions of the forms morality takes, to see where alternatives are possi- ble, and so to raise and intensify problems of evaluation and reconstruction. In many areas it opens fresh avenues where before was only "the fixed order of nature." We saw that this possibility of constant evaluation has reached the point in contemporary theory where a marked rest- lessness characterizes the very picture of evaluation itself in analyses of justification.

On the whole, in this book, we have not engaged much in actual evaluation. This was not avoided on prin- ciple, as if there were a yawning chasm to be crossed before one could approach the process. It was more a matter of division of labor. Wherever an obvious evaluation stood out, we did not hesitate to make it. Thus we took it for granted that many needs would survive the most critical evaluation, and that some common goals would receive substantial reflective acceptance: that it is better for children to get good maternal care than to be neglected; that a distribution system is better insofar as it satisfies the hunger of all the people; that aggression minimized is better than aggression expressed in open violence and killing, though there may be a cost for muting aggression that still needs to be studied; that the widening of the moral community, at least in the sense of treating all people however different or alien as human individuals who count, is a human good; that inner sanctions are preferable to sheer imposed external force, but that the dictatorial voice of conscience is perhaps not the ultimate means of human self-regulation; that justification in terms of satisfactions is a nobler base for human moral consideration than fear of demons or of malice, though perhaps harder to implement. Admittedly, however, to pursue any such evaluations fully would be a large task. They would have to be set in a fuller scientific theory of man, and in a concrete presentation of contemporary needs and problems and value patterns, either for particular societies or for mankind at large, and that too in a developmental perspective. And this obviously was beyond our present scope.

Although we have not engaged in many specific evaluations, we have learned a great deal about evaluating as a process. Now the study of evaluating is not itself evaluating in the same sense; it is rather describing, analyzing, explaining or finding causes—and this is clearly what on a comparative basis we have been doing. But this in turn gives us tools for pursuing evaluation. The study of a language's vocabulary and structure is not equivalent to using the language, but it may reveal more clearly what you are doing when you use the language, and what the limits are of what you can do under the given structure. It is precisely such a study which, by taking the *prescriptive* and the *ought* to pieces, by seeing what determines the way they function, makes it possible to discern the threads that tie them to the *descriptive* and the *is*. And so, while it does not belie what has been seen—that the enterprise of evaluating can be carried on in every context where a description has been provided—it shows that the transcending character of evaluation is only one face of the coin.

Why is it then that any evaluation appears to *transcend* the presently existing situation? What is the "detached" element that constitutes the normative? This is a question of a highly technical sort in philosophical deliberation, and one which has been extremely controversial in contemporary thought. We cannot enter into all its issues here, but we can outline the kind of answer that emerges from our comparative inquiries and analyses. When we evaluate virtues and ideals in a given culture, or types of sanctions and forms of conscience, our question is always which are *desirable, preferable* or *better,* which *ought to be* chosen as a guide to our efforts, and so on. And with these concepts on each occasion go some criteria. A given virtue is less desirable because it *frustrates* certain other *needs*; a given sanction is better because it involves *less violence*; violence against humans should be a last resort because it is contrary to *the ideal of the dignity or worth of every man.* And so on. These concepts and criteria appear to come from a wholly different, an external realm, and to be exercising a transcendent rule.

But the general lesson of our inquiry would seem to be that ethical concepts, no matter how detached they are felt to be in consciousness, have cultural roots and cultural functions, and their meaning is to be found in the offices they perform. And criteria would seem to have a similar character. The criteria in any evaluation of virtues, goals, ideals, needs, and so on, are other virtues, goals, ideals, needs, more abstract or more concrete, which have become enlisted on behalf of the ethical concepts to carry out their office in the given context. Evaluation thus represents the interaction and the interplay of phases of life in the on-going processes of human living rather than the application of an external standard.

On this view there is a kind of *double dialectic* in the ethical process. Evaluation does transcend each presently existing situation, but the detached elements whereby it does so are found in turn to have their own connections with the existential context. The detachment lies, as we have seen, in the continuous possibility of asking as we take our stand in time and look forward, "Where do we go from here?" The attached connections are seen in the local reference in "we" and "from here." It is always in the light of what we are, what needs we have, what aspirations characterize us, what resources are available, that we—taking our stand in time and looking forward—pose the problem of reconstruction.

In the light of such a conception, the role of science in ethics may be a more permeating one than it has hitherto been conceived to be. To ask "Can science tell us what is really and truly good, or only how particular people regard the good and what causes them to go one way or the other?" is very much to over-simplify the question. It is to speak as though one had to deduce ethical conclusions from scientific premises (a straw man easily blown away), or else as if science had to come hat in hand to be given values in the validation of which it had previously had no hand. But actually the assistance that science gives us need not be wholesale and of one type. It may be retail, and vary in its impact. Sometimes it may bring a fairly complete determination through showing that the possibilities are genuinely limited. Sometimes it may open up a field of new possibilities hitherto not even envisaged. But more pervasively it may enter in a way that is intimate yet direct—by contributing to the understanding of the very terms in which ethical questions are formulated.

To show how this can come about has been one of the aims of the present work. At first we looked for the ways in which philosophical formulations might be helpful in suggesting scientific possibilities. We took ethical theories into the philosophical workshop and saw how they could be fashioned into models. Thus instead of arguing whether moral discourse is "really" cognitive or prescriptive, we suggested looking to see what a cognitive organization of morality would be like, or a prescriptive one. Instead of arguing about the correctness of Kant's or Mill's or Adam Smith's analysis of obligation, we ushered them all into the workshop and proposed to see what would be the model of a Kantian conscience, a Millian conscience, a Smithian conscience. From Platonic and Hobbesian and Stoic ethical theories too we saw we could extract pictures of possible whole moralities. We suspected, of course, that we were dealing with real human possibilities, not merely abstract speculations. The philosopher is after all a sensitive participant reflecting as well as reflecting upon the ways and problems of his life and times:

Mill's theory expresses the aspirations of the liberal character of his day, and the rigor of Kant's conscience is aptly characterized by Marx's comment that every Prussian carries his *gendarme* within his breast. Our initial concern, however, was not with particular cultural or subcultural roots and causes, but with the projected moral type embodied in the theory. In this way the philosopher serves as an informant and the extracted model is the model of a possible morality which might or might not correspond to an existent or partially existent pattern.

Scientific processing of these speculative suggestions goes on in the laboratories of the special sciences of man. The anthropologist will look to see if there are actual examples of these models, and will add to the list from his own canvass of actualities. He will then use these actual systems to study how they function and intermesh with the whole of life. In addition to the anthropological laboratory there are psychological, historical, and other special science laboratories, which may join in probing for the assumptions of the various models, and assessing them in the light of current scientific findings. What assumptions of the nature of cognition, of will, of feeling, of person and self, are implicit or expressed in a given model, and how do these relate to current psychological research results and concepts? What structure of social relations is embedded in a particular whole-morality model, and how does it fit the changing structure of human relations? By such procedures we can be helped to determine whether our models are largely speculative abstractions or realistic possibilities under some set of given conditions, and what would be the contours of a human society in which they were or might come to be embodied.

In this processing of philosophical materials we come

to realize how much moral, cultural and social content
there is stowed away not merely in the remote recesses
but in the very core of abstract ethical concepts. And we
learn that this material is not simply to be stripped away,
for some material of that sort plays a constitutive role
within the theories. The question is not whether scientific materials have a place within ethical theory, but
whether by denying that they have we shall find ourselves
using scientific results that are out of date instead of
consciously pursuing the most advanced data and theories
available. To operate upon specific ethical theories as
specimens has not then reduced their philosophical function. As a matter of fact, philosophers have always probed
in this way in criticizing ethical theories. They have
looked to contexts of usage in deciding how moral discourse was really operating, they have examined theories
of obligation for their consistency and accuracy in their
presentation of man, and in dealing with the "adequacy"
of total ethical theories they have telescoped under this
notion a whole host of bases of criticism, logical and
methodological, factual and purposive. We propose to
keep this more consciously part of our enterprise; thus, by
locating the exact points at which psychological and social
science assumptions enter into the configuration of an
ethical theory, philosophy can carry on its analytic and
evaluative functions more explicitly, and make these more
effectively oriented to the growth of human knowledge.

Where would we stand if the kinds of tasks for ethics
that come clearly within the scope of scientific inquiry
were successfully carried out? We would know a great
deal more about the moralities of the past and present,
their systematic character and relations to man's basic biological and psychological equipment and social and cul-

tural conditions. Under favorable conditions, we would know what human aspirations were perennial and recurrent; which problems had to be faced under all conditions and which under analyzable particular conditions; what means were essential to what ends; what ends we have, as it were, built into us, and which ones we grow as we go along depending on conditions, and which ends are arbitrary or of chance occurrence. We would know how aspirations shape obligations, and we would be able to distinguish genuine limits from spurious necessities, and basic human needs from transient desires. We would know the different kinds of qualities in moral experience and the psychological and cultural conditions of their growth and selection; how they could be muted or intensified, which could stand alone and which went in teams. We would know the effects of different types of sanctions, the human costs of restrictive negative sanctions and the degrees of effectiveness to be expected in what cultural settings from positive rewards. We would have a natural history of different ethical concepts, and an understanding of the different ways in which ethical expressions have been employed, in what use-contexts they serve what purposes, where they direct or trigger action, where they commend, where prompt appraisal, where they persuade, under what conditions they become standardized and informative; we would see, in short, how concepts express and are geared to perspectives of inquiry, need and practice, and what they are capable of doing in reformulating and refashioning moral outlooks. We should understand more clearly the careers and relations of criteria or standards of morality—how a need or a goal or a trait rises in the cultural economy to a position of moral power and authority, fusing behind its claims strong feelings and sanctions, dominating the processes of criticism and evaluation. We would understand how different pictures of the world and of man serve in many different ways to stabilize policies of action, furnishing comfortable rationalizations to cling to, or guiding principles for reconstruction. We would know these not only as separate items, but in systematic configurations. And if we could know all this, we surely would have come a long way in the tasks of evaluation. This is not wholesale dictation of values. It is always men who get this enlightenment and who can use it in their decisions. Understanding any particular situation does not necessarily mean approving it; on the contrary it may mean intensified effort to reconstruct it. Knowledge can make the difference between enlightened and unlightened decision.

It is worth summarizing briefly the impact of such an approach upon the old fear that a scientific outlook means the end of absolutes in morals. The question itself must be taken to pieces and the notion of "absolute" itself set in the contexts of its use. There is a great deal of vagueness in the general appeal to moral absolutes. The term can refer to: fixed goals for all men, fixed goals for all conditions, unqualified rules, completely established answers in each particular situation, and so on. Appeal to absolutes does not, in any case, remove the problem of further evaluation. It simply shifts the indeterminate element to another area. A rule may be unqualified, but as we saw in considering the systematic organization of morality, one will not know whether it is the rule to apply here, or whether to apply another absolute that will yield a different particular decision. Those moral theories that try to equate absolutes with "moral truth" are likely to find that the heavens of moral truth may be endless.

There are always fresh values that may come into sight, just as the view changes as you climb the mountain higher and higher. A clearer understanding is likely to come only if the study of absolutes is itself carried out in context. Thus it may become more apparent what stable ends are to be found for all men, whether any are so firm that they can be taken for granted, what reasons might justify the use of all-or-none absolutistic rules in some domains and under what conditions, what kinds of built-in moral feelings will yield sharp commands and what the advantages and disadvantages of such a morality may be, and so on.

We need not attempt to recapitulate the detailed treatment of illustrative proposed invariants in the early part of the book, nor the possible generalizations about elements of structure and their functions in the later part. But it is clear that even in the present state of our knowledge, some trans-cultural evaluation is possible. We have already seen the way in which particular strands in a culture, or particular elements in its moral configuration, could be evaluated in terms of the whole system of goals and values in the culture, and in terms of widely accepted human ends. We saw, for example, that we could map the effectiveness of different kinds of sanctions with respect to the achievement of the goals for which they were intended, and at the same time estimate their social and psychological costs from a wider perspective. In the same way, one could carry out the analysis and evaluation of a whole morality or a whole culture in terms of how well it is doing its many human jobs. And indeed such larger evaluations and reconstructions need not be carried out only from the vantage point of an outsider. One could make many case studies on the contemporary scene in which evaluations of such a type have been carried out by the people themselves, spurred by those who have gone through processes of culture contact—whether one looks to the history of the Asian countries' adoption of western industrialism or the current experience of West African countries with democratic political forms, or the total restructuring of life recently described by Mead for Manus. That we are dealing in most cases with evaluations and not just outside "influences" is clear both from the selective character of the diffusion and from the usually conscious recognition of what is being sought and what is not wanted. The western world has thus almost as much to learn about the merits and weaknesses of its own ways from the experiments of other peoples with its values and institutions as they have to learn—though with greater immediacy—in undergoing the transitions.

There are, of course, dangers of ethnocentrism in the pivotal judgments of basic needs and values on which trans-cultural valuation may rest. But these are not general a priori barriers so much as particular dangers that have to be brought under the survey of advancing knowledge. Take, for example, the judgment that one set of institutional values would make a given people "happier" than another set. This criterion has been prominent in the whole history of ethical theory—in the Aristotelian outlook, where happiness is a kind of well-being, and in the ancient and modern hedonisms, in which it is more localized as pleasure and the avoidance of pain. But these views, though all in the western tradition, are even so hardly unanimous. How far would the criterion of happiness offered by an American be genuinely trans-cultural, and how far deeply ethnocentric? To discover this would require a comparative survey and this would rapidly show that happiness has not always been consciously sought as a goal, that where it has its content has varied and that diverse human needs have been brought into play in its consideration and pursuit. Such comparative study, turning back upon the American conception of happiness, would realize that much of it is an extremely local view which heavily weights physical comforts, individual achievement, successful mastery of obstacles; which gives a central place to an ideal of forward movement or progress; and which tends to thrust aside such other candidates as "contentment," contemplation, and any suggestion of spiritual insight through suffering. But in the same fashion, we could turn back upon other cultures in which there is no "pursuit of happiness," or where happiness is regarded as amoral or even as a shrinking from life's duties, or where the bodily is scorned and the possibility of change in man's lot is deemed an illusion. And here too we should find a particular local and limited character in the focus of individual "satisfactions" or in the conceptions of "blessedness."

Such an inquiry need not, however, come to an end in such comparative portraits. For one thing, even at a surface level there may come to be an appreciation of some elements in others' ways. Usually this is a clue to a point of strain in our own set-up, an area of need or problem or possible value that we sense but have not faced (cf. Benedict, 1934a, p. 249). And so we are led to try to see the different portraits in their fuller rootedness—ours as well as others. We need not recapitulate this process here; it is simply doing for the concept of happiness and the family of its alternatives the same kind of job that we have suggested throughout the book in area after area. As the scientific picture of man becomes clearer on the psychological, social and historical side, we develop concepts and techniques for comparative evaluation on a trans-cultural scale, sometimes in a bit-by-bit fashion, sometimes, as theory grows, in a more unified way. So, for example, we come to be able to distinguish positive, happy expression, whether active or quiet, extrovert or reflective, from surface calm based on inhibition or gaiety rooted in escape from anxiety; this may enable us to give a proper evaluation to our own culture's sometimes hectic pursuit of "peace of mind" or its insistence on "keeping busy" or such phenomena as "Beatle-mania" or deviant "hippie" processes of "drop-out" and "turn-on." At least in some of these concepts we can see a definite value difference between conceptions of losing oneself and expressing oneself, although the full scope of such distinctions requires a more comprehensive theory of the self than we yet possess. Similarly, we can track down, in other cultures, conceptions of blessedness, those elements of rejection of the bodily which stem from poverty and hopelessness. Or again, we can see the shortcomings in our own conceptions of interpersonal relations, which tend to be extremely self-oriented and exploitative as compared to those of many other cultures. And if this leaves us with a a number of viable and satisfying alternative kinds of happiness—so much the better. This is not a moral dilemma. The advantages of choice can be substantiated on a more secure basis than that of just an arbitrary liberal preference, although we still need to understand more about how differences in goals, for individuals and for whole cultures, can be achieved in a total world of interacting peoples.

It may be suggested that the proper term for the trans-cultural criteria we are discussing is not "happiness" at all. It is tempting to slip into some other terms such as "well-being" or "self-fulfillment." But such alternative concepts have their own complex history of ethical usage and are equally studded with their own complex ethnocentrisms. In any case, whatever the terms, we can expect to reach trans-cultural criteria only by the patient growth of the knowledge of man. And it may be that at the present stage of our knowledge we may have to be satisfied with negative trans-cultural criteria of unhappiness—or ill-being or non-fulfillment—rather than positive criteria of happiness. As we have seen, we do not expect to find common human value-atoms—although we may find some specific joys in physical expression and in aesthetic appreciation, in intellectual activity and in human relations, that are typically human no matter how diverse their expressive forms. We expect rather to find similar needs, structures, problem-situations, mechanisms, modes of functioning, necessary conditions with respect to the development of personality and of effective social functioning. The outcome from the growth of knowledge is thus not a simple set of invariant relations, but a complex framework, a *valuational base* (A. Edel, 1955, ch. 9), which includes universal or recurrent needs, perennial aspirations and major goals, central means and necessary conditions, and special factors geared in a systematic way to the stage of development of mankind, its knowledge and ability to utilize resources, its existent forms of organization, and the specific possibilities of their development. It is to the stabilization of such a basis for evaluation that the kind of studies described in this book seem to us, if pursued systematically and intensively, to be able to contribute.

This does not mean that we must tremble for morality or fear that its basis is too shaky for safety. How

shaky a particular morality turns out to be depends on
how it is functioning in its full cultural and social setting,
how it is in fact serving basic needs and meeting the
fundamental aspirations, helping to support and organize
a satisfying total way of life. Basic moral principles need
not lose strength if they are thus interpreted modestly to
serve as guides for evaluation, and on the theoretical
level as guideposts for research. And we can sharpen our
evaluation technique while using it, just as, in the familiar
analogy, we use our existent tools to make better tools.
Neurath (1944, p. 47) has suggested that the whole body
of our knowledge can be compared to a boat that is never
in drydock, that must be constantly repaired and rebuilt
while in action. Suppose we went further, and had the
boat carry the very soil by which it grew the trees from
whose timber it made its repairs. Of course, the globe itself is such a boat! A model of this kind could hold for
morality as well. As a matter of fact, this might help us
remember that what we want is not so much a safe harbor
in which to anchor as good instruments for charting a purposeful course.

Nevertheless, the net impact of these various considerations calls for a changed conception of morality. This
is clear today on a wide front in ethical theory. There
are many signs in many schools of thought of a greater
emphasis on sensitivity, a receptivity to possibly new qualities, a recognition of emergents in human life, an insistence on clearing the path for creativity. There are many
basic concepts in terms of which this trend is expressed.
In liberalism there is the appeal to liberty and the scope
it gives for originality. Evolutionary views, in spite of
their determinism, leave a gap for the emergent, as in the
Marxian recognition that quantitative changes reaching a

critical point bring sharp and not wholly predictable alterations in society. Much of religious ethics in the 20th century has shifted emphasis from rationalist legalism to a kind of existentialist uncertainty and a stress on decision, or on man's capacity for self-transcendence (cf. Niebuhr, 1943). Existentialism itself (e.g., Sartre, 1948) often couples its stress on the completeness of freedom with a stress on the depth of responsibility. A Deweyan naturalism thinks in terms of growth as a basic category (1948). Whitehead finds a prominent place for the category of Adventure (1933). Even biological ethics, which was once used to fix man's nature, now preaches—for example, in Julian Huxley's ethical writing (1947)—lessons on the dangers of foreclosure, in reference to species that died out. Among sociologists and anthropologists, we find Ginsberg (1957, ch. 7) stressing emergence of ethical values, Redfield (1953) calling attention to moral innovation in sensitive discovery or breaking through, Mead (1943) proposing as a goal of education that the future should be able to set its own goals.

In such a convergence among so many different points of view there is evidence of a widespread tendency —a demand that morality take a more creative form, a resistance to foreclosing of evaluation. This is the theoretical restlessness we noted in considering contemporary accounts of justification. A social scientist analyzing it would, of course, seek to attach it to the shape of contemporary social forces and problems. It may be seen in its basic impetus as a varied reaction to present needs for change, a response on the theoretical level to the sweeping transformations in modern life. And while occasionally the reaction takes the form of an anti-scientific obscurantism, for the most part perhaps it expresses the need

to overcome lags and resistances in bringing man's social and intellectual and moral life in line with the new
world in which he lives. But it is also possible that the
phenomenon before us contains more than a reaction to
breaking with the past. It may be a growing up at long
last, in which man has become conscious of the inevitably
changing character of his world, and—more than that—in
which he has also become conscious of the scope of his
creative possibilities. Whichever it is, it carries us far
beyond the confines of our present study. But whichever
it is, it also shows that ethics today conceives itself to be
on the frontier of human life, and that it has to be
wedded with knowledge in the effort to face man's future.

Chapter XVI

SOME PHILOSOPHICAL CONSIDERATIONS IN THE DIALOGUE OF ANTHROPOLOGY AND ETHICS

In the first chapter of the book, three aims were set forth. They were: "to establish 'coordinates' for the more systematic mapping of particular moralities, to explore more explicitly the relations of morality to cultural patterns and social processes, and to see how philosophic issues of ethical theory become refined and reformulated when their cultural content is made manifest." The reflections that follow center primarily around the logic of these tasks.

1.
DESCRIBING MORALITIES

The world has had thousands of religions and thousands of languages. Has it had thousands of moralities? To ask such a question presupposes that a morality can be identified and described, that it can be treated in some systematic way, that in spite of its ramifications in the culture of which it is a part, it does constitute a "department" that can be isolated for descriptive purposes. Such an approach, although referring to a variety of moralities, does not, it should be noted, settle in advance controversies about ethical relativism or ethical absolutism. The plurality of moral "codes" is a fact, not a speculation or a problem. The interpretation of these—whether one believes them to differ on details rather than on fundamentals, on garb rather than on substance, or whether one interprets them as constituting varying hypotheses about one truth or, on the other hand, as showing that the concept of truth is inapplicable to moral judgments—is a quite separate matter. The initial formulation, the search for dimensions in description, stands on its own. From an anthropologist's point of view some dimensional scheme has to be worked out, if he is expected in his field work to ascertain the morality of a people as well as its religion, economics, kinship system, and so on, if—thinking concretely in terms of a book on the culture—he is to have a chapter headed "Morality." He has to know what to look for. The philosophical counterpart of the problem is to determine the meaning of "moral," a matter of considerable traditional controversy.

Our proposal in Chapter II ("The Mark of the Moral") was to cast a wide net, round up variegated phenomena that might fall in the category of "morality," and look not to preliminary or initial ideas but to the results of research—relations and functions that had already been discovered or would hopefully be discovered—to determine what unity there was in the field and what phenomena should be discarded. In adopting this policy we were following the sort of procedure that seemed to us best to fit the history of concepts in human inquiry as far apart as the physical concept of electricity, the medical concept of health, and the anthropological concept of religion. The book carried the delineation of morality as far as to spot a set of constituents, of both content and structure, which would be elements or problems in any morality. Types of content covered rules of enjoined or proscribed behavior, character-traits encouraged or discouraged, goals selected for approval or disapproval. The elements of structure included the indicated community or "congregation" of the morality, concepts and modes of organization, modes of justification, sanctions and feelings utilized in the morality, and general features and configurations. "Structure" is, of course, a word used in many senses in the philosophical literature. We intended it not as an abstraction, but as a term denoting those parts of a given morality that give it shape or form or organization for the carrying on of its work. If one wished to break up the concept, one might distinguish constitution (the moral community), mechanisms (e.g., sanctions), conceptualization (concepts and generalization forms), and even extend the scheme to add processes (application, decision, evaluation). To understand a morality requires a grasp of all the constituents, not just the selection of some favorite. Hence a concept of morality must include them all, in their mutual relations.

This was proposed as a working concept of morality, in the hope that it would prove useful for research and broaden understanding. It did not claim to be simply an explication of ordinary use of the term "morality" or to be intuitively self-justified or to correspond to dominant present professional use. Perhaps the purposes underlying this working concept and the considerations warranting it can best emerge from a comparison with possible alternative ways of dealing with morality. In the following pages four anthropological options (A1–A4) and three philosophical options (P1–P3) will be examined briefly and critically. These may be stated as follows (cf. A. Edel, 1962):

(A1). We know well enough for our purposes what "moral" means. We can get along sufficiently in anthropology with such marks as what people feel outraged about, what they approvingly tell their children, and so on.

(A2). Morality can be handled best within some existent department, or perhaps by a slight enlargement of one. The most likely is "social control."

(A3). Morality appears in *every* department in the importance attached to the basic goals or aims of that department. It cannot therefore be treated as an independent department.

(A4). Morality is a sentiment binding men to one another. It is therefore quite different in type; it is not an institution or category of culture at all, but quite *sui generis*.

(P1). A term means, after all, what we, the users, mean by it. Let us mean by "morality" just what we find in *our own* linguistic use. After that is analyzed, we can ask whether what we find at other times and among other peoples is anything like our concept or is something else.

(P2). Philosophy in the 20th century has developed a general concept of "value," and anthropologists and sociologists have recently carried on many inquiries into values. If "morality" is to be investigated, it should now find its place as a species within that genus.

(P3). Most of the traditional ways of cutting up a culture have proved to be barriers to theoretical progress. Why not look for fresh categories rather than try to resuscitate a concept of the moral and force precision on it?

(A1). Relying on a variety of indices of the moral without attempting to work out a theoretical concept corresponds to an early stage of inquiry in which the material is dispersed and different marks are used in different areas. But one cannot rest indefinitely on indices without going on to explore what they are indices of, whether they all point to the same thing, and so on. For example, if people are outraged at a given marriage, we have to explore their underlying concept of incest; and if they are outraged at a man's accepting an apology for an unintentional hurt or affront, we have to understand why in that culture his act would be seen as weakness and what is the special meaning of honor. Such inquiries lead on, and though it does not mean that we necessarily end up with a single unified concept of the moral, it does mean that we cannot rest on the variety of indices alone.

(A2). If the phenomena and processes of morality are to be taken care of within some already existing or possibly some enlarged department, the chief candidate would be a field of "social control" in which law and politics, some aspects of education, and morality would be merged, for the purpose of studying different ways of regulating human beings. The advantage of such a procedure is that it allows constant attention to the functional aspects of moral concepts and processes, to the jobs that morality is doing in society and in the socialization of the individual. It has the merit of focussing on the social character of morality, and of showing continuities between moral processes and other psychological and social processes. These lessons, however, can equally well be conveyed in the concept of morality formulated in the preceding chapters, as can be seen readily in the detailed illustrations of moral content in the earlier chapters and in the treatment of sanctions.

The dangers of viewing morality wholly in terms of

social control are twofold. There are parts of morality—for example, many ideals and aspirations, or value-orientations that arise in the development of the self (such as attitudes toward creativity)—which do not fit comfortably, in fact tend to be neglected, under the rubric of social control.

Even more significant is that a treatment of morality purely under social control will tend to emphasize the processes and deal only obliquely with the ends, and ends are surely an important part of morality. This danger can be compared to the damage that was done to contemporary political science when the concept of power, though useful in many respects, cut itself adrift from the concept of men's purposes; power came to be reckoned as the end, and purposes only as bases for the manipulation of power. In this strange inversion, "power" meant primarily a capacity to control others, and not a capacity to accomplish ends.

It is not, therefore, a sound theoretical policy to force the study of morality into any one other department, even though it is useful in considering its relations to look at it through the perspective of many departments. In the same way, it is useful to look at religion in its economic phases or its phases of social control without defining it as an economic phenomenon or a phenomenon of social control.

(A3). There is a certain plausibility about refusing to treat morality as an independent department or category of culture on the ground that it is found in every department. Any phase of culture, whether kinship or distribution systems or religious institutions, marks out a particular mode of organization which is felt to embody what is important. Morality thus seems too pervasive to be lined up alongside other institutions, as if it could intersect with others rather than be constitutive in them all.

However, the fact that moral components may occupy

a strategic place in every field of human life by no means militates against a separate analytic treatment of morality. Economic or religious phases of life may in some or many cultures be equally pervasive, and yet still be quite capable of analytic separable treatment. So, too, in a highly authoritarian society even a political structure may permeate all life. The separate analytic treatment may indeed be the best way to estimate the extent of the permeation. For example, the chapter on "Distributive Justice" shows how a rudimentary basic need finds expression and develops channels of satisfaction in a variety of institutional and social forms. Again, in an obvious sense, morality does interact with other phases of life in the specifics of a culture, and affects or is influenced by them. Sometimes, however, it is shut out from them, as in our culture it has been shut out from vital social decisions, and relegated to isolated inner feelings and comparatively narrow personal choices.

Suppose we take this approach quite literally. Morality becomes equated by initial stipulation with what is felt to be important in all fields. A systematic elaboration of this proposal cannot then rest content with the mere sense of importance; it would be compelled to render in explicit terms the basic goals in various fields—in effect, to delineate the content of a morality as we have conceived it, with an emphasis on approved goals or the good. It need only become more sensitive to problems of structure to find itself treating morality in much the same way as we have done here.

(A4). To see morality as a pervading bond or spirit among men which holds them together appears to be a quite different path. Morality is taken to be a matter of feeling, and our knowledge of it to be direct and introspective. Now, although the phenomena referred to are apparent enough, the theoretical objection to this view is that in taking morality to be so universally familiar it risks ethnocentrism. Enough has been learned in anthropology itself about the different ways in which feelings are patterned in different cultures, and enough has been seen, especially in depth psychology, to raise as a problem the precise nature of the bonds that tie men together. To rely on unanalyzed feelings may serve as a useful occasional index, but scarcely as a basis for theoretical progress. Moreover, the assertion that morality is a bond is not ignored in our formulation; it finds its place in the treatment of sanctions and moral feelings, where there is an attempt to probe the linkages among men that are pertinent to morality both in their ongoing smooth processes and in their critical or hesitant phases. Thus this proposal, like the three preceding ones, turns out to be one that stresses a particular part of the more comprehensive concept we proposed.

(P1). The first of the philosophic options, that inquiry should start with what "morality" means in our own usage, and work outward from that, sounds like common sense, and it has the strength and weakness of common sense. One does have to start with something, and meanings are indeed what *we* mean. But the attempt to analyze precisely what we mean has yielded, in moral philosophy, a large and varied set of proposals, about which there has been little agreement. This state of affairs suggests that the varied proposals have fastened on different features of a complex domain for which a descriptive inventory is at present more appropriate than an arbitrary selection of essence. Again, where we settle on a specific meaning, there is the danger that this may harden so as to produce ethnocentrism when we compare other cultures to our own. For example, in the history of the concept of religion there was long the view that *we* had religion, *others* had superstition! Something like this has happened in political theory in the concept of democracy. Here, starting with what we mean has often entailed building our own particular political forms into the concept. An alternative would be to develop a more comprehensive concept in which the ideals and the basic social aims that are found in democracy are joined with possibly varied forms of political organization capable of fulfilling these under varied conditions. The fact that a penumbra of interests is tied to the concept actually leads many contemporary political philosophers to give up any theoretical formulation and to declare the concept itself to be primarily emotive or practical or propagandistic. In the case of morality, then, the occurrence of disagreements and conflicts over determining a generally acceptable set of marks, and the dangers of enthnocentrism prompt the more comprehensive working concept of the type we proposed.

(P2). A merging of the idea of morality with the wider notion of "value" is the implicit recommendation of a considerable part of 20th century philosophy. This procedure has to be judged by its results up to this point. In the social sciences, such a concept of value has been used in recent decades on a broad front in anthropology, sociology, and social psychology. It has brought a greater sensitivity to the study of men's existent attitudes and orientations, and given values a place alongside the ecological, the economic, the socio-institutional and so forth, as explanatory. It has paid off, for fresh phenomena have been discovered and functional relations revealed. But the result has not been a systematically developed concept bringing an elaborated theory with it. At most it has meant permission to go with scientific tools into a field that had hitherto kept aloof as "spiritual" and not "natural." It may be that the concept of value is too broad, and embraces too varied a content, to yield a *general* theory.

Its career in philosophy suggests a similar outcome. For in philosophy a general theory was sought from the outset, on the basic assumption that one could deal in wholesale fashion with problems of meaning, validation, justification, in the analysis of value and valuation. But when value as a whole was equated with some general feature such as interest or emotive expression, the result was to fasten a single model on the analysis. It took a long development in contemporary linguistic analysis to cultivate instead the habit of looking for the specificity of uses of terms in value discourse rather than concentrating on the abstract concept and assigning one interpretation, one mode of validation or justification. The growing lesson is an eminently reasonable one when we look at it squarely. For if the field of value embraces phenomena in or phases of everything from morals and religion to law and economics, from art to physical activity and gastronomy, why should we expect uniform "laws" of value or single modes of verifying value or justifying acceptance of value? Even in morality itself, philosophers today may not expect a similar analysis for obligation and for goodness. The penchant for the abstract concept and the assumption that it would prove a key to general laws of valuation were long common; the search was modelled on the physical sciences and hoped for quick success. The abstract concept may bring results eventually, but only after a fuller study is made of the separate phenomena in all the "provinces." It does not look as if it will provide a shortcut. To treat moralities as fields of exploration is thus in no way incompatible with the more general value inquiries. In fact it could enrich them.

(P3). The third philosophical argument—which advises experimentation with wholly fresh categories rather than tinkering with an old concept such as morality—is

cast in terms of general theoretical policy. Many of the
traditional categories of culture have indeed turned out to
be barriers to theoretical progress—for example, at times,
the sharp division between the political and the economic.
In the present flux, where emphasis falls on seeing the
unity within a whole socio-cultural matrix and analyzing
its complex operations, there might seem little point in
trying to reinterpret the old category of morality rather
than devising new constructs that cut across hitherto isolated fields. For morality, of all things, has perhaps suffered most from isolation; in the preceding chapters we se-
verely criticized the isolationist character of traditional
moral philosophy, and we also raised the possibility, in
considering definitions of "moral," that the unity of the
concept may lie not in some felt quality of consciousness
but in a battery of socio-cultural functions and processes.

The spirit of this argument is indeed admirable. It is
important that new categories be tried out, that different
groupings and organization of material be attempted, and
that in general an experimental attitude be taken to cate-
gorial selection in which justification lies in its light as
well as in its fruits. But such a spirit need not run counter
to the working concept of morality we have offered. For it
is not the old isolationist concept in which the moral is
identified by introspection, in which it is said to have its
own distinctive vocabulary set off from all other vocabular-
ies and with its meanings intuitively clear. It is a comprehensive concept so fashioned as to *reveal*, not overlook, the
human processes at work, and to encourage understanding
by tracing relations to other phases of socio-cultural life as
well as deeper inner psychological processes. Despite its
continuity with older uses, the working concept of morality we have proposed is not simply a resuscitation of an
older category, but a construct geared to research and em-

bodying the lessons of cross-cultural inquiry. It may prove most fruitful at this point of theoretical development precisely because it may bring more varied phenomena under scrutiny and so encourage the search for both wider and more intimate relations. At some future time, when it has done its work, the results achieved might prompt a theoretical restructuring of the field.

New categories may, however, also be necessary for historical reasons. It would certainly appear that categories for description of human life undergo some change as the socio-cultural character of life itself changes. Political science here again offers an instructive parallel. In dealing with earlier periods it may well find no distinctive phenomena of ruling and being ruled, and so its material might be scattered, consisting principally of whatever patterns of authority occur in all phases of life, from production to religion. At a later period, what we have come to regard as distinctive political phenomena are seen to emerge; certainly this happens with the formation of states. In modern times, the sharp separation of political science from economic science (which has been prevalent up to very recent thought) reflects the stage in which the state was separated from economic life. Now much of this separation of disciplines may have an "ideological" character. But such a history does raise the question whether useful categorical distinction may not to some degree reflect actual or growing distinctness of phenomena. It is thus quite possible that morality may be emerging as a distinctive modern phenomenon without having been, always, everywhere, an independent dimension of human life. Concepts of "moral autonomy" common in the 19th and 20th centuries were not wholly unrelated to the growing separation of morality from religion. The dominant individualism of the modern period no doubt accentuated the trend. Today, as we suggested in Chapter XV, the rapidity of change in human life is reflected in the need for more basic decision. This social need, and the fact that it cannot be satisfied in terms of one isolated field of life, has made us conscious of the need for a more systematic theory of decision, for a better developed concept of rationality in decision. The concept of morality itself is often projected in terms of wisdom in decision, problem-solving, creative choice. Whatever the merits or disadvantages of these formulations, they do reflect the growing phenomenon of decisions that require wide knowledge and concern the whole of life, and so cannot be dictated by partial standards from some entrenched or isolated domain. It is this base, grounded in the complexity of problems and the rapidity of change, which seems—whatever other factors may also work in the same direction—to support the emergence of, and likely to render permanent, a concept of autonomous morality. But if such a concept is not to go astray, or to become a fresh individualistic ideology, it must follow the lines which reveal, not disguise its relations to the whole of social and cultural life.

2.

RELATIONS OF MORALITY TO CULTURAL
PATTERNS AND SOCIAL PROCESSES

Twentieth century philosophical analyses of morality have, for the most part, turned their back on socio-cultural relations for historical reasons—the remnants of the traditionally sharp separation of spirit and freedom from nature and causality, and the fact that the social disciplines were formulated as sciences with scientific aims. When pressed, philosophy attempted to settle the question by wholesale logical formulae: to interpret moral concepts in naturalistic terms would be a "naturalistic fallacy"; to justify genuinely moral statements (not simply judgments of efficacy of means to considered ends) in terms of genetic context would be a "genetic fallacy." The assumption was, clearly, that morality was an isolated domain with its own vocabulary and its own methods of justifying its pronouncements.

The detailed history of 20th century analytic ethics has itself, however, exhibited the disintegration of this outlook. The revolution of philosophical positivism was sharp and peremptory, and brought it to a crisis: since scientific knowledge and its modes of verification were taken as paradigmatic both for meaning and justification, the terms and statements of morality were meaningless—on their own showing they could not be interpreted in empirical terms or verified by sense-experience. They could therefore be only emotive expressions. There was no sense in attempting an inductive or deductive proof of the truth of moral assertions; modes of proof in morals were themselves expressions of attitude in the practical effort to influence attitudes of others. Moral problems were not solved rationally; they were dissolved practically by causal change of people's attitudes.

In the analytic developments of the mid-20th century this practicalism mellowed considerably. The meaning of moral terms was explored in a fuller range of uses, and emotional expression was seen as merely one function. The belief in a unified meaning for a term was itself questioned, and the search turned rather to "uses" of the term in diverse linguistic contexts. There was a shift from studying uses of moral terms—as if the terms themselves were distinctively moral—to moral uses of terms. Thus the separateness of the moral vocabulary was questioned.

Again, the diversity of uses was exhibited by an increasingly fuller exploration of contexts, and the contexts were described by a presentation of non-formal conditions. Thus, to say "It ought to add up to 45" is clearly to use "ought" in a non-moral sense. "What ought I to do?" uses "ought" to ask for advice. "He ought not to have done it" is an evaluative use of "ought," because it makes an assertion about someone not addressed, and probably sums up a reckoning. "You ought to do it" involves a prescriptive use of "ought," because it is addressed to someone directly and attempts to exert pressure on him in an imperative sort of way, but at the same time suggests that reasons can be given for the recommended course of action. And so on.

Now, once we have carried the exploration of meaning all this way into non-formal conditions in the context in which the term is used, there is no sound reason for stopping short of fuller contextual exploration. The same kind of effect as is secured by the prescriptive use of "ought" among us may be secured in another culture by telling a story of what happened to So-and-so under similar conditions (perhaps a culture which carefully avoids direct pressure on another as infringing his dignity), with the implication that such happenings would be the rule. Or in another culture, a comparable effect might be secured by saying "People would laugh at you if you didn't do it" —not as prediction of ridicule as a sanction, but as an index of the right and proper. In short, without attempting at this point to evaluate 20th century analytic trends, it does seem that, having once embarked on the practical interpretation of moral discourse, moral philosophers have too long hovered on the brink of a fuller socio-cultural and psychological description of contexts. Thus we suggested, in dealing with ethical concepts (Chapter X), that even a simple imperativistic interpretation of moral terms requires for its fuller understanding an exhibition of the extent of authoritarian structures in the personality and culture of the society.

The same teetering on the edge of a fuller reference to cultural contexts is seen in the development of the theory of justification. While emotivism denied that there was any logical way of validating moral statements, subsequent analytic trends took a more lenient view of "logic." There were, it was argued, definite patterns in the interrelationship of factual claims and moral assertions; and the analysis of these patterns could properly be regarded as exhibiting the logic of moral discourse. Thus it is a good reason for doing something to recognize that it falls under a moral rule, and it is a good reason for not doing something to perceive that it would hurt someone else. (Exceptions are similarly patterned.) The analysis of moral discourse has as a major task the exploration of such basic patterns of "good reasons." Now, since these patterns have been built into the language of the culture during its historic development, such a search is a partial anthropological investigation of cultural norms of justification as revealed in language. Insofar as the search for such patterns is identified with the exhibition of logic of moral discourse we have, in effect, justification by linguistic custom. The obvious next step is to throw the inquiry open to actual mapping of different modes of justification as cultural acts —along such lines as we attempted in the chapter on justification. A great philosophical advantage in this procedure is that the frankly anthropological approach involves less danger of smuggling evaluations into the results, for an acknowledged descriptive intent sets off issues of evaluation as subsequent or separate.

Having seen the way in which philosophy has been pushed toward including in its province an inquiry into cultural context, we have now to ask what kinds of relations are to be found between moral elements and cultural context. In this book, the kinds are not labelled and classified. But it is philosophically interesting, in the many specific analyses and illustrations of how moral rules and virtues and goals are understood more fully in their bio-social relations, to see how varied these relations actually are.

Some of them are *causal*. But causality is not of any one sort. Causes of origin are different from causes of perpetuation, which apply after something has come into existence. Some causation may be direct and compelling—where there is only one moral answer, rule, or virtue to a situation, such as social cohesion in an otherwise impossibly hard environment. More often, there is instead causation by limitation of possibilities, or a kind of evolutionary model in which alternative moral forms were possible but markedly adaptive ones won out. Causality in moral phenomena is certainly no less complex than in historical phenomena generally. One would expect a richer inventory of types to be the outcome of continuing research in the field —distinctions along many further lines, perhaps, such as between what causes something to become a moral problem and what causes it to have a specific answer, between what causes an issue to be morally central in the life of a society and what causes it to be simply one among many moral problems, between what causes an ordinary issue to flare up with moral quality and what causes the moral quality of an issue to evaporate, and so on.

Bulking larger than explicit causal relations are *functional* ones. That these are involved in some of the causal relations is seen in the evolutionary models, for to find one moral form more "adaptive" than another is to say that it does a required job more adequately. The concept of function refers simply to doing jobs, and to different ways of doing different kinds of jobs—as a virtue of charity, or a set of rules of obligatory distribution of products of the hunt, does the job of getting people fed; it may also do the job of enhancing the status of the giver.

No general functionalism was presupposed—as, for example, the view sometimes held that every item of culture serves some role in supporting a total pattern. This is a separate empirical issue, or should be. Similarly, the question of direction in functional relations is an empirical matter. For example, reversibility is often possible: thus financial manipulations enhancing status may in a given culture do the job of encouraging production beyond subsistence needs, while producing the surplus does the job of enhancing status. On the whole, a bio-social outlook of an evolutionary sort would underline the first of these functions; but such an outlook need not constitute a selective bias. It expresses an overall theory of human development, but it may be verifiable in the particular case in some long-range prediction, such that if the financial operations limited the expansion of productivity they would give way rather than issue in a permanent acceptance of limitation. Again, the question of how far there is consciousness of function is a wholly empirical matter. Some of the responses quoted in the discussion of incest, like "If a man were to marry his sister, what would he do for a brother-in-law?" (p. 48), show clear consciousness of the social relations that the incest tabu makes possible in such cultures. Sometimes functions are covered, and it requires careful anthropological or psychological analysis to reveal them. Or else they are partially misassigned in consciousness, as is so common in political ideologies, or in deeply grounded psychological reactions such as ours to cleanliness, which cannot be seen wholly in terms of our knowledge of germs.

Finally, functional relations may be sought both for items and for whole configurations. In the latter case, functions may be complex and multiple, as can be seen for example in the discussion of the Puritan syndrome in its several occurrences (Chapter XIV). Of course, such judgments of functional relations, as of causation, require thorough research and are not to be read off from even plausible appearances (cf. M. Edel, 1960).

The question of consciousness carries us beyond questions of causality and function to what may be called the *cultural meaning* of an idea. This expression is sometimes used to indicate the fact that our understanding of terms—in this case, moral terms—is enlarged or becomes fuller when we see the conditions, applications, and concomitants of their use in a given culture. Obviously, to understand the meaning of "adultery" in a given culture, we need to know the marriage rules concerning permissible intercourse beyond that with the spouse; but also, to understand the conception of "justice" in the culture, we have to be aware of its distribution modes; to understand "gratitude," we have to know the specific relations of giving and supporting and to perceive interpersonal situations typical of the culture. And it is doubtful whether we could really understand "honor" for most moralities in which it is central, without reference to the familial system and its place in the whole culture, or in some contexts the class system which supports an aristocracy. Hence relation to cultural context is required not merely for understanding causality and function, but for gaining a fuller understanding of the meaning of moral expressions and judgments.

Here again, more detailed analysis is needed to appreciate the variety of relationships covered in this loose formulation. A term is properly seen as a term in a given language. Statements about the term having the same meaning in different languages are complex assertions of equivalence of uses for translation from one language to another. So too, statements about the same word having different meanings in two languages, or even in two contexts of one language, have to be analyzed as to whether the reference is to equivocation (as in "hood" of an automobile and "hood" for a hoodlum) or to some rough analogy ("hood" for a kind of head-cover and automobile "hood" as radiator cover), or to some more complex construction. Thus we can speak of one term as having two somewhat different meanings, both concerned with roughly the same act or situation, but each selecting different features for additional stress—for example, we may distinguish between the ordinary use of a term and its legal use, which makes careful qualifications and distinctions. There may be in other cases a common core within which there are blanks for cultural specification—as in the case of "incest," which includes the idea of limits for the occurrence of marriage or intercourse but leaves a blank for the limits to be specified in different cultures, either directly or through variant use of some kinship term. Sometimes the common core may lie in a common psychological attitude, but the content may be left open—for example, "jealousy" might be used with reference to sex in one culture, property in another, both in a third. Sometimes, again, differences of attitude toward an act minimally described may be of sufficient consequence to be added to the minimal marks to yield two different "cultural meanings" —for example, there is Margaret Mead's illustration somewhere that "compromise" means to an American an agreement in which one abandons principle, but to an Englishman it means a realistic agreement that two sides may make without surrender of principle in a context where

neither could win. Or again, when we pointed to phenomenological differences in the idea of custom—one people stress the lessons of experience, another the burden of
the past, and so on—we could either construe this as the
same idea with different responses to additional features,
or as different cultural meanings of "custom."

Philosophers have often in the past avoided the job of
analyzing the complexity of such types and relations of
meanings, by insisting that the meaning of a term be specified by a unique set of marks giving the necessary and sufficient conditions for the use of the term—a strict requirement obviously suited to the formal disciplines such as
mathematics—and that all else be regarded as association,
diverse application, concomitant attitudes, and so on. But
since meanings are, after all, in some sense human con-
structions, there is no guarantee that the requirements of
mathematics will necessarily fit all other fields. And philosophers themselves have been led to a greater awareness
of the problem by looking more systematically to "uses" of
terms to clarify "meaning" of terms, and by grappling with
problems of identity and difference in the expressions of
natural as well as artifically constructed languages. Hence,
only a short step is needed to turn their analytic energies
toward the variety of relationships that culture bears to the
meaning of moral terms.

It should be added here, too, of course, that this approach does not prejudge the extent of unity that may be
found in any particular moral concept. This becomes a
question of inquiry rather than a Platonizing presupposi-
tion of an "essence." Thus, those who insist on defining
"charity" by winnowing out some essence, antecedently asserted for all possible cultures, must either designate the
result a matter of pure postulation or else show by investigation that there is some (probably phenomenological) in-

variance across culture lines. Methodological differences in interpreting moral terms may be seen as reflecting different hopes or predictions about the eventual outcome of trans-cultural investigation. The next question is whether the lessons we have been concerned with in the case of moral terms and moral content extend also to reflective or theoretical inquiry in moral philosophies.

3.

IMPACT ON ETHICAL THEORY

The question was posed above how philosophical issues of ethical theory become refined and reformulated when the cultural context is made evident. This is the most controversial issue for philosophers, since on the whole the tendency has been to assume that ethical theory, like physical theory or theory generally, is an attempt to establish a truth unrelated to cultural context. And, indeed, we did not seek to "relativize" ethical theory, nor to regard it as cultural "ideology" or as an example of any of the other familiar stereotypes which rouse the intellectual fears of philosophers. The aim was, and remains, to bring ethical theory to a fuller self-consciousness of what it is doing, so that as its nature and office becomes clearer it can refine its criteria for self-evaluation.

It is not wholly inappropriate in considering these questions to raise the curtain here on some of the stages of the dialogue out of which the book emerged. For they do carry some philosophical lessons. The original thought had been that since ethical theorizing (or reflective moral philosophy) was so definitely distinct from actual morality (or moral "codes"), it should be independently mapped. Hence the relations between codes, theories, and cultural factors could be more clearly studied on the historical scene. We could see how far changing ethical theories in the western tradition embodied changes in the scientific, religious, and social scene, and how far they influenced these areas in turn; whether changes in theory preceded or followed changes in the actual moral code; how far ethical theory could really function, as propounders of "meta-ethics" claimed that it could, as a neutral logical discipline. By making the variables distinct, their relations could more readily be explored. From the anthropological point of view, however, it was felt that this might be imposing a distinction on the primitive materials which they would not bear. It might be that, as contemporary analysts, we could separate phases of theory in the moral field of preliterate peoples in the light of later-developed distinctions, but the attempt might produce confusion and controversy such as attended the example given above, the search for "political" institutions in societies that had authority patterns here and there but no state form. The dangers were that we might impose a lineal development by seeing the primitive materials as immature stages of the later, and that we might force the field into organizational lines dictated by later theoretical problems. On the other hand, it would be useful to take insights from the diversity of problems and answers in the history of ethical theory as clues, and apply them as questions in order to reveal aspects of the cultural material that might otherwise be overlooked (cf. A. Edel, 1963, ch. 9).

The resolution of this problem lay in recognizing the continuity of theory and morality, and the continuity of specific theories and specific moralities. A morality already contains pre-theoretical elements, precursors of theory, in its structure—in the conceptualization and organization of its content, in its processes of sanctioning and decision, and especially in its mode of justification. In the history of man, as reflection grew, stimulated by inner conflicts in the morality and its culture, by contact with other peoples with contrasting ways, by the growth of general knowledge affecting morality, and by the emergence of systematic knowledge in science and philosophy which became an immanent source of raising questions, moral philosophy or ethical theorizing came into being as a distinct discipline. It did not always see its roots in specific moralities; it has sometimes been harder to recognize the morality in an ethical theory than to see the cultural content in a morality. Yet particular ethical theories, in their historical origin and development, could almost be regarded as particular moralities undergoing systematization, stabilization, or reorganization, in a theoretical growth or extension of themselves. To trace the relations of theories and moralities, however, is a complex matter, involving all the types of relation discussed in the preceding section.

The guiding maxim for research that emerged from these considerations may be expressed as follows: Every moral structure gives shape to an embryonic ethical theory, and every ethical theory can be regarded as a model for a possible moral structure. It proved increasingly fruitful, as we went along, to try translating lessons about differences in ethical theories into lessons about possible varieties of structure. For example, philosophical discussions about the syntax of moral utterances—whether they were to be construed as imperatives or as indicatives, as individual expressions or as some form of socially cooperative expression —came to life when they were regarded as furnishing different models for the actual character of a culture in its moral processes: that is, a morality cast in an authoritarian mold, a morality treated as a kind of knowledge, a morality individually structured in a loose (sometimes anarchic) way or organized with tight communal bonds. Theoretical disputes about whether "right" is definable in terms of "good" seemed the obvious counterpart to different modes of justification—a distinction was made between moralities which felt their injunctions and prohibitions justified when these led to some approved goals, and moralities which justified their rules in terms of tradition or the commands of supernatural beings. Theoretical disputes about whether feelings belonged in the analysis of moral concepts or were merely external associations led to distinguishing where a morality used a feeling as a mode of identification (as feeling proud or ashamed may be used to tell what is right or wrong), and where a morality used a feeling chiefly as a sanction.

If such a counterpart relation is discernible between ethical theory and moral structure, then it is likely that many of the presuppositions about the world and man that enter into the structure of a morality will be found built into an ethical theory. Every ethical theory could thus be examined for its presuppositions about the nature of man and the human predicament, about the critical human problems to which it was addressed, about the kind of community to be recognized, about the organization of moral content, about the character of moral experience, and so forth. In a later paper, we introduced for this purpose the concept of "the anthropological transcription of an ethical theory" (M. and A. Edel, 1963). Such a transcription would enable us better to see what was built into an ethical theory, and by its dissection discover how much of it was amenable to evaluation on factual or scientific grounds, how much embodied men's purposes or even moral content, how much rested on specific linguistic tradition, and so on. As a result, criteria for evaluation of an ethical theory would be markedly refined.

I should like to underscore this point by offering a few central examples of the way in which the cultural lessons gained in the comparison of moral structures may help our understanding of problems of theoretical ethics. The first example is taken from contemporary controversy about universalization in ethics. It is said that the very meaning of "I ought to do this" includes the idea that anyone in a like situation has a like obligation. There is considerable discussion that attempts to fix this meaning as in some sense a logical property of the concept, and many enlightening things have been said in comparing this requirement for "ought" to the use of descriptive predicates, and many questions have been raised about the impact of such a logical requirement on egoistic theories of morality or on the conception of the self as revealed in moral consciousness. But a wholly new dimension emerges when we see this requirement in terms of the comparison of moral structures on the extent of the moral community (Chapter IX). The element of universalization alleged to reside in "ought" begins to seem much more like a theoretical counterpart built into the concept only recently, in a modern world in which demands have emerged for a global community, for the removal of discriminations based on partial group bases of nation, race, or class. It seems to embody a postulate of the moral equality of men; the justification is complexly normative or moral, not simply logical or linguistic. Of course, serious analytic issues remain about precisely how this element of universalization is to be built into morality and how it is to operate.

As a second example, take the very conception of "ought." It is a striking phenomenon, the historian of ethics will note, that the kind of conception so prevalent in modern ethics since Kant had little or no place in the ancient Aristotelian ethics. We find there, instead, a notion of what is "fitting" to the particular situation, as judged by a sensitive man of practical wisdom. We dare not say that Aristotle's *Nichomachean Ethics* is not a work on ethics! It is fairer to recognize instead that the kinds of jobs our concept of "ought" carries out in a morality can be divided up and parcelled out in other ways, and that a careful study of Aristotle's theory will show this is done. But if this is so—and the lesson can be multiplied from comparative study of moral structures—would we not understand the meaning of "ought" better not by purifying it of all content, by thinning out its meaning by abstraction, or assigning to it a set of bare general functions (such as guiding conduct), but by exhibiting the full range of feelings operative in its use or serving as indices in its work, by studying the complexity of its logical relations to other moral terms, by analyzing the structure of interpersonal relations it specifies or calls for in the given culture, by probing for any implicit models in its use—in short, by making an analysis that is psychological and socio-cultural, not merely linguistic or phenomenological? The evaluation of the resultant obligation-structure would again be a complex matter with logical, scientific, and purposive components.

The same lesson emerges in problems of justification. It has already been suggested here that to look for good reasons for doing acts in the logic of moral discourse is a kind of justification by custom. For, obviously, the non-formal rules built into a language for the use of the concept of good reasons have a great deal packed away in them, and only an unpacking can make a thorough or critical justification possible. Paradoxically enough, as we saw, a fuller anthropological perspective here is more philosophical than the partial anthropology of linguistic custom. For it makes clearer the normative job still to be done in the theory itself when the analytic-descriptive inquiry is over.

In general, an anthropological transcription of an ethical theory can dig up the basic problems to which it is addressed, and which it incorporates into its formulation of the tasks of morality. Thus we can see which theories view the tasks of morality as transmitting a stable system of rules from one generation to another, and which restructure the whole conception of morality (as was suggested above) in terms of facing novel or crucial situations and in terms of establishing modes of making creative decisions in regard to changing problems. The very conception of morality's nature and tasks is thus seen as clarified by concern with socio-cultural relations.

On the whole, as one looks back on the past decade, it appears that the basic need for the fuller cooperation of philosophy and the socio-cultural sciences (for that matter, all the sciences of man) has not changed. In fact, it has intensified. From the side of philosophy, the trend may be described as a reaching for a fuller context without quite grasping it. And what can be accomplished when philosophy does grasp the fuller context remains as a hypothesis for the next decades.

BIBLIOGRAPHICAL REFERENCES

ALBERT, ETHEL (1956). The classification of values: A method and illustration. *American Anthropologist,* Vol. 58.

ARISTOTLE. *Nicomachean Ethics,* trans. W. D. Ross. Oxford Univ. Press, 1925.

ST. AUGUSTINE (1948). *The City of God,* trans. Marcus Dodds. Hafner Publishing Co.

AYER, ALFRED J. (1936). *Language, Truth and Logic.* Gollancz (republished Dover Press, 1946).

BENEDICT, RUTH (1934a). *Patterns of Culture.* Houghton Mifflin Co.

—— (1934b). Anthropology and the abnormal. *Journal of General Psychology,* Vol. 10.

—— (1939). Some comparative data on culture and personality with reference to the promotion of mental health, in *Mental Health,* American Association for the Advancement of Science, Publication No. 9.

—— (1946). *The Chrysanthemum and the Sword.* Houghton Mifflin Co.

BENTHAM, JEREMY (1823). *Principles of Morals and Legislation* (new edition corrected by author). Republished, 1907, Oxford: At the Clarendon Press.

BERGSON, HENRI (1935). *The Two Sources of Morality and Religion.* Henry Holt & Co.

BETTELHEIM, BRUNO (1954). *Symbolic Wounds.* The Free Press.

BOAS, FRANZ (1930). Anthropology, in *Encyclopedia of the Social Sciences.* The Macmillan Co.

—— (1932). *Anthropology and Modern Life* (2nd edition). W. W. Norton & Co.

BOHANNAN, PAUL (1958). Extra-processual events in Tiv political institutions. *American Anthropologist,* Vol. 60.

BRANDT, RICHARD B. (1946). Moral valuation. *Ethics.* Vol. 56.

—— (1954). *Hopi Ethics.* Univ. Chicago Press.

BUTLER, JOSEPH (1726). *Fifteen Sermons Preached at the Rolls Chapel, London.*

COLLINS, JUNE (1952). An interpretation of Skagit intergroup conflict during acculturation. *American Anthropologist,* Vol. 54.

DEWEY, JOHN (1922). *Human Nature and Conduct.* Henry Holt & Co.

—— (1927). Anthropology and ethics, in *The Social Sciences and Their Interrelations,* ed. Ogburn and Goldenweiser. Houghton Mifflin Co.

—— (1929). *The Quest for Certainty.* Minton, Balch & Co.

—— (1939). Theory of Valuation, in *International Encyclopedia of Unified Science,* Vol. II, No. 4, Univ. Chicago Press.

—— (1948). *Reconstruction in Philosophy* (enlarged edition). Beacon Press. (Also available in Mentor edition, 1950.)

DEWEY, JOHN, and TUFTS, JAMES H. (1932). *Ethics* (revised edition). Henry Holt & Co. (Dewey's part is separately published as: Dewey, John, *Theory of the Moral Life,* ed. Arnold Isenberg. Holt, Rinehart & Winston, 1960.)

DuBOIS, CORA (1944). *The People of Alor.* Univ. of Minnesota Press.

DUNCKER, KARL (1939). Ethical relativity? (An inquiry into the psychology of ethics). *Mind,* n. s., Vol. 48.

EDEL, ABRAHAM (1953). Ethical reasoning, in *Academic Freedom, Logic, and Religion,* edited by Morton White. Univ. Pennsylvania Press.

—— (1955). *Ethical Judgment: The Use of Science in Ethics.* The Free Press.

—— (1962). Anthropology and ethics in common focus. *Journal of the Royal Anthropological Institute,* Vol. 92, Part I.

—— (1963). *Method in Ethical Theory.* Bobbs-Merrill Co.

EDEL, MAY M. (1957). *The Chiga of Western Uganda.* Oxford Univ. Press for the International African Institute.

—— (1960). Punitive and nonpunitive ancestors in Africa. *Proceedings of the Sixth International Congress of Anthropological and Ethnological Sciences.*

EDEL, MAY and ABRAHAM (1963). The confrontation of anthropology and ethics. *The Monist,* Vol. 47, No. 4.

EGGAN, DOROTHY (1943). The general problem of Hopi adjustment. *American Anthropologist,* Vol. 45. (Available in Kluckhohn and Murray: *Personality in Nature, Society, and Culture.* Alfred A. Knopf, 1948.)

EPICTETUS. *The Enchiridion* or *Manual.* (Available in Liberal Arts Press edition, 1948.)

ERIKSON, ERIK H. (1950). *Childhood and Society.* W. W. Norton & Co.

EVANS-PRITCHARD, E. E. (1956). *Nuer Religion.* Oxford: At the Clarendon Press.

FEIGL, HERBERT (1950). De principiis non disputandum . . . ? in *Philosophical Analysis,* ed. M. Black. Cornell Univ. Press.

FENICHEL, OTTO (1945). *Psychoanalytic Theory of Neurosis.* W. W. Norton & Co.

FERM, VERGILIUS (1956). *Encyclopedia of Morals.* Philosophical Library.

FORDE, DARYLL (1954). *African Worlds: Studies in the Cosmological Ideas and Social Values of African Peoples.* Oxford Univ. Press.

FORTES, MEYER (1945). *The Dynamics of Clanship.* Oxford Univ. Press.

—— (1949). *The Web of Kinship among the Tallensi.* Oxford Univ. Press.

FORTUNE, REO (1935). *Manus Religion.* American Philosophical Society.

FREUD, SIGMUND (1918). *Totem and Taboo.* Moffat, Yard & Co.

—— (1933). *New Introductory Lectures on Psychoanalysis.* W. W. Norton & Co. Ch. 3.

FROMM, ERICH (1947). *Man for Himself.* Rinehart & Co.

GINSBERG, MORRIS (1957). *On the Diversity of Morals.* The Macmillan Co.

GLUCKMAN, MAX (1956). *Custom and Conflict in Africa.* The Free Press.

GOLDMAN, IRVING (1937). The Ifugao, and The Zuñi of New Mexico, in *Cooperation and Competition among Primitive Peoples,* ed. Margaret Mead. McGraw-Hill.

—— (1956). Zuñi Indians, morals of, in *Encyclopedia of Morals,* ed. V. Ferm. Philosophical Library.

GOLDSCHMIDT, WALTER (1951). Ethics and the structure of society: An ethnological contribution to the sociology of knowledge. *American Anthropologist,* Vol. 53.

HALLOWELL, A. IRVING (1955). *Culture and Experience.* Univ. Pennsylvania Press.

HARE, R. M. (1952). *The Language of Morals.* Oxford: At the Clarendon Press.

HARTMANN, NICOLAI (1932). *Ethics,* trans. S. Coit. The Macmillan Co.

HARTSHORNE, HUGH, AND MAY, MARK A. (1928). *Studies in Deceit.* The Macmillan Co.

HERSKOVITS, MELVILLE J. (1958). Some further comments on cultural relativism. *American Anthropologist,* Vol. 60.

HOBBES, THOMAS (1651). *Leviathan.*

HOIJER, HARRY (ed., 1954). *Language in Culture.* American Anthropological Association Memoir No. 79.

HONIGMANN, JOHN (1954). *Culture and Personality.* Harper & Bros.

HSU, FRANCIS L. K. (1953). *Americans and Chinese.* Henry Schuman.

HUXLEY, T. H., AND HUXLEY, JULIAN (1947). *Touchstone for Ethics.* Harper & Bros.

KANT, IMMANUEL (1879). *Kant's Critique of Practical Reason and Other Works on the Theory of Ethics,* trans. T. M. Abbott. Longmans Green & Co.

KARDINER, ABRAM (1945). *The Psychological Frontiers of Society.* Columbia Univ. Press. Chs. 6-9.

KLUCKHOHN, CLYDE (1949). *Mirror for Man.* Whittlesey House, McGraw-Hill.

—— (1953). Universal categories of culture, in *Anthropology Today,* ed. A. Kroeber. Univ. Chicago Press.

—— (1955). Ethical relativity: Sic et Non. *Journal of Philosophy,* Vol. 52.

—— (1956a). Some Navaho value terms in behavioral context. *Language,* Vol. 32.

—— (1956b). Navaho morals in *Encyclopedia of Morals,* ed. V. Ferm. Philosophical Library.

LABARRE, WESTON (1954). *The Human Animal.* Univ. Chicago Press.

LADD, JOHN (1957). *The Structure of a Moral Code.* Harvard Univ. Press.

LEE, DOROTHY D. (1948). Are basic needs ultimate? *Journal of Abnormal and Social Psychology,* Vol. 43.

LEVI-STRAUSS, CLAUDE (1956). The family, in *Man, Culture, and Society,* ed. Harry L. Shapiro. Oxford Univ. Press.

LEWIN, KURT; LIPPETT, R.; and WHITE, R. (1939). Patterns of aggressive behavior in experimentally created "social climates." *Journal of Social Psychology,* Vol. 10.

LINTON, RALPH (1939). Marquesan culture, and The Tanala of Madagascar, in *The Individual and His Society,* by Abram Kardiner. Columbia Univ. Press.

—— (1952). Universal ethical principles: An anthropological view, in *Moral Principles of Action*, ed. R. Anshen. Harper & Bros.

LOWIE, ROBERT H. (1925). *Primitive Society.* Boni and Liveright.

LYND, ROBERT S. (1939). *Knowledge for What?* Princeton Univ. Press.

MACBEATH, A. (1952). *Experiments in Living.* Macmillan & Co., Ltd.

MALINOWSKI, BRONISLAW (1927). *Sex and Repression in Savage Society.* Kegan Paul.

—— (1944). *A Scientific Theory of Culture and Other Essays.* Univ. North Carolina Press. Chs. 7-11.

MEAD, MARGARET (1935). *Sex and Temperament in Three Primitive Societies.* William Morrow & Co.

—— (ed., 1937). *Cooperation and Competition among Primitive Peoples.* McGraw-Hill.

—— (1943). Our educational emphases in primitive perspective. *American Journal of Sociology,* Vol. 48.

—— (1949). *Male and Female: A Study of the Sexes in a Changing World.* William Morrow & Co.

—— (1950). Some anthropological considerations concerning guilt, in *Feelings and Emotions,* the Mooseheart Symposium, ed. Martin L. Reymert. McGraw-Hill.

—— (ed., 1953). *Cultural Patterns and Technical Change.* UNESCO.

—— (1956). *New Lives for Old.* William Morrow & Co.

MILL, JOHN STUART (1859). *On Liberty.*

MOORE, G. E. (1903). *Principia Ethica.* Cambridge Univ. Press.

MORRIS, CHARLES (1956). *Varieties of Human Value.* Univ. Chicago Press.

MURDOCK, GEORGE PETER (1949). *Social Structure.* The Macmillan Co.

NEURATH, OTTO (1944). Foundations of the Social Sciences, in *International Encyclopedia of Unified Science,* Vol. II, No. 1, Univ. Chicago Press.

NIEBUHR, REINHOLD (1943). *The Nature and Destiny of Man.* Charles Scribner's Sons.

NIETZSCHE, FRIEDRICH (1887). *The Genealogy of Morals.*

NORTHROP, F. S. C. (1952). Natural science and comparative law. *Proceedings and Addresses of the American Philosophical Association,* Vol. 26.

PIERS, GERHART, and SINGER, MILTON B. (1953). *Shame and Guilt.* Charles C Thomas.

PLATO. *The Republic of Plato,* trans. F. M. Cornford. Oxford Univ. Press, 1945.

PLUTARCH. *Life of Lycurgus.*

PRICHARD, H. A. (1949). *Moral Obligation.* Oxford: At the Clarendon Press.

RADIN, PAUL (1927). *Primitive Man as Philosopher.* D. Appleton & Co.

READ, K. E. (1955). Morality and the concept of the person among the Gahuku-Gama. *Oceania,* Vol. 25.

REDFIELD, ROBERT (1953). *The Primitive World and Its Transformations.* Cornell Univ. Press.

RIESMAN, DAVID (1950). *The Lonely Crowd.* Yale Univ. Press.

RÓHEIM, GÉZA (1950). *Psychoanalysis and Anthropology.* International Univ. Press.

ROSS, W. D. (1930). *The Right and the Good.* Oxford: At the Clarendon Press.

RUSSELL, BERTRAND (1935). *Religion and Science.* Henry Holt & Co.
——— (1955). *Human Society in Ethics and Politics.* Simon & Schuster.

SANTAYANA, GEORGE (1905). *Reason in Society.* Charles Scribner's Sons.

SARTRE, JEAN-PAUL (1948). *Existentialism and Humanism.* Methuen and Co., Ltd.

SELIGMAN, BRENDA Z. (1950). The Problem of Incest and Exogamy: A Restatement. *American Anthropologist,* Vol. 52.

SMITH, ADAM (1759). *The Theory of the Moral Sentiments.*

STEVENSON, CHARLES L. (1944). *Ethics and Language.* Yale Univ. Press.

SUMNER, W. G. (1906). *Folkways* (2nd edition, 1934). Ginn & Co.

SUN CHIEF (1942). *The Autobiography of a Hopi Indian,* ed. Leo W. Simmons. Yale Univ. Press.

TAWNEY, R. H. (1926). *Religion and the Rise of Capitalism.* Harcourt, Brace & Co.

TOULMIN, S. E. (1950). *The Place of Reason in Ethics.* Cambridge Univ. Press.

WEBER, MAX (1930). *The Protestant Ethic and the Spirit of Capitalism,* trans. T. Parsons. Charles Scribner's Sons.

WESTERMARCK, EDWARD A. (1932). *Ethical Relativity.* Harcourt, Brace & Co.

WHITEHEAD, ALFRED NORTH (1933). *Adventures of Ideas.* The Macmillan Co. Ch. 19.

WHITING, JOHN W. M. (1954). The cross-cultural method, in *Handbook of Social Psychology,* ed. G. Lindzey. Addison-Wesley Publishing Co.

WHITING, JOHN W. M., and CHILD, IRVIN L. (1953). *Child Training and Personality: A Cross-Cultural Study.* Yale Univ. Press.

WILSON, MONICA (1951). *Good Company: A Study of Nyakyusa Age-Villages.* Oxford Univ. Press.

INDEX